TRAILS OF THE
TRIANGLE

OTHER TRAIL BOOKS BY THE AUTHOR

Adventuring in Florida, Georgia Sea Islands, and Okefenokee Swamp (1991, 1995)
Hiking and Backpacking (1979, 1983, 1989, 1994, 2004)
Hiking and Backpacking Basics (1985, 1992)
Hiking North Carolina's Mountains-to-Sea Trail (2000)
Hiking the Mountain State: The Trails of West Virginia (1986, 1997)
Monongahela National Forest Hiking Guide (1988, 1993, 1999, 2006)
North Carolina Hiking Trails (1982, 1988, 1996, 2005)
South Carolina Trails (1984, 1989, 1994, 2001)
The Trails of Virginia: Hiking the Old Dominion (1984, 1995, 2003)
Trails of the Triad (1997)

Second Edition

Trails of the Triangle

Over 400 Trails in the Raleigh / Durham / Chapel hill Area

by Allen de Hart

John F. Blair
PUBLISHER
Winston-Salem, North Carolina

Second Edition, 2007

The paper in this book meets the guidelines
for permanence and durability of the Committee on Production
Guidelines for Book Longevity of the Council on Library Resources.

PRINTED ON RECYCLED PAPER

All photographs were taken by the author unless otherwise noted.

COVER PHOTOGRAPH
Big Lake Trail in William B. Umstead State Park
by Paul Magann, courtesy of Raleigh *News & Observer*

Library of Congress Cataloging-in-Publication Data

De Hart, Allen.
    Trails of the triangle : over 400 trails in the Raleigh/Durham/Chapel Hill area / by Allen
de Hart.—2nd ed.
        p.   cm.
    Includes index.
    ISBN-13: 978-0-89587-349-1 (alk. paper)
    ISBN-10: 0-89587-349-4
    1. Hiking—North Carolina—Raleigh Metropolitan Area—Guidebooks. 2. Hiking—North
Carolina—Durham Metropolitan Area—Guidebooks. 3. Hiking—North Carolina—Chapel
Hill Metropolitan Area—Guidebooks. 4. Trails—North Carolina—Raleigh Metropolitan
Area—Guidebooks. 5. Trails—North Carolina—Durham Metropolitan Area—Guidebooks.
6. Trails—North Carolina—Chapel Hill Metropolitan Area—Guidebooks. 7. Raleigh Metropolitan Area (N.C.)—Guidebooks. 8. Durham Metropolitan Area (N.C.)—Guidebooks.
9. Chapel Hill Metropolitan Area (N.C.)—Guidebooks. I. Title.

GV199.42.N662R354 2007
796.5109756'55--dc22
                                2007035799

Table of Contents

Acknowledgments

Without the assistance from the staffs of the U.S. Army Corps of Engineers, N.C. Wildlife Commission, N.C. Division of Parks and Recreation as well as the staffs from various cities, towns, counties, and private organizations, I would not have attempted or completed the research necessary for this book.

Some of the preliminary work began in 2003 when I was exploring and taking notes on new trails in the Triangle for the fourth edition of *North Carolina Hiking Trails*. That work brought to my attention the rapid development and expansion of outstanding new parks and trails throughout the area. I regularly queried some of the parks-and-recreation staffs to learn about changes that occurred during a research period of nearly four years. Assistance came from the following:

Victor Lebsock, park and greenway planner for Raleigh Parks and Recreation; Karen Berry at Durant Nature Park; John Brown, director of Apex Parks, Recreation, and Cultural Resources; Joe Godfrey, park planner for Cary Parks, Recreation, and Cultural Resources; William Royston, park planner for Durham Department of Parks and Recreation; Len Bradley, director of Holly Springs Parks and Recreation; Steadman Sugg, parks and greenway planner for Morrisville Parks, Recreation, and Cultural Resources; Pete Armstrong, director of Rocky Mount Parks and Recreation; Willard Leonard, director of Rolesville Parks and Recreation; Bill Wester, director of Chapel Hill Parks and Recreation; Larry Bailey, director of Clayton Parks and Recreation; Susan Simpson, director of Wake Forest Parks and Recreation; Larry Philpott, director of Cumberland County Recreation and Parks; Bob Jones, director of Orange County Recreation and Parks; Michel DiFabio, conservation technician for Little River Regional Park and Natural Area; Chris Snow, director of Wake County Parks and Recreation; Tim Maloney, community services manager for Wake County Parks and Recreation; Bill Bussey of the Chatham County Trails Committee; Jessica Poland of the

Triangle Land Conservancy; Paul Hart, superintendent for Raven Rock State Park; Donny Taylor, site manager for Bentonville Battleground State Historic Site; David Cook, superintendent for Eno River State Park; and Betty Anderson, naturalist for William B. Umstead State Park.

Providing assistance with vehicle shuttling, note taking, using measuring wheels or GPS equipment, sorting maps, and keeping me company were Jeff and Amy Brewer, Jessica Burnett, Josh Carpenter, Andre Chappell, Megan Cornell, Eric Crouch, Allison Culley, Shawn De Priest, Don Flowers, Jeffrey Horton, Marcus Huiet, Wade Montgomery, Kyle Perkins, David Perlman, Adam Sharpe, Aaron Smith, Chris Southard, Jalena Spikes, David and Tim Straw, Rett Townsley, Mark and Kristi Trinks, Matt White, Garry Willie, Bruce Wisely, and Reid Zimmerman. Joe Miller of the Raleigh *News and Observer* provided frequent updates.

I am also grateful for the professional assistance provided by John F. Blair, Publisher's staff, and particularly Carolyn Sakowski, whose editorial wisdom and examination of my research made this book possible.

Introduction

How This Guidebook Is Organized

In the Table of Contents, you will notice that this book is divided into sections according to what type of agency owns the trail property. Although most of the trails are owned by federal, state, county, or city agencies, there is also a section that covers trails owned by universities or private individuals. The last chapter covers trails in counties that adjoin what is officially known as the Triangle.

Within each chapter, the individual locations are listed in alphabetical order unless otherwise noted. For most trails, you will find trail lengths, difficulty ratings, directions to trailheads, and descriptions of the trails. Frequently, you will find contact information for the park or recreation area where the trails are located, but additional resource information can be found in the "Resource Information Appendix." Maps are provided for many of the trails, particularly if there is a network. The maps are not all drawn to scale.

What is the Triangle?

The term *Triangle* was first used in the 1950s to describe Raleigh, Durham, and Chapel Hill. It identified an area that had established diverse but complementary relationships to exchange economic, cultural, and scientific benefits. The three cities also exchanged educational benefits through their three major research universities: Duke University in Durham, the University of North Carolina at Chapel Hill, and N. C. State University in Raleigh. Thus, the term *Research Triangle* was born.

The universities provided a surplus of graduates in technology, science, medicine, and related disciplines for the local job market. To prevent many of the outstanding graduates from leaving North Carolina, metropolitan leaders conceived the idea of Research Triangle Park (RTP). The result was the creation of a 7,000-acre tract adjoining southeast Durham (traversed by I-40), near the west side of Raleigh/Durham International Airport (RDU). By 1959, research companies were moving in; IBM located in Research Triangle Park in 1965. Today, RTP proudly has more than 132 research companies and more than 36,000 employees.

Geometrically, today the Triangle is shaped more like a parallelogram than a triangle. Chapel Hill/Carrboro and Durham have adjoining boundaries, and Cary, which has a population of more than 130,000 and for the past few years has been among the state's fastest-growing cities, adjoins Raleigh on the southwest. With rapid development in Morrisville, Apex, Holly Springs, Wake Forest, and Garner, the triangular shape is now becoming more like a fat circle.

The Triangle area is in Region J of the state's 17 regions of government. The counties included in Region J are Chatham, Durham, Johnston, Lee, Orange, and Wake. Near the turn of the 21st century, Moore County was included in the Triangle. Geographically, that addition made the Triangle look like a crescent. Granville and Franklin counties adjoin Wake County, but they were technically in Region K. As the population spreads, especially out of the capital city of Raleigh, it is obvious that using the word *Triangle* for educational, governmental, and geographical identifications is becoming fused and confusing. If a vote were taken, it is likely the residents of all these counties would care less about boundary lines and simply think of the Triangle as a great place to live.

The Triangle reached a population of one million in the summer of 1996. The U. S. Census Bureau revealed that half of that population (517,639) lived in Wake County alone. Wake's population increased 20 percent from 1990 to 1995. In May 1996, the U. S. Bureau of Economic Analysis predicted that the Triangle population would grow to 1.2 million by 2005. This prediction came true.

Also during this period, the Triangle had the fifth fastest-growing workforce in life-science industries and biotechnology research in the nation, according to a Milken Institute study. This growth helped contribute to the 196,300 new jobs in the area.

Quality of Life in the Triangle

Residents of the Triangle area have known for a long time that the metropolitan area is an outstanding place to live, work, and enjoy recreational options. Supporting this judgment are the accolades bestowed by major business publications and various surveys. In the past five years, Expansion Management's Quality of Life Quotient has listed Raleigh as one of the top fifty five-star cities for its quality of life. They ranked it number two in the category of best educational system. *Forbes Magazine* ranked the area number two for the best place for business and careers; *USA Today* ranked the Triangle number one for diversity of college cities and towns, and *Kiplinger Report* ranked the area number one for the best educational options for the dollar. *House and Home* and *Employment Review* magazines listed the area as the nation's best place to live. *Business Magazine* predicted the area would be number nine in growth in the nation by 2006. *Sporting News* listed it eighteenth in the nation for sports; *Runners World* recognized the area as seventeenth in the country for urban trails. The Triangle has also received high rankings for its quality of life from the *Wall Street Journal* and *Fortune* magazine.

Although residents feel pride in these high rankings, there are additional factors that make life pleasurable in the Triangle. Two factors are the area's excellent recreational facilities and its protection of the natural environment. Those of us who have lived in the Triangle for a long time may accept our parks, preserves, botanical gardens, forests, and greenways as routine places to visit and enjoy, but visitors and new residents are quickly taking note of the rapid development in the Triangle's trail system.

Variety of Trails

The Triangle area offers a choice of over 400 trails. Diverse in length and emphasis, the trails may be limited to foot travel or may be shared by pedestrians, bicyclists, equestrians, in-line skaters, and the physically impaired. On residential trails such as Shelley Lake Trail in Raleigh (Chapter 4), you may see walkers, runners, bicyclists, in-line skaters, and people pushing baby strollers. The trail is so popular that it has a speed limit of 10 miles per hour and a centerline to separate traffic. On trails such as Summit Loop Trail at Medoc Mountain State Park in Halifax County (Chapter 6) or Weaver Creek Trail in the New Hope Game Lands near B. Everett Jordan Lake (Chapter 1), you may not see anyone.

In addition to hiking trails, the major mountain-bike and equestrian trails—even those designed exclusively for those uses—are described in this guide. For example, the trails at Beaver Dam Recreational Area (Chapter 1) and Little River Regional Park and Natural Area (Chapter 3) are mountain-bike trails designed and constructed by volunteers. At Harris Lake County Park (Chapter 3), there are trails exclusively for mountain bikers. An example of trails that are reserved for equestrians is in the northern section of Raven

Rock State Park (Chapter 2). An example of a trail designed specifically for use by the physically impaired is Big Lake Handicapped Trail in William B. Umstead State Park (Chapter 2).

Trails range in distance from a few yards, such as the 92-yard-long Honeysuckle Lane Trail in Fuquay-Varina (Chapter 4), to the area's longest, Falls Lake Trail (Chapter 1), which is also part of the Mountains-to-Sea Trail.

Some trails, such as Woodland Nature Trail at Sandling Beach Recreation Area near Falls Lake (Chapter 1) and Shepherd Nature Trail in the Durham Division of Duke Forest (Chapter 5), are interpretive trails. Trail surfaces can be made of gravel, sand, concrete, asphalt, various combinations of these materials, or natural substances. Swift Creek Recycled Trail in Cary (Chapter 4) uses unique materials, including recycled asphalt for the treadway and plastic for the bridges. Concrete or asphalt trails, which are located mainly in urban areas, are called greenways, not because the pathway is green but because the grass, trees, and shrubs bordering the route are green. The city of Raleigh lists all of its trails as greenways.

Trails of the Triangle not only describes the foot trails for day hikes in the metropolitan areas of the Triangle, but also foot trails within 55 miles of the center of Raleigh. (See Chapter 6.) Comparatively short distances between sites allow hikers to visit more than one trail during a day's outing. A few parks, mainly those in state parks, allow overnight camping. Routes along streets and designated bicycle routes also provide a large network in the Triangle area. Detailed maps for these trails are available from the N.C. Department of Transportation (NCDOT). (See the address in "Resource Information Appendix.")

Some trails, particularly greenways in the cities, are in planning or construction stages. Some of these future projects are listed in this guidebook, but you should check the listed addresses for the most recent developments. There are two long trails with ongoing planning and construction—The American Tobacco Trail, which will go from central Durham south toward U.S. 1, and Falls Lake Trail, which will go from NC 50 west to West Point on the Eno.

Health and Pleasure

Walking has always been a natural way to exercise, and its value to human health has long been known. Some physicians suggest that exercise, such as walking, is an activity that not only prevents disease, but one that can be a prescription for treating and managing disease. A clinical psychologist at Duke University's Center for Living has stated that exercise can be an "alternative or complementary treatment for a wide range of medical disorders." Additionally, a family physician at the University of North Carolina in Chapel Hill, who is also an avid runner, believes in the therapeutic effects of physical exercise.

Research specialists in outdoor sports have surveyed those who walk and asked why they walk. Eighty percent walk to enjoy the natural scenery, 75 percent for exercise and health, 40 percent for errands, and 17 percent for commuting to work or school. For urbanites, even a walk on the sidewalk is good for health and pleasure. This is one reason the sidewalk design continues to be an important part of the overall plans for Research Triangle Park (RTP). Visitors will notice the RTP planning has left plenty of natural green space and wide walkways for walking and jogging. Some sidewalks provide a way to view birds, squirrels, flowers, trees, streams, and lakes. Some cities combine sidewalks and nature paths through their historic districts. The networking of greenways, a product of the 1980s, is also enhancing options for walkers.

Health therapist Paula Alder claims that we can "walk out" our problems. Walking helps a person stay active, shave off calories, and deal "more positively with issues." On urban greenways, walkers are likely to see a high percentage of pedestrians walking fast, running, or jogging to lose weight. Health specialists advise that regardless of modern medical treatments, we cannot substitute having a healthy diet and getting plenty of exercise for maintaining our health. The most natural and inexpensive way to acquire and maintain physical and mental health is to take a walk every day. One of the purposes of this book is to emphasize how close you are to places that will allow you to do just that.

Trail Selection and Planning

Experienced hikers can usually make quick decisions about where to go and what to take on a hike. Beginners may need some assistance from experienced hikers, sports specialists, scoutmasters, or outdoor-sports coaches. Outdoor sports that can incorporate walking or hiking include backpacking, camping, canoeing, and fishing; the latter may require a license. Some parks that have hiking trails may also offer fields for baseball, football, and soccer; courts for basketball and tennis; and beaches for swimming. You may wish to incorporate bicycling in your hiking plans, since some trails are designated for multi-use.

With such a variety of options and combinations available, advance planning about what gear to take and what size vehicle you will need is important. Even with the use of this guidebook, you may have additional questions about the services or schedules at the various parks. It is likely that the parks will have brochures or signs to assist in your decisions after your arrival, but contact information is provided here if you want to call in advance.

For parents taking their children on trails and picnic outings, part of the planning may involve choosing a park with playgrounds or a nature museum. If taking senior citizens or those who need wheelchairs, you may need to call in advance. Many of the greenways are ideal for those who have special needs to accommodate physical disabilities. This guidebook also identifies parks that have boat, bike, or horse rentals. A few parks even have nature-tour guides.

Hiking Alone or in Groups

An important question in making the selection of where to go is who is going on the trip. The issue of hiking alone has become more important in recent years as emphasis on safety has increased. Research and statistics indicate that having a hiking companion is a good policy. If hiking alone is your choice, you should know the trail's safety record and know how to get help if needed. For those in a hurry, a solo hike can be defended as the best choice.

If taking children along on a hike, you should always have them within sight of one adult, even at children's playgrounds in established parks. Having at least two adults along to supervise a walk with two or more children is not only a good safety precaution, it also gives the adults the opportunity to interact with children in a natural environment. Children usually like to be outdoors regardless of whether they are hiking, playing games, or exploring. They will enjoy the trails even more if accompanied by siblings or friends in the same age group.

Group hiking is another alternative. It is a common activity among scout, church, or school groups. Those planning for groups have to consider how many are going, what kind of transportation they will need, what food they will need, how that food will be prepared, and what to do in case of bad weather.

When hiking a long trail, it may also be necessary to arrange for a shuttle to be available from the end of the hike back to the point of origin.

Trail Footwear

Blisters on your feet can spoil a hike. Specialists in footwear can help you avoid such problems. A study made by the American Podiatric Medical

Association revealed that about 62 percent of Americans assume that it is normal for their feet to hurt, and that about 80 percent endure some type of foot pain regularly. Yet hardly three percent visit a podiatrist to determine the cause. A large percentage of people buy shoes from salespeople who are not trained in recommending the best shoes for their customers. A frequent comment is that after you "break them in," shoes will be comfortable. If the shoes are of poor quality, do not have proper toe-box space or arch support, or are in need of custom foot beds and cushioning, you are likely to have discomfort or damage to your feet. When replacing good shoes, take the pair with you to a qualified salesperson to assist in the choice of your new shoes. Usually, one foot is larger than the other. The thickness of socks is also an important factor in proper fitting.

If you are a walker, runner, and backpacker, you will need different shoes for each activity. Walking shoes do not need as much heel cushion as running shoes. For most walkers, the heel buildup on running shoes can cause shin muscles to be strained or pulled. When buying backpacking boots, you may wish to examine the "Gear Guide" edition of *Backpacker* magazine or discuss your wishes with a specialist at an outdoor outfitter. When being fitted, ask the salesperson to use a Brannock measuring device.

For foot maintenance, wear two pairs of socks (one wool or synthetic and one lightweight liner acrylic); wear ankle-high gaiters to prevent skin erosion; protect sore spots with moleskin; wash and dry your feet daily on long trips (there are about a quarter-million pores in the sweat glands); and use foot powder occasionally.

Where in the Triangle will you need hiking shoes? On all the trails where the surface is natural, rocky, and steep. For some longer trails, you may have to walk through water or wet places, thus making a waterproof hiking shoe preferable. Also, for some hikers, the hot and flat surface of some greenways takes a toll on the metatarsal part of the foot.

Trail Clothes

In *The Complete Walker III*, Colin Fletcher wrote that the best trail clothes are none at all. In his long hike through the Grand Canyon, he lived by that principle, wearing only boots to protect him against rattlesnakes and a big hat for shade. With all due respect to one of America's most authoritative writers on walking, Mr. Fletcher's fashions are not appropriate for the Triangle trails. Instead, hikers should first consult the weather forecast and wear what is comfortable. Clothes should keep you warm and dry, in thermal equilibrium. If it is cool and you are sweating due to fast walking, jogging, or running, you may need both an absorbent garment and a Gore-Tex shell.

Whatever clothing you choose, be aware of the risk of hypothermia when cooling down too rapidly in cold weather.

Long-sleeve shirts and trousers are recommended for brushy trails, such as locations around Jordan and Falls lakes. In these places, ticks and other biting bugs can easily get on your skin. Some experts also recommend light-colored clothing. If you are hiking on game lands or hunting preserves during hunting season, you should wear an orange-blazed jacket and cap. If backpacking on long or overnight trails in the Triangle, choose extra clothing appropriate for the season. Local trail-supply stores have an outstanding diversity of trail clothes and gear and can provide counsel on what is best for your excursion.

Daypacks

Famed hiker Grandma Emma Gatewood carried her food, clothes, and a blanket in a gunnysack on her first Appalachian Trail journey. John Muir said that a knapsack small enough to jump over a fence, filled with bread and cheese, was all you needed for a trek, but that was years ago. Now you have choices far beyond anything our grandparents ever imagined. A daypack (carried around your waist or on your shoulders) is desirable when you are on a trail long enough to need water, food, rainwear, or first aid. Some trail consultants insist that you should take a daypack if you are going to be out of sight of your home or vehicle at all. Among the basics items you need to carry are maps, water, nutritional food, a first-aid kit, a pocketknife, insect repellant, a flashlight, a whistle or other alarm, a handkerchief, spare clothing, a rain jacket with a hood, and notepaper. You should also carry "FastAid," a small first-aid card that provides instructions for dealing with 31 potential emergencies; there is a place on the card to include emergency telephone numbers for ambulance, rescue squad, personal doctor, hospital, and family members. A cellular telephone? Of course. Had Grandma Gatewood had a cellular she would not have been lost four days the first week.

Nature outing or not, take a camera to record your hike. If taking children, make a daypack for each of them. And finally, if the family dog is large enough, provide it with more than a leash. With a dogpack, your pet can carry its own food and water.

Trail Security

Trails are usually open only between sunrise and sunset. The first rule of security is not to hike the trails after dark. Many of the signs at the trailheads specifically state that the trails are closed after dusk. Often the only lights on some trails are those in tunnels and even they frequently have missing bulbs.

Very few urban trails have designated police patrols during the night, except at parking areas. Only a few trails have emergency telephones—the Al Buehler Cross Country Trail at Duke University (Chapter 5) and Black Creek Trail in the Lake Crabtree County Park in Wake County (Chapter 3) are exceptions.

Other security tips include locking your vehicle and not leaving valuable items where they can be seen through the windows. You should also inform someone in your family or a friend where you are going and when you expect to return. Always keep your eyes and ears alert (headsets with loud music may interfere with the sounds of impending danger); take a cellular telephone with you; and, of course, have one or more partners with you whenever possible. Walking on a wide, scenic greenway, seeing so many happy faces, hearing laughter from children playing, and sharing friendly greetings with strangers may make you wonder how anything could go wrong. But criminal behavior has happened in the past and will happen again. Residents of the Triangle and other urban areas are justified in their concern over security and safety.

Trail Courtesy

Some trail courtesy rules are distinctive to a locality, some are written on signs in parks and subdivision greenways, and others are unwritten but generally understood. One basic rule, which applies to sidewalks and streets as well as trails, is to share space. On multi-use trails used by equestrians, cyclists, and hikers, equestrians have the right of way. Pedestrians have the right of way, unless otherwise posted, on trails also used by cyclists. Signs indicating that trails are for foot travel only should be respected. Pets must be kept on a leash and the owner should remove the pet's waste. Follow the usual trail code of not leaving any trash on the trails. Do not damage plants, harass wildlife, or play loud radios to disturb the tranquility of the natural areas. Try to avoid having loud cellular telephone conversations at park benches where others are reading or resting.

There are many ways to meet people on the trail. How friendly you are with strangers depends on your personality and the reasons for starting a conversation. Aggressively trying to establish a conversation with others on the trail is not recommended. Sometimes trail users choose the trail for seclusion and that should be respected.

Maps and Locating Trailheads

Although the maps in this guidebook may prove helpful, it is essential that you have a state and city map if you are unfamiliar with the area. Free state maps are available at interstate welcome centers, chambers of commerce, some state and city park offices, and the Highway Map Office (N.C. Department of Transportation, 1 South Wilmington Street, Raleigh, NC 27601; 919-733-7600).

Delorme's detailed *North Carolina Atlas and Gazetteer* is available at bookstores and many convenience stores. County maps can be helpful for rural and isolated areas; these are sold by the NCDOT, chambers of commerce, and county register of deeds offices.

This guidebook describes trailhead locations under the heading "Trailhead(s) and Description." The location of the trailhead is limited to giving you the directions to a nearby street or parking area. Larger and more expansive maps may be needed to locate some areas.

Triangle Traffic

After you have decided which trails to hike and who will go with you, made preparations, listened to the weather report, and acquired your maps, it is time to face Triangle traffic. One reporter from the *News and Observer* described it this way: "Triangle drivers still feel the need for speed . . . they have a taste for heart-stopping lane shifts around slower traffic, the high-speed drift across multiple lanes with no turn signal flashing and other Thunder Road moves." The stress will be less if you leave and return between rush hours. Weekend traffic should be less of a problem. If you have recently moved to the Triangle from other metro locations, you will adjust easily. If you moved here from less populated areas, well, you may have more of an adjustment.

As if we did not already know, the Urban Mobility Study of the Texas Transportation Institute (the nation's largest transportation research organization) reports that traffic congestion will become worse. The study predicts that Triangle drivers will spend 52% of their driving time in congested conditions during rush hours. It is recommended that before you leave your house, you know what interstate or street you can use to avoid congestion. If you miss a turn, be prepared to use your map for guidance and options.

If you arrive at a trailhead and find that parking is not allowed, be prepared with other options. When you finally park your car and see the trailhead sign, you will feel the stress disappearing. The birds are singing, the pine boughs are gently soughing, and if you did not lock your keys in the car, all is right with the world.

Future Trails

Trail planning and construction is going on somewhere in the Triangle every working day. The Mountains-to-Sea Trail, described in the "Mountains-to-Sea Trail Appendix" and the American Tobacco Trail described in Chapter 4 are two of the larger ongoing projects.

Most Triangle cities and towns have long-range plans for greenway networks that offer unlimited options. For example, the Raleigh Parks and Recreation staff continues to work on sections of "Circle the Triangle"—a network of greenways that will offer options of hiking 100-135 miles of trails. Two trails included in that network are Honeycutt Creek sections of Falls Lake Trail (Chapter 1) and Neuse River Trail (in Raleigh section of Chapter 4). Longer-range plans call for Walnut Creek Greenway to connect with Neuse River Trail. The Neuse River Trail, part of the Mountains-to-Sea Trail, will continue downriver into Johnston County. (See "Mountains-to-Sea Trail Appendix" for more details.)

The city of Cary continues to work on Black Creek and White Oak Creek greenways. Proposed future trails will connect Apex, Durham, Raleigh, Morrisville, and Holly Springs. In Morrisville, construction continues on Indian Creek, Crabtree Creek, and Cedar Creek greenways and their connections. In Chapel Hill, proposed trails include Wilson Creek, Meadowmont, Little Creek, and Rail trails.

Trails are also included in the plans for new parks. Cary appears to be the leader with proposals for 18 new parks. Garner has plans for the 96-acre White Deer Park; Chapel Hill for Southern Community and Pritchard parks.

Raleigh has the new Horseshoe Farm Park beside the Neuse River on its northern perimeter. The city is also searching in the same general area for another park, which would offer more athletic facilities. Raleigh's largest park now in planning stages is the 586-acre Forest Ridge Park, which will be located immediately north of Falls Lake Dam. Although the land is owned by the U.S. Army Corps of Engineers, Raleigh and the N.C. Department of Environment and Natural Resources (NCDENR) have a partnership agreement to manage the park. In addition to having more hiking trails, this park will offer more miles of mountain-biking trails than any other area of the Falls Lake system. The initial phase of the park's construction will cost about $2.9 million. It is estimated that the park will cost over $17 million when completed.

A 155-acre farm was bequeathed to the city in 2006. It lies between the U.S. Army Corps of Engineers property on the south side of Falls Lake Dam and Raven Ridge Road. The benefactor, Annie Louise Wilkerson, left specific requests that the land be developed as a nature and wildlife education center. The park will be named Annie Louise Wilkerson, MD Nature Preserve Park.

On the edges of the Triangle, more work is planned on the Haw River trail system to the west and the proposed 70-mile All American Trail through Fort Bragg properties to the south. North of Raleigh, the master plan is drawn for Smith Creek Greenway, which will run from the Neuse River north to NC 98 in Wake Forest.

If you have comments about this guidebook, you can write to:

John F. Blair, Publisher
1406 Plaza Drive
Winston-Salem, NC 27103

You can also email the author at adh4771@aol.com.

The Triangle Area

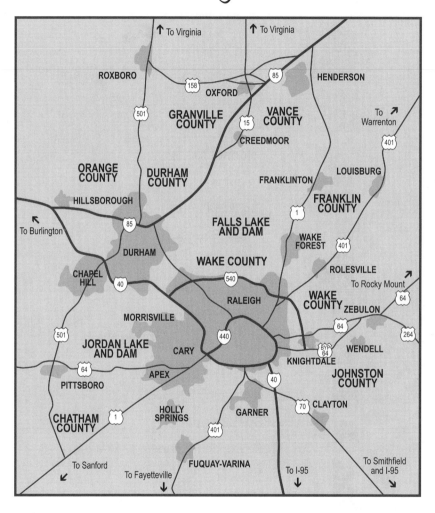

LEGEND FOR MAPS

🚶 - - - - -	Hiking Trail
🚲 🏇 - -	Bicycling, Equestrian, or General
ⅠⅠⅠⅠⅠⅠ	Railroad
P	Parking Lot
?	Information
☏	Telephone
⅋ ⅋⅋	Picnic Table(s)
🏠	Picnic Shelter
🚻	Restroom
▲ ▲▲	Camping / Group Camping
🚶▲	Walk-in Campsite
▣	Amphitheatre
🐟	Fishing
🏊	Swimming
🚤	Boat Ramp
🛶	Kayaking / Canoeing / Boating
🚿	Shower
♿	Wheelchair Accesible

Hikers on Falls Lake Trail near Falls Lake

CHAPTER 1
Trails on U.S. Government Properties

Formed during the early years of the nation as part of the Continental Army, the U.S. Army Corps of Engineers had its beginning at West Point, a garrison on the Hudson River. In 1798, the Corps was enlarged, and in 1802 Congress made West Point a military academy. Since then, Congress has authorized a wide range of Corps projects. Among them have been blazing and building roads, clearing waterways and harbors, building dams for flood control and hydroelectric power, protecting and restoring shorelines, providing natural-disaster relief, ensuring fish and wildlife development, and enhancing recreational opportunities. While emphasizing diversity in recreational usage, the Corps enforces zoning regulations to protect the ecology.

There are four major Corps projects in North Carolina: B. Everett Jordan Dam and Lake (Haw and New Hope rivers), Falls Lake (Neuse River), John H. Kerr Dam and Reservoir (Staunton/Roanoke and Dan rivers), and W. Kerr Scott Dam and Reservoir (Yadkin River). Two of these projects are in counties considered a part of the Triangle and one is in the adjoining region. All were constructed for the major purpose of preventing downstream flood damage. With the exception of the Scott project, acreage is leased by the N.C. Department of Environment and Natural Resources (NCDENR) for recreational purposes and is managed by the Division of Parks and Recreation. These properties are described by the NCDENR as state recreation areas (SRAs). The Corps also leases acreage to the state's Wildlife Resources Commission for wildlife management and motorboat registration on all four projects. Examples of other types of leases are Wilkes County Park at the Scott project and Blue Jay Point County Park at the Falls Lake project and commercial leases such as marinas on all the projects (usually subleased by the NCDENR). All three Corps projects have trails that are described in this book. The first two are in this chapter. Because the third lake project is located outside the central Triangle area, it is described in Chapter 6.

Fishing boat on Jordan Lake

B. Everett Jordan Dam and Lake

B. Everett Jordan Dam and Lake
P.O. Box 144
Moncure, NC 27559
Telephone: 919-542-4501 or 919-542-2227
www.saw.usace.army.mil/jordan/index.htm
To contact rescue squads, the sheriff, or report a fire, call (919-542-2911); for boating and wildlife violations, call (I-800-662-7137); and for weather information, call (I-800-992-7433).

After a hurricane caused a major flood in 1945, the United States Congress instructed the Corps of Engineers to study the historic Cape Fear

River basin for flood control. A lake, known then as New Hope Lake, was authorized in 1963 and constructed in 1967. In 1973, it was renamed in honor of United States senator B. Everett Jordan. In 1982, the lake covered 13,900 acres of the project's 46,768 total acreage. The area is now located in Chatham, Durham, Orange, and Wake counties.

Since then several governmental agencies have shared the management of this land for recreational purposes. This chapter will detail areas controlled by the U.S. Army Corps of Engineers; the North Carolina Division of Parks and Recreation through its State Recreation Areas (SRAs); the North Carolina Division of Forest Resources, and the North Carolina Wildlife Commission. A fifth agency—the Triangle Rails-to-Trails Conservancy—manages five sections of the American Tobacco Trail, which runs through the Corps property. That trail is discussed in detail on pages 149–55. Other than hiking, popular recreational activities in these areas include boating, fishing, water-skiing, sailing, windsurfing, camping, and swimming.

U. S. Army Corps of Engineers

Poe's Ridge Recreation Area

The U.S. Army Corps of Engineers' Visitor and Management Center is more than a headquarters for Jordan Lake. The visitor center is a great source for information. You can pick up a map here that shows the trail network. You can also request a trail map through the mail. The center is open from 8:30 A.M. to 4:30 P.M., Monday through Friday.

Near the visitor center, there is a major observation platform where you can view the dam and lake. A paved walkway descends from the parking area to the dam, where a 0.5-mile round-trip walk begins across the dam. You can also drive to the parking lot at the dam and walk from there.

To access a group of trails, there is a road that descends from the dam's parking area to another parking area at the Tailrace Area and fishing pier. In addition to the trails accessed from the fishing pier, the U.S. Army Corps of Engineers has proposed *Poe's Ridge Trail*, a 3.5-mile natural-surface trail that will travel west from the visitor center to the boat-ramp parking area. The trail plans call for a combination of three loops and two shortcuts through a forest of loblolly pine and hardwoods.

Other facilities at the recreation area include picnicking and fishing at the Tailrace Area, which is open 24 hours a day. No camping, hunting, swimming, bicycling, or horseback riding is allowed in the visitor-center area.

Highland Trail	Fishermens Trail
Midland Trail	Jordan Dam Loop Trail
Creek Side Trail	

Length and Difficulty: 2.1 miles combined; easy

Trailheads and Description: From the junction of U.S.1/U.S.64 in Cary, drive south on U.S. 1 to Exit 79. Turn right and travel west onto Moncure/Pittsboro Road. After 0.3 mile, turn right on Jordan Dam Road and arrive at the visitor center after 2.4 miles. (It is another 0.3 mile to descend to the tailrace.)

Highland Trail is a loop that ascends on a ridge. After descending for 0.3 mile to an old road, the trail connects with *Midland Trail* in the heart of the loop. Both trails connect with *Creek Side Trail*, whose length may vary from 0.5 mile to 1.0 mile, depending on whether you follow part of Highland Trail. Along the hike, there are bridges over ravines, steps, a grove of shagbark hickory, and quartz rock that is located on a ridge.

Creek Side Trail connects with *Fishermens Trail* near the Haw River, downstream from the fishing pier. Although the signboard and map may state the trails have red blazes, you may also find blue and white markers. To hike the 0.5-mile *Jordan Dam Loop* follow the scenic road across the dam and then backtrack. (Another trail is in the planning stages.)

N.C. Division of Parks & Recreation

The N.C. Division of Parks and Recreation oversees the State Recreation Areas (SRAs) in this project. All SRAs require fees for camping and reserved picnic shelters. Day-use fees are charged only between Memorial Day and Labor Day, although there may be some fees on weekends in late spring and early fall. The four SRAs described below have specifically named foot trails. As facilities continue to develop, visitors are requested to call in advance for an update on services.

There are five campgrounds in the Jordan Lake project. Vista Point and New Hope Overlook SRAs have detailed trail information below. Vista Point has group camps and RV sites; New Hope offers a boat ramp, fishing, and hike-in tent camping. Of all the SRAs, New Hope has the longest hiking trail.

Poplar Point SRA and Crosswinds SRA provide tent and RV sites with hot showers. Unnamed, but connected, walking trails for registered campers are between A, B, and C campgrounds and boat ramps. For Crosswinds campers, there is a beach. At both campgrounds, the facilities are open only to registered campers.

Parker's Creek SRA has tent, RV, and group campsites, with boat ramps for campers only. Walking trails are for registered campers only, except for the 0.5-mile *Children's Nature Trail* at picnic shelter #3.

> Jordan Lake SRA Office
> 280 State Park Road
> Apex, NC 27523
> Telephone: 919-362-0586; fax: 919-362-2621
> www.ils.unc.edu/parkproject/visit/jord/home.html

Ebenezer Church State Recreation Area

Old Oak Trail (0.9 mile, easy)
Ebenezer Church Trail (1.0 mile, easy)

Trailheads and Description: From the junction of U.S. 64 and NC 751, drive 3.7 miles west on U.S. 64 and turn left (south) onto State Park Road, the last road before crossing a causeway/bridge on U.S. 64. Access is off U.S. 64 at the junction with Beaver Creek Road (SR 1008) in Wilsonville. Drive south for 2.1 miles and turn right. Take the first road to the right after the entrance and park on the east side of the parking lot at a trail sign.

Hike the red-blazed *Old Oak Trail* past a bamboo grove at a sign about diving ducks at 0.4 mile. Complete a loop of 0.9 mile through a pine forest and tall oaks. Return to the entrance road, drive right, and park at the nearest access to the lake on the left at a picnic area; there is a sign for Ebenezer Church. Follow the red-blazed *Ebenezer Church Trail* (for foot traffic only) on an old road. After nearly 0.2 mile, the former site of the historic church is to the right, but turn left off the road. Walk through a young forest, cross a paved road at 0.4 mile, curve around a tranquil small pond, cross the road again, and return to the parking area at 1.0 mile.

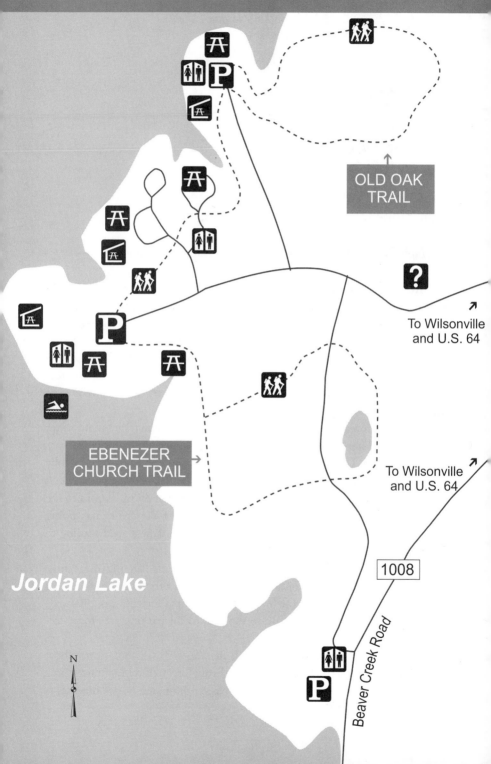

OLD OAK
TRAIL

To Wilsonville
and U.S. 64

EBENEZER
CHURCH TRAIL

To Wilsonville
and U.S. 64

1008

Jordan Lake

N

Beaver Creek Road

New Hope Overlook Trail at Jordan Lake

New Hope Overlook State Recreation Area

New Hope Overlook Trail (5.4 miles round-trip; moderate)

Trailhead and Description: From Cary/Apex, drive south on U.S. 1 to Exit 81 (Pea Ridge Road). Turn right on Pea Ridge Road (SR 1972) and drive 2.9 miles. Turn left onto W.H. Jones Road (SR 1974). Drive 0.5 mile farther on W. H. Jones Road to the entrance-fee station where there is a fork. Continue right to a parking area and restroom on the left. Ahead is an access to a boat ramp. The trail is exceptionally well designed and constructed. It makes a loop between Areas A and B—two walk-in campgrounds. The mileages listed below are cumulative.

Enter the forest at the trail sign and follow the red markers in a former tobacco field. After 92 yards, begin the loop. If hiking counterclockwise, pass an old homesite. The forest is composed of hardwoods and scattered loblolly pines. The understory is chiefly holly and sparkleberry. There are scenic views of the lake at 0.5 mile. At 0.8 mile, an overlook spur of 85 yards goes to the right. A bench is there for a peaceful observation of the peninsula's point. Ascend and then descend until you cross the gravel access road leading to Area A's walk-in campsites at 1.0 mile.

For the next mile, gentle trail undulations are situated among rock cairns. At 2.2 miles, there is a junction with a blue-blazed shortcut on the left, which will take you around half of the loop. (If taking this shortcut, it is 140 yards to another left, which returns you to the trail to the parking area for a 2.7-mile loop.)

If continuing on the full-loop trail, the route crosses occasional short footbridges, parallels the lake, and passes through scattered mountain laurel. At 3.5 miles, cross a ravine in a holly grove. At 3.6 miles, notice the trail is

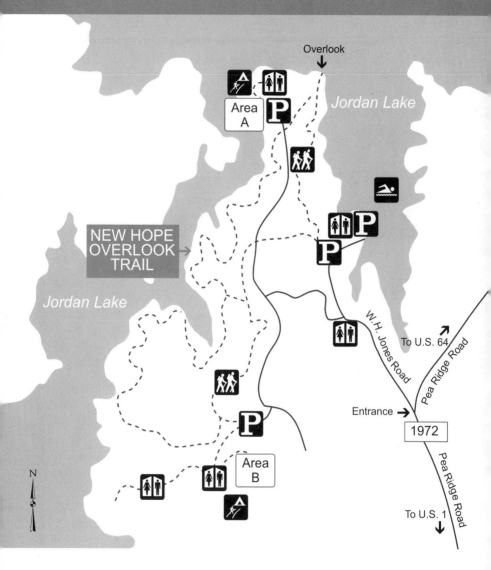

Overlook

Jordan Lake

Area A

NEW HOPE OVERLOOK TRAIL

Jordan Lake

W. H. Jones Road

To U.S. 64

Pea Ridge Road

Entrance

1972

Pea Ridge Road

To U.S. 1

N

Area B

SEAFORTH STATE RECREATION AREA
POND TRAIL

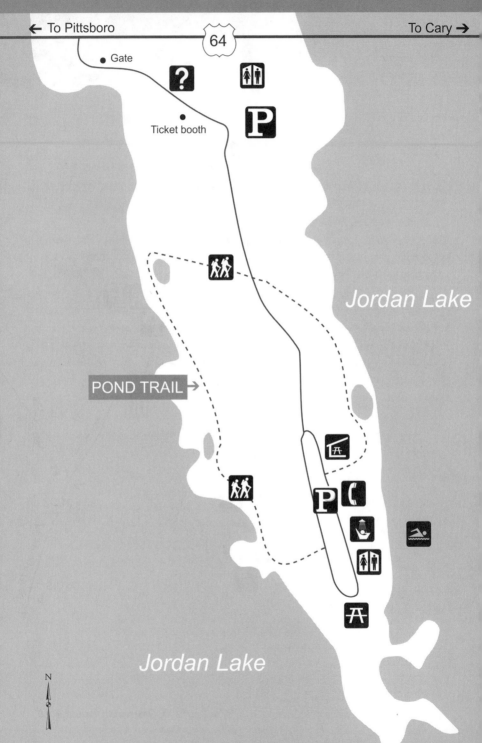

curving away from the lake. By 3.8 miles, there is a steep ascent. At 4.0 miles, there is a gravel road on the right that leads to the parking area and walk-in campsites in Area B. At 4.8 miles, arrive at the blue-blazed connector trail for the short loop mentioned above. At 5.1 miles, cross the gravel road, which was crossed earlier. It leads to Area A walk-in campsites. Ascend steps and make a gradual descent to complete the loop.

Seaforth State Recreation Area

▓ Pond Trail (1.6 miles, easy)

Trailhead and Description: From Wilsonville, drive 2.4 miles west on U.S. 64 to the intersection of Beaver Dam and Farrington Point roads. Continue on U.S. 64. After crossing the lake's causeway/bridge, turn left (south).

Park near the end of the parking area across from the beach bathhouse and enter the red-blazed trail through an oak forest mixed with loblolly pine. At 0.2 mile, cross a boardwalk for an exceptionally beautiful view of the lake. By the boardwalk are lizard's tail, marshmallow, and fragrant buttonbush. Circle left of a pond with an active beaver hutch at 0.6 mile, then pass through a field of lespedeza, cross the entrance road, walk through a loblolly-pine forest, pass a former pond site with willows, and exit at a picnic shelter. Cross the parking area for a return to the point of origin.

Vista Point State Recreation Area

▌ Vista Point Red Trail (2.7 miles, easy)
▌ Vista Point Blue Trail (1.2 miles, easy)

Trailheads and Description: From Wilsonville, drive west on U.S. 64 for 3.4 miles to Griffins Crossroads, which is 5 miles east of Pittsboro. Turn left onto North Pea Ridge Road (SR 1700). Drive 2.5 miles to Vista Point SRA. Park on the right before the entrance-fee booth.

The red-blazed *Vista Point Red Trail* is for foot traffic only. It begins at either the RV group campground's shower house or picnic shelter #7 for a loop through a mixed forest of oak, maple, and pine. At 0.7 mile, there is a proposed loop extension. At 0.8 mile, there is a lake view to the left. At 1.1

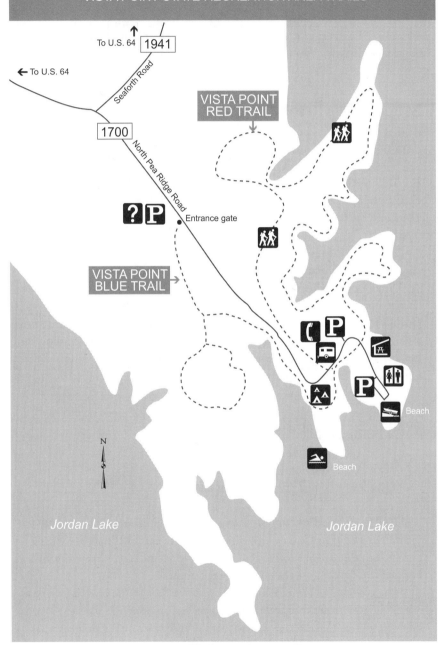

VISTA POINT STATE RECREATION AREA TRAILS

To U.S. 64
1941

← To U.S. 64

Seaforth Road

VISTA POINT
RED TRAIL

1700

North Pea Ridge Road

Entrance gate

VISTA POINT
BLUE TRAIL

Beach

Beach

N

Jordan Lake

Jordan Lake

miles is evidence of former tobacco rows. At 1.2 miles, curve in and out of a series of coves, sometimes passing close enough to view the lake through the trees. Footbridges cross the ravines. Forest growth remains the same, with occasional holly, sparkleberry, and fern beds. Pass left of a group RV campground at 2.3 miles and right of a picnic shelter at 2.5 miles. At 2.6 miles, cross a paved road to complete the loop at picnic shelter #7.

Blue-blazed *Vista Point Blue Trail* is located at the parking area at the entrance gate on the right. Follow it through the forest to make a loop around an old tobacco barn and wellhouse. Either return to the parking area or take a linear route to parallel the entrance road, going toward a field near the campground ticket booth. Backtrack.

N.C. Division of Forest Resources
Jordan Lake Educational State Forest

Like other state forests in North Carolina, this one serves as a living environmental center, providing information to improve the understanding of forest values. It has a network of trails to illustrate its mission. The state forest is leased from the Jordan Lake U.S. Army Corps of Engineers. Usage is for hiking only. To hike the trails, it is recommended that you have a map from the center to differentiate the trails from the roads. Other facilities and services are restrooms, shelters, group sites for picnicking, and ranger-conducted classes. The forest is open year-round except Thanksgiving and Christmas Day. Contact the forest office or use the website for office hours. *Note*: a 1.2-mile *Upland Trail* has been proposed on the west side of Big Woods Road, about 0.3 mile south of the forest's entrance.

The four hikes that are available are listed together because they can be combined for one hike.

> Jordan Lake Educational State Forest
> 2832 Big Woods Road
> Chapel Hill, NC 27514
> Telephone: 919-542-1154
> www.ncesf.org/JLESF/home.htm

Lowlands Trail (0.8 mile, easy)
Talking Tree Trail (0.4 mile, easy)

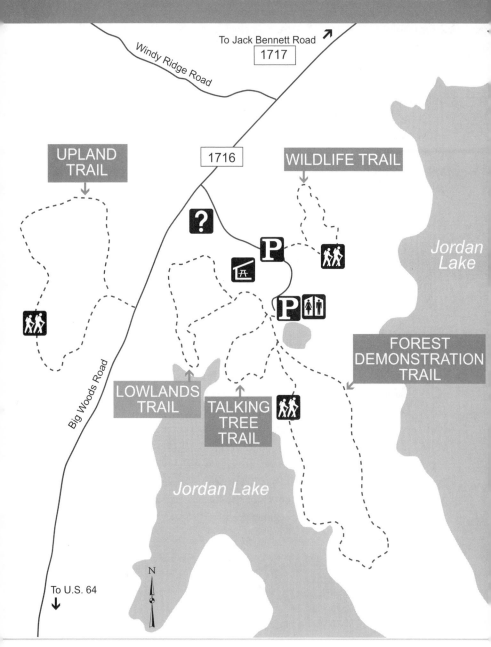

Forest Demonstration Trail (1.5 miles, easy)
Wildlife Trail (0.6 mile, easy)

Trailheads and Description: On U.S. 64, drive 3.3 miles west of Wilsonville to Big Woods Road. Turn right and travel north on Big Woods Road for 2.7 miles. The state forest entrance is on the right.

From the parking and picnic area, look for the trail signs. If choosing the yellow-blazed *Lowlands Trail,* descend and cross a footbridge at 0.1 mile. At 0.2 mile, there is a fork. If walking left, follow the stream. Examples of tree burls are seen along the way. At 0.3 mile, near the lake, there is a kiosk with information about waterfowl. Continuing on the loop, there will be signs about the forest's upland and lowland trees, wildlife, and floodplains.

To access the route to the red-blazed *Talking Tree Trail* from the parking area, walk near the log cabin. The trail makes a short loop of 0.4 mile. It has a few interpretive sites where you can hear recorded messages about tree identifications.

To reach the green-blazed *Demonstration Trail,* walk south of the log cabin about 60 yards to a fork. If walking to the right, slightly descend to a boardwalk at 0.2 mile. At 0.3 mile, there is an example of one cord of wood's measurement. Enter an open forest of loblolly pine, then pass the edge of the lake at 0.4 mile. Turn away from the lake at 0.7 mile. Pass a wildlife food plot at 1.2 miles. Cross a boardwalk and return to complete the loop.

To hike the blue-blazed *Wildlife Trail* from the parking area, walk past the restroom. At 0.4 mile, cross a bridge over an intermittent stream. Old tobacco rows are noticeable at 0.6 mile. After passing a forest-management information sign, complete the loop.

N.C. Wildlife Resources Commission

New Hope Game Lands

With permission from the N.C. Wildlife Resources Commission, environmentally sensitive volunteer organizations created and maintain a few trails in this area. The trails are used mainly by hikers, bird watchers, photographers, and sometimes hunters and fishermen. Two of the trails are described here. Mileage counts are cumulative for each trail.

Weaver Creek Trail (4.0 miles round-trip; easy to moderate)

Trailhead and Description: From the junction of U.S. 64 and Beaver Creek Road (SR 1008) at Wilsonville, drive south on Beaver Creek Road; and cross a bridge over Jordan Lake. At 3.7 miles, turn right on Pea Ridge Road (SR 1972). After 1.1 miles, turn left at the intersection with Lower Thrift Road (SR 1907). Park in the gravel parking area.

At the trailhead, there may not be a trail sign because the first mile of this section of the forest may be scheduled for a selective timber cut. Enter the forest on a narrow yellow-blazed hiking trail. If hiking during hunting season, wear an orange-blazed jacket and cap. The seasons begin with dove and quail around September 1 and last through deer season, which ends on February 28. Call 800-662-7350 for information.

This classic forest path features hardwoods and loblolly pine with an extraordinary understory of holly. Decorating the forest floor are ferns and club moss, wild orchids, ginger, and windflower. Wildlife is prominent, particularly deer and squirrel. Puff adders have been seen. Among the many bird species are downy woodpecker, Carolina chickadee, and song sparrow.

Follow yellow blazes for 0.1 mile to a signboard showing a Jordan Lake map and charts about forest trees and wildlife. At 0.4 mile, the trail begins to meander until it crosses a footbridge, followed by a short boardwalk. At 0.9 mile, reach a fork. (A sign at 1.0 mile may have been moved to the fork because of a nearby forest burn on the left. After the area has been cleared, the sign may be back in its proper location.) Turn left and after a few yards, enter a timber cut and cross a fire rim. On a ridge, cross an old forest road, which is now used by ATVs. To the left of the trail on the old forest road, there are views of and access to the lake. To the right of the road, it is 0.3 mile to access the saddle dam. If you take this access, you can make a shorter loop of this trail.

At 1.3 miles on the main trail, descend to cross a footbridge in a marshy area. Between 1.6 and 1.9 miles, ascend to another ridge and descend to more marsh. After crossing a fire rim, access a wide grassy saddle dam and turn right. To the left are scenic views of the lake. On the saddle dam, there are high views of the terrain. Below the saddle dam are small pools with spring peepers. At 2.3 miles, pass the old forest road on the right for a shorter loop. Arrive at a gate at 2.8 miles. Turn right into the forest and descend at 0.3 mile to complete the loop. Turn left to return to the parking area.

NEW HOPE GAME LANDS
WEAVER CREEK TRAIL

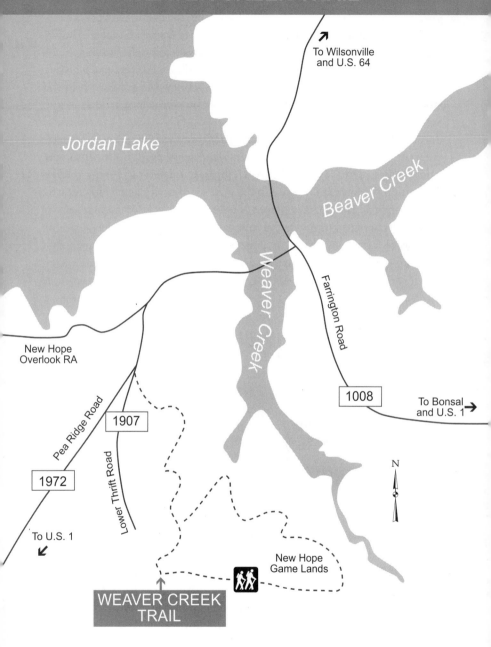

To Wilsonville
and U.S. 64

Jordan Lake

Beaver Creek

Weaver Creek

Farrington Road

New Hope
Overlook RA

1008

To Bonsal
and U.S. 1

Pea Ridge Road

1907

Lower Thrift Road

1972

N

To U.S. 1

New Hope
Game Lands

WEAVER CREEK
TRAIL

▌ Wildlife Observation Trail (1.6 miles round-trip; easy)

Trailhead and Description: To access the trail from I-40, take Exit 274 and go south on NC 751 for 6.5 miles to a sign on the right. From U.S. 64 and NC 751, drive north on NC 751 for 5.6 miles for a left turn, which is a few yards past New Hope Road's west end. Follow the gravel road to the parking site. At the trail entrance, there may be a brochure printed by the New Hope Audubon Society.

At 0.1 mile, a fork for the loop trail leads into the forest. Proceed right if you want to follow the order of the numbered signs. At sign #3, which tells about raptors, there is a kiosk. Approach the lake and curve left to the wildlife observation platform at 0.7 mile. To the west is a view of Eagle Point, located on a peninsula. The point is named for the bald eagles sometimes seen in the area. Between signs #8 (at 0.8 mile) and #9 (at 1.0 mile) is evidence of old tobacco farm rows. After crossing some streambeds that are usually dry, ascend to complete the loop to the parking site.

Falls Lake

> **Corps of Engineers Resource Management Office**
> **11405 Falls of Neuse Road**
> **Wake Forest, NC 27587**
> **Telephone: 919-846-9332**
> **www.saw.usace.army.mil/Falls/index.htm**

Like Jordan Lake, the Falls Lake project is a U.S. Army Corps of Engineers project. It encompasses 38,886 acres in Durham, Granville, and Wake counties—11,620 of water and 27,266 of land. Falls Lake received its name from the Falls of the Neuse, a short section of rapids below the dam. It also serves as the major water source for the city of Raleigh.

The project has 12 public-use locations, seven of which are recreation areas under the auspices of the Falls Lake State Recreation Area, managed by the N.C. Division of Parks and Recreation. They will be discussed in detail below. Boating, water-skiing, sailing, fishing, and picnicking are the major activities.

Hiking the more than 35 miles of *Falls Lake Trail* that are now completed is another significant recreational activity. This trail, which has been designated as part of the *Mountains-to-Sea Trail*, is described ahead. It is located on the southern boundary of the lake and passes mainly through game lands of the N.C. Wildlife Resources Commission. It also passes through Rolling View and Shinleaf recreation areas.

The U.S. Army Corps of Engineers' office serves as headquarters for the Falls Lake reservoir and dam area. In addition to administrative offices, it has displays about the history of the project as well as animals and plants in the area. Its location high on the south side of the lake provides scenic views of the lake and beyond. There are picnic sites near the visitors parking area.

To reach an alternate approach to the *Falls Lake Trail/Mountains-to-Sea Trail*, follow the white-blazed Mountains-to-Sea Trail (MST) from the parking area at the tailrace and branch off to the left onto *Blue Dot Trail*, a light blue-blazed alternate MST. It rejoins MST to make a 1.5-mile loop, which passes by the Corps headquarters.

Long Leaf Trail comes from the parking area at the entrance gate at Falls of the Neuse Road. The 0.75-mile (one-way) hike parallels the entrance road to the visitor center. This walk provides access to the visitor center and picnic areas when the entrance gate is locked. Along the way, there are educational panels, which describe long-leaf-pine restoration. This trail connects with a 0.7-mile *Nature Trail* loop designed for children. It circles the visitor center and uses parts of the MST and Blue Dot Trail. The trail features interpretive markers that explain biological topics.

At the southern base of the dam is another parking area. A short, paved trail leads from here to views of the tailrace and scattered boulders in the rapids of the Neuse River. From the parking area, you can also find picnic shelters and riverside fishing options. This parking area is the current eastern trailhead for the Falls Lake Trail. The western route, which avoids ascending to the dam, offers the alternate route, mentioned above. This route crosses the road on top of the dam and leads directly to the management office.

ACCESS: To reach the U.S. Army Corps of Engineers' office from the intersection of Falls of Neuse and Raven Ridge roads, drive north on Falls of the Neuse Road for 1.0 mile. Turn left at a Corps sign or stay north on Falls of the Neuse to a left turn into the Falls Lake parking area below the dam.

To access the parking area at the base of the dam from west of Wake Forest, turn onto Old NC 98 Road at the Falls Lake sign. After driving 0.6 mile, make a sharp left turn onto Falls of Neuse

Road. Follow this road for 2.4 miles. After crossing a bridge, the parking area will be on the right. Farther south on Falls of Neuse Road is the entrance to the Corps office on the right. Coming from I-540, take Exit 14 and drive north on Falls of Neuse Road for 2.6 miles. The turn into the entrance is on the left.

N.C. Division of Parks and Recreation

Falls Lake State Recreation Area

Falls Lake SRA Management Office
13304 Creedmoor Road
Wake Forest, NC 27587
Telephone: 919-676-1027; fax: 919-676-2954
www.ils.unc.edu/parkproject/visit/fala/home.html

The following seven recreation areas are located within the Falls Lake State Recreation Area: Beaverdam, B.W. Wells, Highway 50, Holly Point, Rolling View, Sandling Beach, and Shinleaf.

Highway 50 Recreation Area does not have camping facilities or designated trails. However, it does have a large area for boating. Boat ramps are located at the dock. Nearby, you can find picnic sites, restrooms, and areas for fishing along the banks. It also has a scenic view of Beaver Dam and its spillway. Steps and a switchback path lead to a bridge over the spillway and a walk across the dam. The recreation area is located on NC 50, 2.7 miles north of NC 98.

The only trails that Holly Point Recreation Area has are those that run between camping areas. It does have a campground that accepts reservations. The campground offers electric and water hookups, group campsites, a boat ramp, a fishing pier, a swimming beach, picnic sites, and a children's playground. It is open only from March 15 to October 31. To get to Holly Point from NC 98, travel north on New Light Road (SR 1907) for 2.0 miles. Turn right to reach the park's entrance.

B.W. Wells Recreation Area has group campsites that accept reservations. The campground offers showers, a boat ramp, and picnic sites. The Wells Rock Cliff Farm is in this area, but it is closed to vehicular traffic. The historic farm has a network of short forest and wildflower nature trails that connect to an interpretive center. For information and tour arrangements, contact B. W. Wells Association, Inc., at 919-859-1187.

Rolling View Recreation Area offers camping facilities that offer handicapped-accessible and group campsites. Reservations are accepted. The campground has electric and water hookups, showers, a boat ramp and marina, a boat beach, a swim beach, a fishing pier, picnic sites and shelters, hiking trails, an amphitheater, a community building, a playground, and 3.2 miles (including some backtracking) of well-designed, white-blazed, unnamed connecting trails to the beaches, picnic shelters, the campground, and the community building. From the parking lot for the swimming beach, the trails offer a 1.7-mile round-trip hike in an oak and pine forest to the family campground and a 1.5-mile round-trip hike, also in an oak and pine forest, to the group campground and the community building. On a connector trail between loops A and B in the family campground is a scenic spot with a small waterfall and pool under an overhanging rock. Buckeye and saxifrage grow on the stream banks. To access Rolling View, drive 5.9 miles west on NC 98 to Baptist Road. Turn right onto Baptist Road and travel 4.0 miles to the park entrance.

Shinleaf Recreation Area is a hike-in primitive area for camping only. It has restrooms and showers near the campsites. It is located on the Falls Lake Trail route. (See Section #3 of *Falls Lake Trail* ahead.) To access Shinleaf, drive 1.6 miles east on NC 98 to a left turn onto New Light Road. After 0.6 mile, you will reach the entrance on the right.

Beaverdam and Sandling Beach recreation areas do not have camping facilities, but they do have trails, which are discussed in detail below.

ACCESS: To reach the Falls Lake State Recreation Area Management Office from the intersection of NC 50 and NC 98, drive north on NC 50. After 1.6 miles, turn right at the entrance sign.

Beaverdam Recreation Area

Beaverdam has a boat ramp, swimming beach, picnic sites, picnic shelters (reservations are recommended), restrooms, fishing piers, a bathhouse, a children's playground, two nature trails (constructed by Eagle Scouts and other organizations), and four mountain-biking trails (constructed by members of North Raleigh Mountain Biking Association and other volunteers).

Waterfowl Observation Trail (1.2 miles round-trip; easy)

Trailhead and Description: From the intersection of NC 98 and NC 50, drive north on NC 50 (Creedmoor Road) for 4.0 miles to a right turn into Beaverdam Recreation Area. Pass a gatehouse (no fee is charged in the winter). For mountain-bike trailheads, turn left at all forks. For parking and restrooms, turn right near the trailheads. For the nature trails, stay right on the main road for 1.1 miles. Park at the far side of the loop parking lot. At the wood's edge is a nature sign constructed by Eagle Scout Troop 314 and a footbridge built by Troop 215. Follow the orange-blazed footpath through a predominantly pine forest. There is evidence of former tobacco rows along the way. At 0.2 mile, cross a gravel road. At 0.4 mile, cross the last of four bridges. Ascend to an old forest road, which is located in a mixed forest with a holly and sparkleberry understory. After 0.6 mile, turn left and descend to a waterfowl observation blind. Retrace the trail back to the parking lot.

Beaverdam Loop Interpretive Trail (1.6 miles round-trip; easy to moderate)

Trailhead and Description: From the parking area at the trailhead for the *Waterfowl Observation Trail*, drive back to the main road. Take a right, and curve around the loop that travels by picnic sites and shelters to the last picnic parking lot on the right.

Enter the woods at a signboard and descend left of a picnic table. Follow the orange-blazed trail to where the loop begins but stay right. After 0.2 mile, cross a bridge over a branch. The loop continues to the left but a sign indicates an access on the right to a parking lot and picnic shelters at 0.1 mile. The parking lot is the third lot from the entrance road to that particular group of picnic sites and shelters.

Follow the loop trail upstream, walking among tall pines in a prescribed fire burn. Pass through a large patch of Christmas fern and then ascend a ridge. At 0.7 mile, begin the return. After crossing a bridge, which was constructed by Eagle Scout Troop 215, ascend and descend ridges to complete the loop in 1.4 miles. Turn right, where the loop is completed and return to the parking lot.

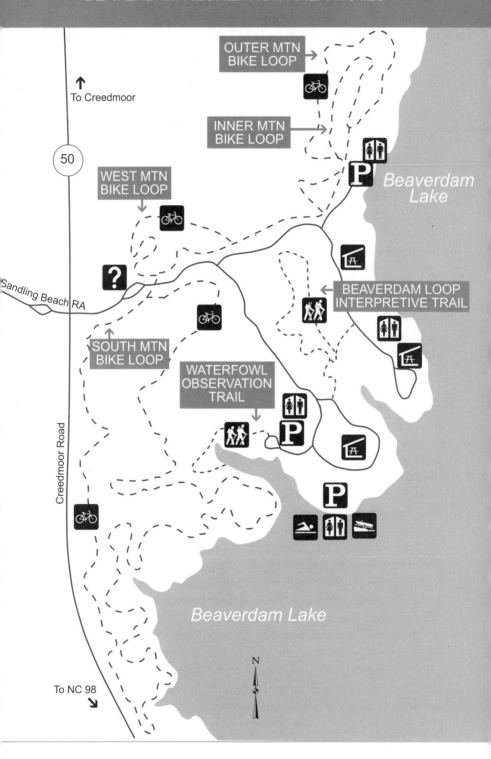

BEAVERDAM RECREATION AREA TRAILS

To Creedmoor

50

Sandling Beach RA

Creedmoor Road

To NC 98

OUTER MTN BIKE LOOP

INNER MTN BIKE LOOP

WEST MTN BIKE LOOP

Beaverdam Lake

BEAVERDAM LOOP INTERPRETIVE TRAIL

SOUTH MTN BIKE LOOP

WATERFOWL OBSERVATION TRAIL

Beaverdam Lake

N

Beaverdam Bike Loop in the Beaverdam Recreation Area of Falls State Recreation Area

Outer Mountain Bike Loop Trail (2.6 miles)
Inner Mountain Bike Loop Trail (1.4 miles)
West Mountain Bike Loop Trail (2.4 miles)
South Mountain Bike Loop Trail (7.2 miles)

Length and Difficulty: 13.6 miles combined; easy to strenuous

Trailheads and Description: From the mountain-bike parking area, cross the access road to the signboard and central trailhead. These four loop trails were constructed by mountain-bikers and are used primarily by cyclists. However, hikers can use these trails. Hikers might want to walk the trails in the opposite direction of cyclists for better visibility.

The outer and inner loops are designed for beginning more than advanced cyclists. Mileages given below are cumulative.

At the central trailhead, go right to reach the green-blazed *Outer Mountain Bike Loop Trail*. Descend through a hardwood forest and infrequent loblolly pines to cross a footbridge at 0.25 mile. In late February and early March, you can hear the mating calls of spring peepers in the streambeds. From 0.6 mile to 1.3 miles, there are occasional views of the lake and the Old Weaver Trail Road bridge. At 1.8 miles, take a sharp left. At 2.0 miles, follow the Corps of Engineers boundary line. At 2.4 miles, there is a connection with the *Inner Mountain Bike Loop Trail* on the left. (If following this yellow-blazed trail, it passes through a hardwood forest with scattered holly for 1.2 miles.) To complete the Outer Mountain Bike Loop Trail instead, stay right of the other trail connections with a different return through a low area and tall trees to the parking area road at 2.6 miles.

To follow the red-blazed *West Mountain Bike Loop Trail*, begin at the information sign and turn left after 80 yards. After 0.2 mile, cross over a small stream on a high wooden bridge with railings. At 0.5 mile, reach a fork. If staying right, at 0.8 mile the trail becomes more rugged and hilly with a few dips. At 1.4 miles, cross a small wooden bridge over a dry ravine. At 1.8

miles, come to a junction with the blue-blazed *South Mountain Bike Loop Trail*, near the park's gatehouse. Continuing to the left, the trail parallels the road to the parking area. At 2.0 miles, the trail crosses a service road. At 2.4 miles, the loop is completed.

The blue-blazed South Mountain Bike Loop Trail is a more advanced route. There is not a parking area near the gatehouse for this access. From the intersection with the West Loop Trail, cross the entrance road. After 45 yards, at the fork, ride to the right. At 0.3 mile, cross a footbridge over a branch. At 0.5 mile, there is a scenic area. At 0.7 mile, cross a gravel service road. At 1.0 mile, curve left on an old road. To the right, you will hear traffic sounds from NC 50. There is a dip at 1.4 miles, followed by an ascent. At 1.8 miles, descend to another dip. At 2.3 miles, turn left near an old homesite. Begin a descent. At 2.4 miles, bikers have carved a flat "skinnie" about 20 feet long on an oak log. There may be some log piles in this area. At 2.5 miles and 2.8 miles, there are views (particularly in the wintertime) of Beaverdam Lake. Turn left at 3.1 miles. At 3.6 miles, there is a log pile on a slope, which can be used for a stunt leap. At 3.7 miles, there is a large spread of Christmas fern. After a bridge at 4.1 miles, there are some steep hills, ravines, and coves. Repeated energy pedaling is necessary for about 0.5 mile. There are more views of Beaverdam Lake at 4.8, 5.0, and 5.3 miles. Some of the views are of the beach at Beaverdam Lake picnic area. At 6.0 miles, cross a ravine and stream. At 6.7 miles, cross a long bridge over a branch in a scenic area of large lobolly pines. Gradually ascend to the entrance road and gatehouse at 7.2 miles.

Sandling Beach Recreation Area

Sandling Beach Recreation Area offers swimming, trails, a boat launch, fishing on the lake banks, and picnic shelters.

▌ Woodland Nature Trail (0.7 mile, easy)

Trailhead and Description: Sandling Beach Recreation Area is located on NC 50, across the road from the Beaverdam Recreation Area entrance. From Creedmoor, go 5.5 miles south on NC 50 before turning right into the entrance.

Across the road from the parking lot of picnic shelter #1, enter the forest for an interpretive loop with 24 stations. The educational trip is through mixed hardwoods of oak, beech, yellow poplar, and hornbeam. Evergreens

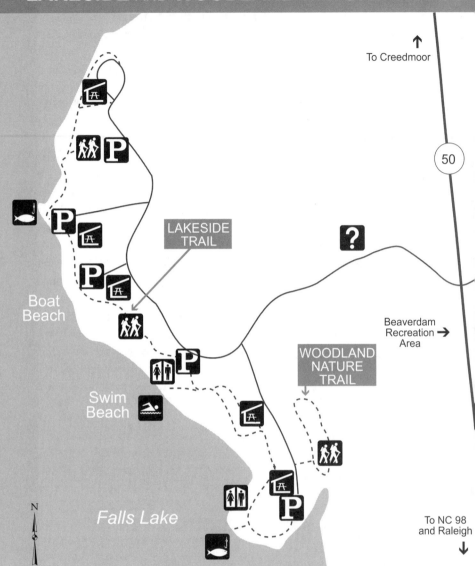

To Creedmoor

50

LAKESIDE
TRAIL

?

Beaverdam
Recreation
Area

Boat
Beach

WOODLAND
NATURE
TRAIL

Swim
Beach

Falls Lake

N

To NC 98
and Raleigh

seen include pine, holly, and cedar. Ferns and club moss are part of the ground cover. After descending, the trail goes upstream among tall trees. At 0.3 mile, a unique sycamore and a maple with pyramid-shaped roots can be seen. After ascending a ridge, complete the loop.

Lakeside Trail (1.7 miles, easy)

Trailhead and Description: Across the road from the *Woodland Nature Trail*, drive to the south parking lot near picnic shelter #1. From the beginning trailhead to the trail's end, the lake scenery and forest cover are appealing. At 0.4 mile, near picnic shelter #2, the trail divides. To the right, the trail passes picnic shelter #3; to the left, it goes closer to the lake but rejoins the other trail at 0.6 mile. At 0.8 mile, pass a parking area and access to the beach. At 0.9 mile, pass access to parking areas at the boat launch near picnic shelters #4 and #5. At 1.6 miles, pass the last picnic shelter (#7). The route approaches the north end of the trail at a parking lot.

Falls Lake Trail

The dream for the construction of the *Falls Lake Trail* began with staff members of the N.C. Division of Parks and Recreation in the early 1970s. The hiking trail would extend for 50 to 60 miles along the south shore of Falls Lake, from the lake's dam at Falls of Neuse Road in Raleigh west to Penny's Bend Nature Preserve at Old Oxford Highway in Durham.

Although the U.S. Army Corps of Engineers and the state would be supportive, the construction was completed mainly by volunteers. The trail's image became more significant when it was promoted as part of the *Mountains-to-Sea Trail*. Well-designed and well-maintained, the first section of 13.2 miles was designated as a state trail as part of the Mountains-to-Sea Trail (MST) on April 11, 1987. Other sections that extend for another 12.9 miles to NC 50 have since been completed and joined the MST designation.

In 2006, the Friends of the Mountains-to-Sea Trail established a Memorandum of Agreement between the U.S. Army Corps of Engineers, N.C. Division of Parks and Recreation, N.C. Wildlife Resources Commission, and Durham County for continuing the trail construction to Penny's Bend Nature Preserve. In the same year the city of Durham and the Friends of the Mountains-to-Sea Trail signed an agreement for extending construction of the MST from Penny's Bend to the West Point on the Eno Park. (See

Bridge building on Falls Lake Trail at Falls Lake
Photo by Arthur Kelley

"Trails in Municipal Parks and Recreation Areas—Durham" and "Trails in N.C. State Parks—Eno River State Park" for more information on the MST routing.)

The trail presently passes through a hardwood forest, weaves in and out of coves, crosses numerous small drainages, ascends to a number of gentle ridges, and offers outstanding scenic views of the lake. The mature forest has a few old-growth trees and some specific evidence of succession. For example, in a few places young growth can be found among former tobacco rows. Holly, mountain laurel, loblolly pine, Christmas fern, wild ginger, and club moss comprise the winter greenery. Among the ferns are royal, cinnamon, sensitive, resurrection, ebony, and southern lady. Wildflowers include three species of wild orchid, coral bell, squirrel cup, mandrake, yellow root, and spring beauty. Some of the more evident mammals are deer, beavers, foxes, squirrels, and raccoons. Wildfowl includes American eagle, osprey, ducks, geese, and dozens of bird species.

The trail is currently divided into at least twenty sections. Twelve of those sections are completed; the others are either under construction or in planning stages. The completed sections are described in more detail below.

From Falls of Neuse Road to Six Forks Road
Section 1: Honeycutt Creek, East
Section 2: Honeycutt Creek, West
Section 3: Neuse Bend Point
Section 4: Cedar Creek
Section 5: Loblolly Point

Length and Difficulty: 13.2 miles; easy to moderate. Mileages given are cumulative for hiking Sections 1-5 together.

Trailheads and Description: The eastern trailhead is at the Tailwater Fishing Access Area parking lot, located below the dam on Falls of Neuse Road (SR 2000) in north Raleigh. To access the trailhead from the junction of U.S. 1 and NC 98 at Wake Forest, drive 0.7 mile west on NC 98 to Old U.S. 98, turn left, then follow the signs 2.4 miles to the parking area across the bridge and to the right. Other access points will be described along the trail route. The trailhead has a white blaze and sign; it is located in front of the restrooms. (Avoid the path leading up to the dam.)

To begin *Section 1 (Honeycutt Creek, East)*, follow an old service road where white blazes line the route. The trail goes into a forest of loblolly pine, sweet gum, tulip poplar, and oak with an understory of holly and dogwood. At 0.1 mile, turn left on a foot trail. After 110 yards, the trail forks near a unique double tulip poplar. Take either route. (The blue-blazed trail, to the left, goes 0.6 mile before rejoining the main trail.) Turn right and cross the paved dam road to stay on the main trail. Arrive at the parking lot of the Corps' Operational Management Center at 0.3 mile. Follow the lakeside road; at 0.5 mile, reenter the forest, which features scattered jessamine and redbud. At 0.9 mile, cross a Corps service road and a junction with the blue-blazed alternate route described earlier. Turn right at the junction with the blue-blazed trail. At 1.5 miles, cross a pipeline right-of-way. At 2.0 miles, there is a scenic stream area. At 2.3 and 2.6 miles, cross footbridges over streams. Pass some fine views of the lake between the streams. At 3.4 miles, arrive at Raven Ridge Road (SR 2002) to complete Section 1. If you turn left onto Raven Ridge Road, it is 3.9 miles to the intersection of Raven Ridge Road and Falls of Neuse Road and the eastern trailhead.

To continue on *Section 2 (Honeycutt Creek, West)*, turn right at 3.5 miles and cross the Honeycutt Creek causeway to reenter the woods. At 4.4 miles, enter a clear-cut area, followed by a series of small stream crossings and an old power-line clearing at the edge of a residential area. At 5.0 miles, pass an old farm pond and farm area, followed by a cove and large beech trees.

At 6.1 miles, arrive at a residential area and an exit to Possum Track Road for the completion of Section 2. (To the right, the road is barricaded, but to the left onto Possum Track Road, it is 6.2 miles on a road with vehicular access to the trail's origin. Traveling 1.4 miles on Possum Track Road, turn left onto Raven Ridge Road. After 2.9 miles on Raven Ridge Road, turn left onto Falls of Neuse Road. After traveling 1.9 miles on Falls of Neuse Road, turn left to the dam's parking lot.)

Continuing on *Section 3 (Neuse Bend Point)*, cross the road into a grove of loblolly pine. At 6.4 miles, cross a paved road. At 6.6 miles, enter another pine-forest grove. At 7.7 miles, pass lake views. Cross a couple of ravines before crossing a footbridge at 8.5 miles. At 8.8 miles, reach an old woods road. Turn right. At 9.0 miles, arrive at Possum Track Road. (The junction with Raven Ridge Road is 0.2 mile to the left.) This completes Section 3.

To continue on *Section 4 (Cedar Creek)*, turn right on Possum Track Road and cross the Cedar Creek causeway. At 9.2 miles, turn right into a pine forest, which has honeysuckle near its edge. At 10.1 miles, pass remnants of an old homestead on the right, then enter a scenic area of large beech trees. At 10.2 miles, cross a footbridge. After enjoying views of the lake at 10.7 miles, enter a section of mountain laurel for the next 0.6 mile. At 12.0 miles, arrive at Bayleaf Church Road (SR 2003). This completes Section 4. (To the right is the Yorkshire Center of Falls Lake State Recreation Area; to the left on the gated road, it is 1.0 mile to Bayleaf Baptist Church and a junction with Possum Track Road.)

To continue on *Section 5 (Loblolly Point)*, cross the road at the exit sign of the Yorkshire Center and reenter the forest. Cross a number of small streams in rocky areas, and arrive at the end of the guardrail on Six Forks Road (SR 1005). To the right at 13.2 miles is the Lower Barton Creek causeway. This completes Section 5. (To the right, on Six Forks Road, it is 2.2 miles to NC 98. To the left, it is 7.9 miles back to the parking lot below the dam. To return to the dam using a vehicle, go left 0.7 mile on Six Forks Road, where a left turn follows Possum Track, Raven Ridge, and Falls of Neuse roads, as described above.)

From Six Forks Road Through Blue Jay Point County Park
Section 6 (Blue Jay Point)

Length and Difficulty: 3.4 miles, moderate

Trailhead and Description: From the trailhead on Six Forks Road (described at the end of Section 5), follow the road to the right (north) across the Lower Barton Creek causeway for 0.3 mile to the end of the causeway railing at the parking area on the shoulder of the road.

Turn right and enter Blue Jay Point County Park through the forest. Follow an old woods road for 0.1 mile before descending on a footpath to cross a footbridge. Wildflowers and a maple tree with a unique root formation are seen here. Ascend and descend in and out of coves and cross footbridges. At 0.9 mile, there are patches of spicebush, wild ginger, and hepatica. At 1.6 miles is the first of four color-coded spur trails encountered in the next

0.7 mile. The spur trails cross or join Falls Lake Trail from the recreational areas near the center of the peninsula. *Blue Jay Point Trail*, which is 0.2 mile in length, is the first trail that crosses. *Laurel Trail*, also 0.2 mile in length, follows. The next trail leads to a trail for the physically disabled. The last trail, *Sandy Point Trail*, another 0.2-mile-long spur, originates at the park lodge. At 2.0 miles on the main trail, there are rock piles left by early farmers. Exit the forest at 2.3 miles and arrive at a display board and a parking lot between a ball field and the park lodge. Cross the paved road and descend to footbridges. Follow the undulating trail through hardwoods and loblolly pine to reach Six Forks Road and a trail sign at 3.4 miles. This completes Section 6. (Turning right onto the road, it is 1.0 mile to NC 98. To the left, it is 1.3 miles to the western trailhead of Section 5.)

From Six Forks Road to NC 98
Section 7 (Upper Barton Creek)

Length and Difficulty: 2.7 miles, moderate

Trailhead and Description: From the end of Section 6 (Blue Jay Point), turn right on Six Forks Road and cross the causeway to a roadside parking space on the right. At the upper end of the parking space, enter the forest at 0.3 mile, following white blazes. Arrive at an overflow parking lot for Upper Barton Creek Boat Ramp. Cross the lot and go straight into the woods on the other side.

At 0.7 mile after entering the forest, cross under a power line, where there are multiple species of wildflowers and large hardwoods. Cross two bridges, one of which crosses a stream near a large beech tree. At 1.0 mile, cross an old road. (The road descends right to a scenic sandy beach area.) At 1.2 miles, exit the forest to follow a power line as it parallels the forest a few yards before descending into a cove and turning into the forest. Ahead are wildflowers such as trillium, wild quinine, and blazing star. At 2.4 miles, arrive at the paved Old NC 98. Turn right. At 2.5 miles, turn left into a grove of oaks at an old home site. Near a guardrail, descend to NC 98 and turn right. After a few yards, cross the highway to a roadside parking space near a causeway to complete Section 7. It is 1.5 miles west on NC 98 to the junction with Six Forks Road.

From NC 98 to NC 50
Section 8: Shinleaf Peninsula
Section 9: Twin Creek
Section 10: Quail Roost

Length and Difficulty: 6.8 miles, moderate. The mileage given is cumulative for hiking Sections 8-10 together.

Trailheads and Description: From the roadside parking space at the end of Section 7, begin *Section 8 (Shinleaf Peninsula)* by descending and then ascending an embankment. At 0.1 mile, pass under a power line, located among redbuds, sumacs, and blackberries. Cross a number of footbridges in coves. At 0.7 mile, enter a grove of large beech trees and tulip poplars. The scattered understory contains dogwood, holly, and sparkleberry. There are also enjoyable views of the lake here. At 1.1 miles is a scenic area with large beech trees and wildflowers. At 1.5 miles, there is a skillfully designed footbridge, located near a cove. Another scenic area along the lake features infrequent tawny pinesap. At 2.6 miles, Indian pipe and tawny pinesap are found along the path. After a number of footbridges and hilly climbs, at 3.0 miles, you reach Shinleaf Recreation Area, a walk-in campground with central restrooms and showers. To access the recreation area by vehicle, travel 0.5 mile north on New Light Road from its junction with NC 98. (This junction is located opposite the north end of Six Forks Road.) Cross the parking lot and enter the forest. To the left is Norwood Cemetery. Descend steeply and then ascend. At 3.5 miles, exit to New Light Road to complete Section 8. (To the left of this trail exit, it is 1.5 miles to NC 98.)

To continue on *Section 9 (Twin Creek)*, turn right onto New Light Road. After 0.1 mile (3.6 miles in cumulative total), turn left and go up an embankment; watch for the trail's roadside sign, as the turn may be easy to miss. At 3.9 miles, enter a low area with large ironwood trees and spots of yellow root. At 4.0 miles, ascend to cross paved Ghoston Road. This completes the short Section 9.

To continue on *Section 10 (Quail Roost)*, descend from Ghoston Road to banks of mayapple, foam-flower, and crested dwarf iris. At 4.6 miles, cross the dam of a small pond. At 5.1 miles, the trail passes around a rocky knoll, where there are former tobacco field ridges on the hillside. At 5.3 miles, pass to the right of an unnamed cemetery near an old home site. On an old road of red clay, approach a junction with a grassy road at 5.6 miles. At 5.7 miles, turn left (avoid the grassy road to the extreme left) and then exit the old road to the right. After the right turn, the trail goes through a pine grove, and then follows a grassy, open road, bordered in sections with orange cow-itch vine.

At 6.6 miles, cross two paved roads (the latter road goes right to the Falls Lake Information Center). At 6.8 miles, exit at a kiosk and gravel parking area on NC 50 to complete Section 10.

From NC 50 to NC 98
Section 11: Boyce Mill
Section 12 : Lick Creek

Length and Difficulty: 7.1 miles, easy to moderate. The mileage given is cumulative for hiking sections 11-12 together.

Trailheads and Description: From the graveled parking area on NC 50 (described above), walk across NC 50 and turn right on the road shoulder. Go a few yards to a Falls Lake causeway guardrail. Turn left to enter a forest dominated by beech and oak trees, which begins *Section 11 (Boyce Mill)*. To the right, there are scenic views of Falls Lake. After 0.2 mile, enter a grassy area in a cove and go under a power line. At 0.4 mile, reenter the forest on the right. Cross a small stream at 1.0 mile. On an approach closer to the lake, there are views of a long island to the right. At 1.8 miles, there are scenic views to the northwest of Rolling View Marina and Lick Creek bay. Pass a cascading stream, which is on the right at 2.4 miles. There is an abundance of wildflowers among the large rock formations.

Pass through the site of an old homestead at 4.0 miles. Among the remains is a stable tobacco barn with an extended roof, which can provide shelter during inclement weather. Cross a footbridge at 4.3 miles and another one at 4.5 miles. At 5.0 miles, wade or rock-hop Laurel Creek, one of the most scenic sites on this section. After following an old roadbed, ascend on a switchback to a ridge top. Exit the forest at 5.6 miles. There is sparse roadside parking at the end of graveled Boyce Mill Road. This is the western end of Section 11. (From here, it is 0.6 mile on Boyce Mill Road to NC 98. If you go east on NC 98, it is 1.9 miles to a junction with NC 50).

To continue on *Section 12 (Lick Creek)*, walk past the gate at the end of Boyce Mill Road and go left into a grassy field. Descend to cross the dam of a small pond at 5.8 miles. In a forest of tall loblolly pines, follow an intermittent footpath and old forest road through a flat area. To the right, there are swamps. At 6.7 miles, there are frequent sightings of waterfowl in Lick Creek cove. Exit at the roadside parking on NC 98 at 7.1 miles. (East on NC 98, it is 0.8 mile to Boyce Mill Road on the left. It is another 1.9 miles to a junction with NC 50.)

Note: Parts of *Section 13 (Rolling View)* are either in the proposal or construction stage. Section 13 will begin west across the Lick Creek bridge. The finished segment may be approximately 3.5 miles from NC 98 to the entrance gate of Rolling View Recreation Area. From there a new segment of approximately 3.6 miles will go to a former bridge over Little Lick Creek if the bridge can be rebuilt or restored. A new bridge will save about 3.4 miles, since the alternate route would make a loop south to extend to a partial passage on Patterson Road. Proposals for the rest of the trail include another 7.8 miles of trail to go under I-85, northeast of Durham; another 5.5 miles to get to Red Mill Road; and 3.8 miles following the south side of Eno River to reach Old Oxford Road. At that point, Falls Lake Trail would end, but the MST would connect with trails at Penny's Bend Nature Preserve to continue upstream on the north side of the Eno River. For updates on the trail, contact the N.C. Division of Parks and Recreation (919-715-8699; www.ncsparks.net) or Friends of the Mountains-to-Sea Trail (919-841-0088; 919-496-4771; or 919-676-3750; www.ncmst.org).

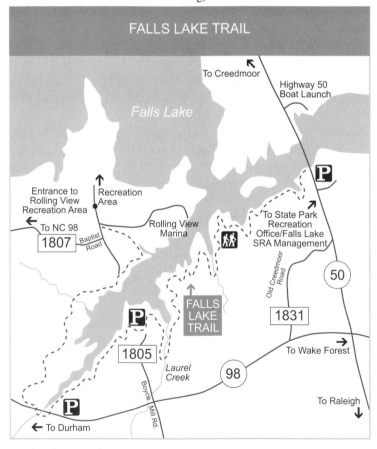

CHAPTER 2

Trails in North Carolina State Parks, Forests, Historic Sites, and Natural Areas

The N.C. Department of Environment and Natural Resources (NCDENR) has seven Natural Resources divisions: Aquariums, Forest Resources, Marine Fisheries, Museum of Natural Sciences, Parks and Recreation, Soil and Water Conservation, and Zoological Park. The current administrative form was created in 1997, but a number of reorganizations preceded the change. For example, in 1995, the state legislature transferred all the state historic sites from the Division of Parks and Recreation to a new Department of Archives and History.

The state parks system is divided into six units of management: state parks, lakes, recreation areas, rivers, trails, and natural areas. Regardless of which department or division of state government oversees each specific trail, all the trails in parks, forests, historic sites, and preserves are covered in this chapter. The trails in the State Recreation Areas (SRAs) or forests are covered in Chapter 1 because they are on U.S. Army Corps of Engineers territory and operate under their regulations.

Interest in the state's natural resources began in the late 19th century.

An example is the establishment of a state geological survey in 1891 to determine North Carolina's mineral and forest resources. In 1905, the legislature reorganized the survey to create the North Carolina Geological and Economic Survey. When the legislature and Governor Locke Craig learned in 1914 that timber harvesting and forest fires were destroying such valuable areas as Mount Mitchell, the governor, a strong conservationist, went to the area for a personal inspection. The result was a bill passed in 1915 to create the state's first park, with a cost not to exceed $20,000. The management of Mount Mitchell State Park became the responsibility of the Geological and Economic Survey.

The state's second park was Fort Macon. Its 410-acre site was acquired in 1924 from the federal government for one dollar. In 1943, Crabtree Creek State Park became the Triangle's first—and the state's ninth—park. In 1955, its name was changed to honor former governor William B. Umstead. Umstead Park is described later in this chapter.

In 1925, the legislature expanded responsibility to fire prevention, reforestation, and maintenance of the state parks and forests when the Geological and Economic Survey was phased into the new Department of Conservation and Development. Acquisition was slow; only three of the Bladen Lakes areas were added to the list in the 1920s. But in the 1930s, federal assistance programs became available, particularly the Civilian Conservation Corps (CCC). Between 1935 and 1943, the state acquired six new parks. The congressional Recreation Area Study Act of 1936 became the blueprint for state parks systems, but the North Carolina legislature appropriated only sporadic funds. From 1945 to 1961, only Mount Jefferson was acquired.

Five state parks and a natural area were added in the 1960s. There was a notable increase in the 1970s, with 11 new parks, eight new natural areas, and the first SRA at Kerr Lake. This decade of growth came under the administrations of governors Bob Scott and James E. Holshouser. Within a three-year period, the parklands nearly doubled with the addition of 50,000 acres. Other advances during this period were the beginning of the state zoo, a trust fund for the natural areas, and the State Trails System Act of 1973, which created a master plan for implementing a statewide network of multiuse trails for hikers, bicyclists, equestrians, canoeists, and ORV users, as well as seven-member citizens' North Carolina Trails Committee (NCTC) to advise the director of Parks and Recreation.

During the early 1980s, three SRAs (Jordan Lake, Falls Lake, and Fort Fisher) were established. In 1987, the state legislature established Lake James State Park. This was the year the state legislature, led by state senator

Henson P. Barnes, passed the State Parks Act. The act created a master plan that "firmly defines the purpose of state parks and requires sound strategy in managing the system."

The creation of other parks followed with Lumber River State Park in 1989, Gorges State Park in 1999, and Haw River State Park in 2004. By 2005, two new state parks were in the planning stages—Hickory Nut Gorge State Park in Rutherford County, which will include the recent purchase of Chimney Rock, and Carver's Creek State Park in northern Cumberland County. The latter will be near Fayetteville and Fort Bragg Military Reservation. The area for the new park, which will be in one of the Triangle's neighboring counties, is described as a longleaf pine savannah with rare plants and aquatic species.

Until the 1990s, North Carolina was at the bottom of national rankings for funding of park construction, staffing, and maintenance for the whole twentieth century. Voters responded to this neglect on November 2, 1994, when they passed a $35 million bond referendum for a Parks and Recreation Trust Fund and Natural Heritage Trust Fund. It was a first in the agency's history and the largest single appropriation since the agency's creation in 1915. Sixty-five percent of the recreation fund goes to state parks; 30 percent to matching funds for local park projects; and five percent to beach access.

In 2007, there were 28 state parks, of which 26 had officially named trails. In the Triangle, the largest and most central is William B. Umstead State Park in Raleigh (Wake County). Also included in this chapter are Eno River State Park, located in Durham, and Raven Rock State Park, in Harnett County, which adjoins Wake County.

Most parks open daily at 8 A.M. They generally close at sunset, which usually means at 6 P.M. November through February; at 7 P.M. in March and October; at 8 P.M. in April, May, and September; and at 9 P.M. June through August.

Rules are posted conspicuously in the parks. Alcohol, illegal drugs, and firearms are prohibited. Fishing is allowed, but a state license is necessary. Camping facilities (including those for primitive and youth-group camping) for individual parks in the Triangle area are described in this chapter. When visiting a park, first go to the park office and request a brochure and maps to make your stay a pleasurable and educational experience.

In addition to the state parks, the Division of Parks and Recreation in the NCDENR administers 12 natural areas, four of which have visitor centers and designated trails. Two of these, Hemlock Bluffs Nature Preserve and Occoneechee Mountain State Natural Area, are in the Triangle. Since 1963, an increase in public pressure influenced the state to adopt principles for the natural-area system: to preserve, protect, extend, and develop natural areas of scientific, aesthetic, and geological value.

For information on state parks and state natural areas, contact the Division of Parks and Recreation, 1605 Mail Service Center (mailing); 512 North Salisbury Street (physical location), Raleigh, NC 27699-1615 (919-733-7275). For information on trails, contact the state Trails Coordinator, Division of Parks and Recreation, MSC 1615, Raleigh, NC 27699-1615 (919-715-8699).

The Division of Forest Resources (another division of the NCDENR) administers five educational state forests. Two of them, Clemmons and Jordan Lake Educational state forests are in the Triangle area. The Jordan Lake location is described in Chapter 1 because of its proximity to other locations with trails on the U.S. Army Corps of Engineers property.

The locations of the forests are diverse, but their purpose and facilities are generally the same. For example, they all have interpretive displays and trails, primitive walk-in campsites (except Jordan Lake), and picnic areas. They serve as outdoor-living and environmental centers that teachers and other group leaders use as classrooms. Arrangements can be made with each ranger station for ranger-conducted programs. Campsites are free but require permits. Open season for Clemmons is March 15 to November 30, but year-round for Jordan Lake, except Thanksgiving and Christmas holidays.

There are 28 state historic sites administered by the Historic Sites Section, Division of Archives and History, and Department of Cultural Resources. The sites offer visitor centers with artifacts, exhibits, and multimedia programs about such historic places as the Duke Homestead, Historic Halifax, and the Thomas Wolfe Memorial. The majority of the sites do not have admission charges. Bentonville Battleground State Historic Site is the only historic site described in this chapter. For more information, contact the Department of Cultural Resources, 2640 Mail Service Center (mailing); 430 North Salisbury Street (physical location), Raleigh, NC 27601 (919-733-7862).

The sections in this chapter are organized in alphabetical order by the name of the location. Although some trails in this chapter are short they are important walks for educational and cultural purposes.

Bentonville Battleground
State Historic Site (Johnston County)

Bentonville Battleground State Historic Site
Box 27
Newton Grove, NC 28366
Telephone: 910-594-0789

After the capture of Savannah, Georgia, on December 20, 1864, General William T. Sherman's troops turned north to join General U. S. Grant's troops in Virginia. On the way, Sherman continued a swath of destruction, particularly in Columbia, South Carolina. The Battle of Bentonville is significant because it was the last major Confederate offensive, the largest battle with the worst carnage of any battle ever fought in North Carolina. A quote from a Confederate, who fought in the battle and recorded his observations, is posted in the Hasting House in Smithfield. It reads: "Scarcely a bird is to be seen or heard—not a flower, not even a wildflower unlocks its fragrant store—no beautiful leaves through which to walk—no broad meadows..." General Joseph E. Johnston, with less than half the number of Union troops, fought bravely but lost the battle, which took place from March 19 to March 21, 1865. The Confederates withdrew toward Smithfield with plans to protect Raleigh, the state capital, but the Union forces did not pursue them.

ACCESS: The entrance is 1.4 miles off U.S. 701 on Harper House Road (SR 1008), 3.0 miles north of Newton Grove.

Bentonville Battleground History Trail (0.2 mile, easy)
Bentonville Battleground Trail (13.4 miles, easy)

Trailheads and Description: *Bentonville Battleground History Trail* is a self-guided walk that begins at the parking lot of the historic Harper House, near the field fortifications exhibit. It leads to the original trenches dug by Union forces on the first day of the battle. There are 29 stations along the route that describe what happened here.

From Harper House, begin *Bentonville Battleground Trail* by crossing

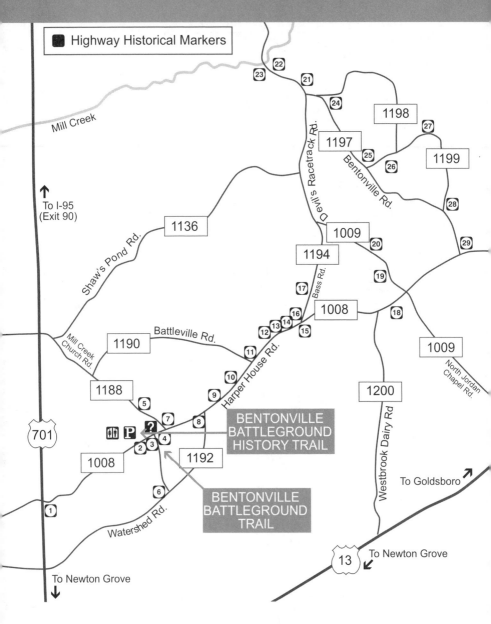

■ Highway Historical Markers

Mill Creek

To I-95
(Exit 90)

Shaw's Pond Rd.

1136

Devil's Racetrack Rd.

Bentonville Rd.

1197

1198

1199

1009

1194

Bass Rd.

1008

Mill Creek
Church Rd.

Battleville Rd.

1190

Harper House Rd.

1188

1008

1192

701

1009

North Jordan
Chapel Rd.

1200

Westbrook Dairy Rd.

BENTONVILLE
BATTLEGROUND
HISTORY TRAIL

BENTONVILLE
BATTLEGROUND
TRAIL

To Goldsboro

Watershed Rd.

To Newton Grove

13 To Newton Grove

To Newton Grove

the public road. At 0.6 mile, turn left on SR 1192. Reach a junction with SR 1008; turn right. The United Daughters of the Confederacy (UDC) monument to the Confederate soldiers is at 2.7 miles. Turn left on SR 1194, which later merges with Devil's Racetrack Road (SR 1009); arrive at the Bentonville Community Building at 5.6 miles. Continue to marker #23 at 5.8 miles; here, Confederate cavalry was halted by the flooded Mill Creek. Return to the Bentonville Community Building and take the road to the left; after 0.1 mile, turn right at marker #24. At 7.1 miles, turn left at marker #25. Pass markers #26 and #27 and turn right on a private dirt road near a feed bin at 7.9 miles. Continue by the field's edge for 0.7 mile to a paved road and turn left at marker #28. Reach SR 1008 at 9.0 miles; turn right and go 0.6 mile to Ebenezer Church to junction with SR 1009; a country store is across the road. Turn right and go 0.5 mile to marker #20. You will return to SR 1008 at 10.6 miles; follow it to the UDC marker at the SR 1194 junction at 11.6 miles. Return on SR 1008 to the starting point for a total of 13.4 miles.

Clemmons Educational State Forest

(Johnston County)

Clemmons Educational State Forest
2411 East Garner Road
Clayton, NC 27520
Telephone: 919-553-5651; fax: 919-550-8050
www.ncesf.org/CESF/home.htm

A forest of 912 acres between Clayton and Garner, Clemmons Educational State Forest has study sites for rocks, trees, wildlife, watersheds, and forest management. Opened in 1976, it represents a transitional zone between the Piedmont and the coastal plain. (There are future plans to add another 600 acres and to create another 10 miles of trails.) A forestry center and exhibits explain the varied facilities of the area. Picnicking and group primitive camping facilities are available, and sections of the trails can be used by the physically disabled. Visitors may choose from 20 ranger-conducted programs.

In addition to the named trails ahead, there is a 3.0-mile loop on a fire maintenance road that is open to the public for hiking. The forest is open from the Tuesday before Arbor Day in March until the last Friday before Thanksgiving in November. During the open season, the forest is open

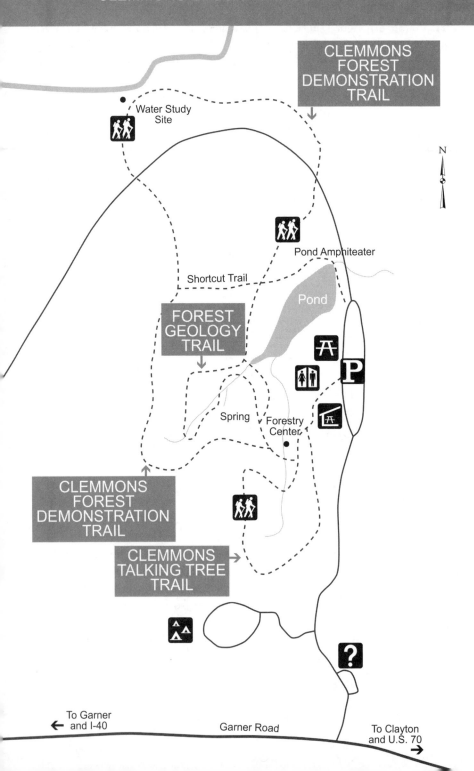

CLEMMONS EDUCATIONAL STATE FOREST

CLEMMONS FOREST DEMONSTRATION TRAIL

Water Study Site

N

Pond Amphiteater

Shortcut Trail

Pond

FOREST GEOLOGY TRAIL

Spring

Forestry Center

P

CLEMMONS FOREST DEMONSTRATION TRAIL

CLEMMONS TALKING TREE TRAIL

To Garner and I-40

Garner Road

To Clayton and U.S. 70

?

Tuesday through Friday from 9 A.M. to 5 P.M. and from 11 A.M. to 5 P.M. on Saturday and Sunday.

ACCESS: On I-40 east of Raleigh, take Exit 306. Follow U.S. 70 east for 3.5 miles to Guy Road (SR 2558) and turn left. After 0.4 mile, turn right on East Garner Road (SR 1004). This road may be called Old U.S. 70 on some maps. Drive 2.0 miles and turn left at the forest sign.

Clemmons Forest Demonstration Trail (2.2 miles, easy)
Forest Geology Trail (0.4 mile, easy)
Clemmons Talking Tree Trail (0.6 mile, easy)

Trailheads and Description: Access to the *Clemmons Forest Demonstration Trail* begins at the parking lot. Enter left of the picnic area and follow the signs for 100 yards to a forest information board and another 100 yards to the Forestry Exhibit Center and trail signboard. Turn right and follow the red blazes. At 0.2 mile, cross a stream near *Forest Geology Trail*. The 0.4-mile Forest Geology Trail is marked with yellow diamond blazes and features seven talking rocks that explain different rock formations seen on the trail. It also goes by a spring. Continuing on the Clemmons Forest Demonstration Trail, cross a shortcut trail at 0.4 mile; pass it again on the left at 1.3 miles. On the trail are examples of forestry practice, particularly longleaf-pine restoration areas. After completing the loop, return to the trail signboard to hike the 0.6-mile green-blazed *Clemmons Talking Tree Trail*. An exceptionally well-designed trail, it provides push-button devices for recorded botanical information. All three trails have easy treadways.

Eno River State Park (Durham and Orange counties)

Eno River State Park
6101 Cole Mill Road
Durham, NC 27705
Telephone: 919-383-1686; fax: 919-382-7378
http://ils.unc.edu/parkproject/visit/enri/directions.html

The park is a popular hiking, canoeing, fishing, and picnicking area along 12 miles of the river between Hillsborough and Durham. Covering 2,738 acres, the park is segmented into four sections—Few's Ford, Cabe Lands, Cole Mill Road, and Pump Station—but the sections are similar, with floodplains, rocky bluffs, and low-range white water. Remnants of milldams and rock piles illustrate the settlements of pioneer millers and farmers. Sycamore, river birch, and sweet gum are prominent on the riverside. Wildflowers are profuse. Among the wildlife are deer, beaver, squirrel, fox, and turkey. Anglers will find Roanoke bass, largemouth bass, bream, redhorse sucker, and catfish. Other activities include picnicking and canoeing. Canoe-launching points are located below Pleasant Green Dam, Cole Mill Road, Few's Ford, and Guess Road. Group camping is allowed by reservation. All supplies, including water and firewood, must be packed in for 0.4 mile. Five backpack sites are available on a first-come basis for small groups or individuals. Accessing these sites requires a 1.0-mile hike.

ACCESS: From I-85, take Exit 173 northwest onto Cole Mill Road (SR 1401 in Durham County; it becomes SR 1569 in Orange County) and drive 5.2 miles to the park office at Few's Ford Access Area.

Few's Ford Section (South)

Eno Trace Trail (0.3 mile)
Cox's Mountain Trail (3.7 miles)
Fanny's Ford Trail (1.0 mile)

Length and Difficulty: 5.0 miles combined round-trip; easy to strenuous

Trailheads and Description: All of these trails connect. From the park office, drive to the parking area at the end of the road, on the right. Follow a well-maintained trail 0.1 mile to a junction on the left with *Eno Trace Trail*. This self-guided trail is also called Eno Trace; it loops 0.3 mile through large hardwoods. Continue on blue-blazed *Cox's Mountain Trail* to cross the swinging footbridge over the Eno River. On the left at 0.3 mile, reach the Wilderness Shelter campsite. At 0.7 mile, the trail forks for a loop. If hiking left, ascend and pass under a power line at 0.9 mile to go to Cox's Mountain. Descend to a stream at 1.2 miles and follow it downstream to the Eno River at 1.6 miles. Turn right and go downriver among river birch and beech. Turn right on an old wagon road at 2.0 miles, pass under a power line, and follow the old road in a forest with beds of club moss. At 2.8 miles, connect with

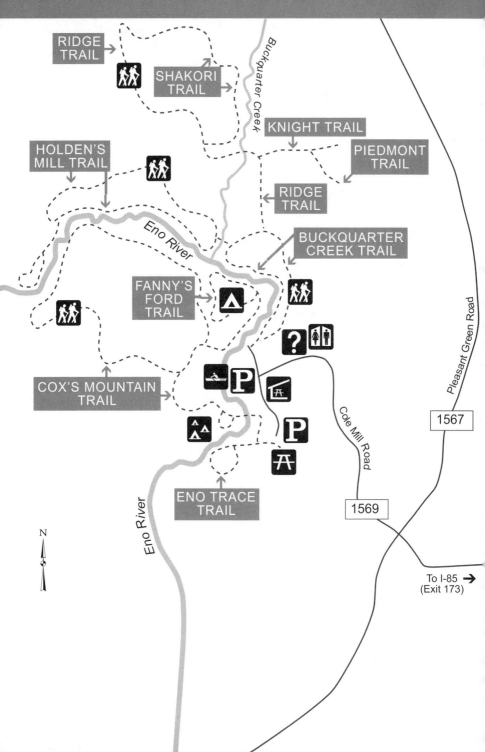

ENO RIVER STATE PARK
FEW'S FORD SECTION

RIDGE TRAIL

SHAKORI TRAIL

Buckquarter Creek

KNIGHT TRAIL

PIEDMONT TRAIL

HOLDEN'S MILL TRAIL

RIDGE TRAIL

BUCKQUARTER CREEK TRAIL

Eno River

FANNY'S FORD TRAIL

COX'S MOUNTAIN TRAIL

Pleasant Green Road

1567

Cole Mill Road

ENO TRACE TRAIL

1569

Eno River

N

To I-85
(Exit 173)

Fanny's Ford Trail, to the left. (Fanny's Ford Trail is a 1.0-mile loop that passes by the riverbank and the pack-in primitive campsite. The trail's name comes from Fanny Breeze, a beloved black midwife and hospitable neighbor to the river community during and after the Civil War. To complete the Cox's Mountain Trail loop, continue on the old road to the fork at 3.0 miles. Backtrack to the parking lot at 3.7 miles.

Few's Ford Section (North)

Buckquarter Creek Trail (1.5 miles)
Holden's Mill Trail (2.6 miles)
Ridge Trail (1.3 miles)
Knight Trail (0.3 mile)
Piedmont Trail (0.1 mile)
Shakori Trail (1.0 mile)

Length and Difficulty: 6.8 miles combined round-trip; easy to moderate

Trailheads and Description: Drive past the park office to the first parking lot on the right. Walk down to the Eno River and turn right, going upriver to a fork at 0.1 mile. (The first trail with steps is not the trail route; this route goes to the park office.) If hiking the right fork of the red-blazed *Buckquarter Creek Trail*, follow an old road through a hardwood forest that was once farmland. Evidence of farm buildings may be seen through the woods on the right. At 0.5 mile, the trail turns left and the blue-blazed *Ridge Trail* goes straight ahead.

If following the Ridge Trail, after 0.2 mile there is a junction with *Knight Trail* on the right. The 0.3-mile red-blazed Knight Trail is a spur trail that ascends a hill to a level area at the park's boundary. The trail connects with 0.1-mile *Piedmont Trail* near the right-of-way for a power line. Both of these trails give a residential area near Pleasant Green Road access to Ridge Trail. Backtrack if hiking these trails. This sidetrip mileage is not counted in the total loop distances.

Continuing on Ridge Trail, descend 0.1 mile to rock-hop Buckquarter Creek. This area has ferns, wildflowers, tall trees, and evidence of former farmhouses. After another 0.1 mile, there is a connection with the yellow-blazed *Shakori Trail* on the right.

Stay left on Ridge Trail and ascend, steeply at a few points, to a park gate and a connection with Shakori Trail. It is a total of 1.8 miles from this point to the parking lot. Follow the Shakori Trail as it descends for 1.0 mile

*Hiker on Ridge Trail in
Eno River State Park*

before rejoining Ridge Trail. Turn left, rock-hop Buckquarter Creek, and rejoin Buckquarter Creek Trail on the right for a total of 3.2 miles. Follow the trail downstream for 0.3 mile to a junction with *Holden's Mill Trail* on the right at a wood-and-steel footbridge over Buckquarter Creek. (If you go to the left, without crossing the bridge, Buckquarter Creek Trail loops back to the parking area for a round-trip of 4.2 miles.)

To hike the yellow-blazed Holden's Mill Trail, cross the footbridge over Buckquarter Creek and come to a fork after 160 yards. If taking the upland route, ascend on an old farm road in a forest of pine and mixed hardwoods. Pass rock piles from early farm clearings, then walk under a power line and descend to the Eno River at 1.0 mile to connect with the lower section of the loop. On the descent, there is a trail on the left where there is another 0.6-mile loop upriver. To the right, there are visible foundations for Holden's Mill. Return downstream, where there are occasional rapids, along a scenic path. The scenery includes rocks, cedar, pine, mountain laurel, and wildflowers. Rejoin Buckquarter Creek Trail at 2.6 miles. Continue down river and complete the trail at 3.3 miles.

Cole Mill Road Access Section

Pea Creek Trail (1.3 miles, easy)
Dunnagan's Trail (1.8 miles, easy)
Cole Mill Trail (1.2 miles, easy)
Bobbitt Hole Trail (1.6 miles, easy)

Trailheads and Description: The activities offered at Cole Mill Road Access include picnicking, fishing, canoeing, and hiking. Access to these trails is the same as described to the park office above, except if you are coming from I-85, go 3.2 miles and turn left on Old Cole Mill Road.

All of these trails connect, many overlap in parts, and all are blazed. From the lower end of the parking area, follow the sign down to the Eno River. At 0.3 mile, reach blue-blazed *Pea Creek Trail* (left) and yellow-blazed *Cole Mill Trail* (right). On Pea Creek Trail, pass under the Cole Mill Road bridge, then under a power line at 0.6 mile. Reach Pea Creek in an area of wildflowers and ferns. At a footbridge is a junction with red-blazed *Dunnagan's Trail*. After crossing Pea Creek, turn right along the Eno River. Turn left at the river and follow the bank downstream. Soon after seeing the stone wall of the old pump station across the river, turn left. Go uphill, circle back to Pea Creek on a ridge above the river, and pass through two old homesites. Complete Pea Creek Trail on a return to Cole Mill Trail.

Hike upriver on Cole Mill Trail. At 0.6 mile, there is a junction with red-blazed *Bobbitt Hole Trail*, which continues upriver. Cole Mill Trail turns right under a power line and rejoins Bobbitt Hole Trail, left, after 300 yards. (To the right, it is 0.4 mile on Cole Mill Trail to the upper parking lot and the picnic area.) If taking the higher elevation of Bobbitt Hole Trail, follow a pleasantly wide trail through pine, oak, and holly on the approach to the river. A right turn leads a few yards to a sharp curve in the river and the large, scenic pool called Bobbitt Hole after 0.9 mile. Return down river. After 0.6 mile, connect with Cole Mill Trail for a return to the parking area.

Pump Station Access Section

Pump Station Trail (1.5 miles)
Laurel Bluffs Trail (2.5 miles)

Length and Difficulty: 5.3 miles, including backtracking; easy to moderate

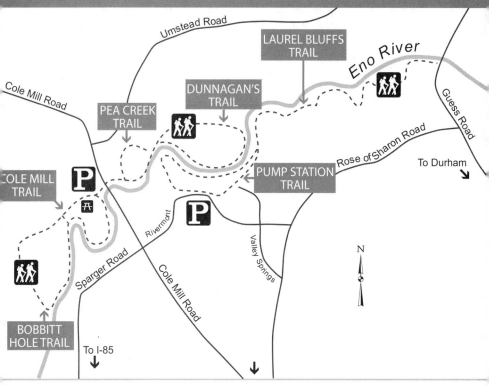

Trailheads and Description: From Exit 173 off I-85, drive 2.3 miles north on Cole Mill Road (SR 1569) to Rivermont Road (SR 1402) and turn right. Drive 0.6 mile to Nancy Rhodes Creek and Bridge. Park on the side of the road. A trail sign on the left is at the trailhead, which goes down an embankment.

To begin *Pump Station Trail*, follow the trail sign; the creek is on the left. Among tall loblolly pine, approach a wide power line opening at 0.22 mile. Descend to cross a small stream and bridge. At 0.3 mile, reach a junction, on the right, with *Laurel Bluffs Trail*. For a loop hike on Pump Station Trail, stay left and pass the remains of the pump station, which supplied Durham with water from 1887 to 1927. Moss covers much of the brickwork. Continue left to parallel Eno River. Cross a footbridge at a former dam. After passing a system of river islands, turn sharply left at 1.0 mile. Gradually ascend, pass under the power line, and curve left to return to the roadside parking on Rivermont Road at 1.5 miles.

From the Pump Station and Laurel Bluffs trails junction, go right on

*Hikers on Pump Station Trail
in Eno River State Park*

Laurel Bluffs Trail. The trail parallels the Eno River, which is generally within sight or hearing the entire distance. Mainly in a hardwood forest, the trail has an understory with groves of mountain laurel and wildflowers on the rocky ledges. The trail follows a few segments of old roads, but the major distance is a hand-dug foot trail that undulates from stream to stream and ridge to ridge. At 0.3 mile, follow the trail over a buried optic cable line. At 0.8 mile, cross a small steel bridge over a stream. To the left is a large island in the river. To the right is a short foot trail for access to Wilderness Road.

After a scenic ridge at 1.4 miles, descend and cross a cascading stream at 1.5 miles. From here, climb to a steep ridge and a pine forest. After a left turn at 2.0 miles, approach an old homesite with a chimney, hand water-pump relics, and coiling wisteria. At the river are rapids and a site of an old dam. After a descent, follow an old mill canal. Mill artifacts may be seen along the way. Ascend an embankment to Guess Road (NC 157) and a bridge over the Eno River at 2.5 miles. Backtrack, or use a shuttle to return to where you parked.

Across the bridge on the left, it is 0.1 mile to *Eagle Trail*, which descends to the right. It goes to the west-end gate of West Point on the Eno Park. Pump Station and Laurel Bluffs trails can be combined with Eagle Trail. These three trails are a proposed part of the *Mountains-to-Sea Trail*. (See "Durham" in Chapter 4 for more about Eagle Trail.)

Cabe Lands Access Section

Cabe Land Trail (1.2 miles, easy)

Trailhead and Description: This loop trail is at Cabe Lands Access. From I-85, take Exit 173, go 2.3 miles and turn left on Sparger Road (SR 1400). Drive 1.3 miles, then turn right on Howe Street (Howell Road on county maps). After 0.5 mile, reach a parking space on the right.

To hike *Cabe Lands Trail*, follow an old service road to the Eno River, passing carpets of periwinkle, ivy, and club moss. Reach the river at 0.4 mile; turn left. Pass beaver cuts and old mill foundations at 0.5 mile, then cross a bridge over a small stream at 1.0 mile. Ascend to the point of origin at 1.2 miles.

Hemlock Bluffs Nature Preserve

(Wake County)

> Hemlock Bluffs Nature Preserve
> P.O. Box 8005 (mailing)
> 2616 Kildaire Farm Road (physical location)
> Cary, NC 27518
> Telephone: 919-387-5980

This 150-acre preserve received its name from eastern hemlock, a conifer usually not found in groves farther east than Hanging Rock State Park, 100 miles northwest of Cary. In both locations, damp, cool, north-facing bluffs encouraged the tree species' survival here from the Ice Age period of 10,000 to 18,000 years ago. In varying sizes, there are more than 200 of these beautiful evergreens, easily viewed from a trail network with observation decks near Swift Creek. (The 0.8-mile *Swift Creek Recycled Greenway* on the north side of the stream is part of the Cary greenway system, not part of the Hemlock Bluffs trail network. See Chapter 4 for more details about the Cary greenway system.)

The hemlock trees, some as old as 400 years, are surrounded by other plant species usually found in the Appalachian mountains, among them yellow orchid, trillium, and chestnut oak.

The state purchased this valuable and unique preserve in 1976. The adjoining property is owned by the town of Cary, whose Parks and

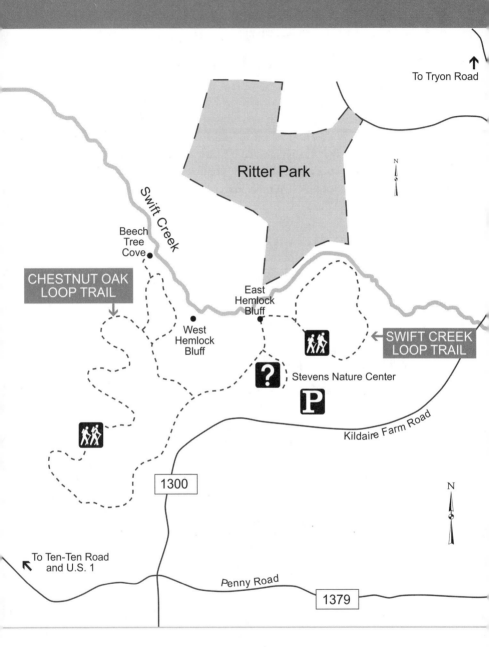

To Tryon Road

Ritter Park

Swift Creek

Beech Tree Cove

CHESTNUT OAK LOOP TRAIL

East Hemlock Bluff

West Hemlock Bluff

SWIFT CREEK LOOP TRAIL

Stevens Nature Center

Kildaire Farm Road

1300

To Ten-Ten Road and U.S. 1

Penny Road

1379

Recreation Department developed and still manages the entire preserve. Some assistance has been received from the Wake County Grant-in-Aid Program. At the entrance to the trail system is the Stevens Nature Center, completed in 1992 and named in honor of Colonel W. W. Stevens and his wife, Emily. The center has a park office, exhibit and classroom space, and a wildflower garden. Hours at the preserve are 9:00 A.M. to sunset daily; hours at the Stevens Nature Center vary according to the season. The exceptionally well-designed and well-maintained trail system is described below.

ACCESS: To access the preserve from the junction of U.S. 1 and U.S. 64, drive northeast on Tryon Road for 0.6 mile and turn right on Kildaire Farm Road. After 1.4 miles, turn right at the preserve entrance and sign.

Swift Creek Loop Trail (0.7 mile)
Chestnut Oak Loop Trail (1.4 miles)

Length and Difficulty: 2.1 miles combined round-trip; easy to moderate

Trailheads and Description: From the northeast corner of the upper level parking lot, enter the forest at a signboard on a concrete walkway. The Stevens Nature Center and floral gardens are on the left. Immediately beyond to the right, there is a wide wood-chip access trail that leads to a T junction. To the right is *Swift Creek Loop Trail*; to the left is *Chestnut Oak Loop Trail*. Trail brochures with marker descriptions are available on post boxes here.

If following Swift Creek Loop Trail, descend on more than 100 steps to two observation decks. The first deck is named East Hemlock Bluff. Eastern hemlock is prevalent here. On the ground, there are carpets of aromatic galax, yellow star grass, trillium, and other wildflowers. At 0.1 mile, the trail reaches the bottom of the steps. The trail begins a loop by going left. On the route, there are markers in a floodplain where tall hardwood trees are prominent. Two long boardwalks provide dry routing. At one point, there are scenic views from the bank of Swift Creek. Complete the loop at 0.6 mile and ascend to the trailhead at 0.7 mile.

The brochure for the upland Chestnut Oak Loop Trail provides information about the preserve's geology and biology, which is highlighted on this trail. In addition to the chestnut oak, which is usually found in the mountains, the more common red, white, and black oaks are also found here. Other trees seen here are red maple, sourwood, American holly, and the occasional loblolly pine. After 260 yards, the trail arrives at a triangle fork. Turn right. At 0.2 mile, there is a side trail to the right that leads 100 yards to another fork. Turn right and go 50 yards to the West Hemlock Bluff overlook. Although the view here is scenic at any time, winter provides the advantage of seeing the bluff's full dimensions. Backtrack and turn right to approach Beech Tree Cove side trail. Descend on steps to an observation deck. An aging American beech, which has been battered by past storms, is ahead. Two yellow poplars, which are younger but equally large, are nearby. Backtrack to the main trail at 0.5 mile and turn right to arrive at the Stevens Nature Center at 1.4 miles.

Occoneechee Mountain State Natural Area (Orange County)

For information, contact Eno River State Park, which administers the natural area, at

6101 Cole Mill Road
Durham, NC 27705
Telephone: 919-383-1686

Comprised of 124 acres on a forested hill, this natural area is located west of the historic town of Hillsborough between busy, noisy I-85 and the solitude of Eno River. Although the elevation is only 867 feet, there are species common to some of the state's western mountains.

ACCESS: At Exit 164 off I-85, drive north onto Churton Street. At the first traffic light, turn left onto Mayo Street. Drive 0.2 mile; at the next traffic light, turn left onto Orange Grove Road. After 0.5 mile, turn right on Virginia Cates Road and drive to a parking lot for the natural area.

Occoneechee Mountain Loop Trail (1.6 miles)
Brown Elfin Knob Trail (0.2 mile)
Overlook Trail (0.4 mile)

Length and Difficulty: 2.2 miles combined, with some overlap; moderate to strenuous

Trailheads and Description: To hike the trails, follow the trail signs from the parking lot.

Follow the red-blazed *Occoneechee Mountain Loop Trail* past a fishing pond at a grassy field, which is bordered with blackberry bushes. At 0.2 mile, enter the forest. At 0.5 mile, there is a junction with the blue-blazed *Brown Elfin Knob Trail*. It ascends left to a rocky knob among chestnut oak, mosses, and lichens before descending as a shortcut to the main loop. Upon reaching the main loop on Brown Elfin Knob Trail, a left turn goes 0.1 mile to the parking area for a short loop of 0.8 mile.

If continuing on the main loop past Brown Elfin Knob Trail, the trail travels among patches of mountain laurel and huckleberry. At 1.0 mile, pass power lines to an overlook of Eno River, where there are steps down to an abandoned quarry. This route ends after a few yards. Backtrack. (Caution signs indicate it is dangerous to go off the trail.)

Ascend to a junction with a scenic spur trail on the right; backtrack. From here, the yellow-blazed *Overlook Trail* runs jointly with the main loop trail to a gravel road, which forks at 1.1 miles. (To the right, it is 0.3 mile to a summit without a view at the park's boundary. Backtrack.)

To stay on the main trail, keep left and descend to a swag. At 1.5 miles, there is a junction with Brown Elfin Knob Trail on the left. Continue the descent on the main trail to the parking and picnic area at 1.6 miles.

Raven Rock State Park (Harnett County)

Raven Rock State Park
3009 Raven Rock Road
Lillington, NC 27546
Telephone: 910-893-4888; fax: 910-814-2200
www.ils.unc.edu/parkproject/visit/raro/home.html

Established in 1970, Raven Rock State Park is a 3,953-acre wilderness-type forest. The Cape Fear River runs through its center. A major geological feature of the area is the 152-foot-high crystalline rock jutting out toward the river. Ravens once nested here, thus the park's name. It is unusual for rhododendron and mountain laurel to grow this far east. The park also features a diverse and long list of Piedmont and coastal-plain plants. Some of the wild birds and animals present are osprey, eagle, owl, squirrel, raccoon, salamander, and deer.

Prominent fish are largemouth bass, catfish, and sunfish. Activities in the park include picnicking, hiking, fishing, and primitive backpack camping. All gear and supplies (including water) must be carried to the camps; registration is required at the park office. There are bridle and hiking trails on the north side of the river. They are described in this section after a discussion of the trails on the south side.

ACCESS: Access the park by driving 3.0 miles off U.S. 421 on Raven Rock Park Road (SR 1314), which is 6.0 miles west of Lillington.

Raven Rock Loop Trail (2.6 miles)
American Beech Nature Trail (0.5 mile)
Little Creek Loop Trail (1.4 miles round-trip)
Group Camp Trail (1.0 mile round-trip)
Fish Traps Trail (1.2 miles round-trip)
Northington's Ferry Trail (2.2 miles round-trip)

Length and Difficulty: 8.9 miles combined round-trip; easy to moderate

Trailheads and Description: From the parking lot, follow the Raven Rock sign on the east side of the lot to begin *Raven Rock Loop Trail*. To the right is a junction with *American Beech Nature Trail*. The 0.5-mile-long American Beech Nature Trail descends and crosses a small stream through yellow poplar, sweet gum, red maple, beech, sweet bay, laurel, and oak. It returns on the east side of the picnic area.

Continuing for 0.8 mile on Raven Rock Loop Trail, there is a junction with *Little Creek Loop Trail*, to the right. (Little Creek Loop Trail descends downstream by Little Creek for 0.7 mile to a canoe camp. Downriver from there, it is another 0.5 mile on *Group Camp Trail* to a group backpack campsite.) Reach scenic Raven Rock at 0.9 mile. Descend on stairways to the riverbank and rock overhangs; return on the steps, but take a right turn at the top.

Arrive at a scenic overlook of the Cape Fear River at 1.1 miles, then junction sharply right with *Fish Traps Trail* and *Northington's Ferry Trail* at 1.7 miles. Fish Traps Trail—named for the trap baskets Indians placed at the rapids to catch fish—leads to a rock outcrop beside the river at 1.1 miles from the junction; backtrack. Northington's Ferry Trail follows a wide, easy route to the mouth of Campbell Creek—also called Camels Creek—the former site of a Cape Fear River ferry crossing, which linked Raleigh and Fayetteville as early as 1770; backtrack.

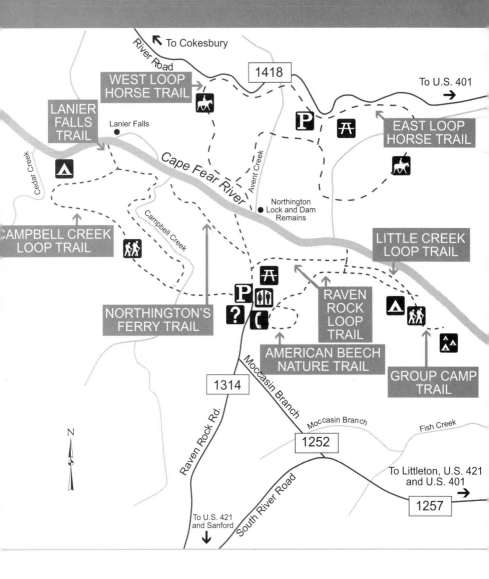

To Cokesbury

River Road

1418

To U.S. 401

WEST LOOP
HORSE TRAIL

LANIER
FALLS
TRAIL

Lanier Falls

EAST LOOP
HORSE TRAIL

Cedar Creek

Cape Fear River

Avent Creek

Northington
Lock and Dam
Remains

CAMPBELL CREEK
LOOP TRAIL

Campbell Creek

LITTLE CREEK
LOOP TRAIL

NORTHINGTON'S
FERRY TRAIL

RAVEN
ROCK
LOOP
TRAIL

AMERICAN BEECH
NATURE TRAIL

GROUP CAMP
TRAIL

1314

Moccasin Branch

Moccasin Branch

Fish Creek

N

1252

Raven Rock Rd.

To Littleton, U.S. 421
and U.S. 401

1257

To U.S. 421
and Sanford

South River Road

Continue on Raven Rock Loop Trail on an old woods road to the parking area at 2.6 miles.

Campbell Creek Loop Trail (5.1 miles)
Lanier Falls Trail (0.4 mile round-trip)

Length and Difficulty: 5.5 miles combined round-trip; easy to moderate

Trailheads and Description: From the parking lot, follow the old service road 45 yards north and turn left into young growth before entering an older forest. Descend gradually in an oak-hickory forest to a footbridge over Campbell Creek at 0.7 mile. Here, *Campbell Creek Loop Trail* goes right or left. If taking the left route, ascend and descend on low ridges through sections of mountain laurel to a junction with the former *Buckhorn Trail* at 2.1 miles. A park service road comes in from the left and joins the trail on the right. Descend to the primitive campsites on the left at 2.3 miles. *Lanier Falls Trail* is located on the left at 2.5 miles. (The 0.2-mile Lanier Falls Trail leads to a scenic rock outcropping at the Cape Fear River; backtrack.) Follow Campbell Creek Loop Trail to the mouth of Campbell Creek and continue upstream to rejoin the access route at the bridge at 4.4 miles for a return to the parking area.

East Loop Horse Trail (3.4 miles, moderate)
West Loop Horse Trail (3.6 miles, moderate)

Trailheads and Description: Because these trails are on the north side of the river, the access is different from the other trails in the park. If approaching from Raleigh on U.S. 401 through downtown Fuquay-Varina (using the junction of NC 24 as a starting point), stay on U.S. 401 for 9.0 miles to Christian Light Road (SR 1412). Turn right onto that road. Drive west 3.9 miles and make a left turn on River Road (SR 1418). After 1.6 miles, turn left to a parking space. If accessing from the south section of the park, return to U.S. 421, turn left and drive 6.4 miles east to Lillington for a left turn on U.S. 401. After 4.9 miles, turn left on Christian Light Road and follow the same directions given above to come from Raleigh. Although these trails are primarily used by equestrians, hikers can also use them.

From the sign for the parking and picnic areas, follow an old road, which may be muddy in the wet season. At 0.2 mile, pass the Arnold cemetery on the right. At 0.4 mile, there is a fork where the *West Loop Horse Trail* goes right and the *East Loop Horse Trail* goes left. If taking the East Loop, descend and cross a streamlet at 0.9 mile and again at 1.1 miles. There is a larger stream at 1.3 miles. The forest is mainly yellow poplar as well as black and red oaks, with some understory of holly and ironwood. At 2.3 miles, pass under a power line. At 2.6 miles, travel over another small stream. Pass under a power line again at 3.1 miles and return to the parking area at 3.5 miles.

The west trailhead for the West Loop Horse Trail is near the parking lot entrance. Descend through the forest parallel with the vehicular road. Pass patches of club moss at 0.4 mile. Immediately leave the road and ascend. At 0.7 mile, there is a level area. Cross an old road at 0.8 mile. Near a junction with an old road is the foundation of an old barn and homesite. Descend to a level area at 2.1 miles, where the trail forks left. (A 0.2-mile side trail on the right leads to an outstanding view of the Cape Fear River. This is the site of the river's former Northington Lock and Dam.)

As the trail continues upstream, there are large river birches, elms, and sycamores, as well as groves of buckeyes. At 2.3 miles, cross a small stream and arrive at Avent Creek crossing; to the left are rock layers and cascades. Except for the river views, this area is the most scenic on the loop. It is a great place for horses to have a drink. Hikers should expect a need to wade. Across the stream is an example of volunteer work—horse riders built cribbing to prevent erosion on the bank and slope. After passing through a hollow, approach a connection with the East Loop Horse Trail at 3.1 miles. Return to the parking area at 3.5 miles; cross the parking area to the trailhead at 3.6 miles.

Equestrians crossing Avent Creek on West Loop Horse Trail in Raven Rock State Park

William B. Umstead State Park
(Wake County)

William B. Umstead State Park
8801 Glenwood Avenue
Raleigh, NC 27617
Telephone: 919-571-4170; fax: 919-571-4161
www.ils.unc.edu/parkproject/visit/wium/home.html

William B. Umstead State Park covers 5,480 acres: 4,026 in the Crabtree Creek (northern) section and 1,454 in the Reedy Creek (southern) section. One of the state's largest parks, Umstead is a valuable oasis in the center of a fast-developing metropolitan area. Adjoining on the west is the Raleigh-Durham International Airport, on the north is U.S. 70, and on the south is I-40. Crabtree Creek flows west to east through the park and separates the two sections.

A former Civilian Conservation Corps camp in the 1930s, the park's original 5,088 acres were deeded to the state by the federal government for a dollar in 1943. The property was designated Crabtree Creek State Park. In 1955, the park was renamed for a former governor and conservationist William B. Umstead. In 1950, a separate park called Reedy Creek State Park had been set aside south of Crabtree Creek for African Americans. In 1966, the sections were united as Umstead Park, with access open to all.

The park is filled with ridges, floodplains, coves, and rocky banks along the creeks and their tributaries. Sycamore Creek, which runs through the park from northwest to southeast, empties into Crabtree Creek. Tributaries such as Pott's Branch, Reedy Creek, and Turkey Creek flow into the main creeks. Quartz rock piles indicate the presence of farmers in the last century and the early part of the 1900s. The park's forest has large stands of mature oaks, yellow poplars, sycamores, and loblolly pines, with an understory of dogwoods, redbuds, mountain laurel, and sourwood.

In the Reedy Creek section is Piedmont Beech Natural Area, a 50-acre tract containing American beech and yellow poplar, some of which are more than 300 years old. The tract is included in the National Registry of Natural Landmarks. Access to the tract is allowed by permit only, which must be obtained from park officials. Beaver, deer, squirrel, wild turkey, and raccoon are among the wildlife in the park.

Recreational activities include fishing, camping, hiking, picnicking, horseback riding, bicycling, and nature study. There are three lakes in the park. From north to south, they are Big Lake, Sycamore Lake, and Reedy

Creek Lake. Fishing for bass, bluegill, and crappie is allowed, but swimming is permitted only at the park's three organized group campsites (Crabtree, Lapihio, and Whispering Pine). Each of these tent campsites is designed to accommodate 25 users. Maple Hill Lodge also accommodates groups of 25 or less. Its facilities include a fireplace, drinking water, and restrooms. Reservations are required for any of these locations. In addition, there is a tent/trailer campground, which has hot showers but no electrical hook-ups. It is usually open from mid-March to mid-October. (It may be open only on weekends. Call 919-571-4170 for updated information. It is open on a first-come, first-serve basis.)

Both park sections offer a multi-use trail network on gated roads with granite screenings. The multi-use roads were formerly called B&B (bridle and bicycle) to designate their use by equestrians and cyclists. These roads are also open to pedestrians. For equestrian usage, the only authorized access is at the horse-trailer parking area at the U.S. 70 entrance. Horse owners must register at the visitor center and present a statement indicating the horses have had a Coggins test. Both hiking trails and multi-use trails (B&B trails) are described in this chapter.

Big Lake Trail, located in the Crabtree section, is a trail specially designed for the physically handicapped. The 0.2-mile paved trail crosses the dam and spillway of Big Lake, leading to the boathouse. It provides scenic beauty and options for fishing. (No bicycles are allowed on this trail.) To access this trail by vehicle, go south of the park office and visitor center; then turn left on Maintenance Road. Take the first right onto Group Camp Road. After crossing a bridge below the dam, park on the right at the dam's edge. (This trail is also accessible by a steep foot trail that leads from the parking lot at the end of Umstead Parkway.)

ACCESS: Access to the Crabtree Creek section is off U.S. 70. From the junction of I-440/U.S. 1 and U.S. 70, drive west on U.S. 70 for 6.0 miles to reach the entrance sign. To reach the Reedy Creek section if driving from the Crabtree Creek section on U.S. 70, drive west on U.S. 70 for 1.5 miles to I-540 (Northern Wake Expressway) and turn left. Drive 4.7 miles to I-40. Turn left (east) and drive 4.9 miles to Harrison Avenue, which is Exit 287. At the top of the ramp, turn left, cross I-40, and go straight to the Reedy Creek parking area. If driving west in Raleigh on I-440, travel to the junction with Wade Avenue. Go west on Wade Avenue for 4.0 miles to the merger with I-40. Turn off I-40 at Exit 287 (Harrison Avenue); turn right at the top of the ramp and drive 0.3 mile to the parking area.

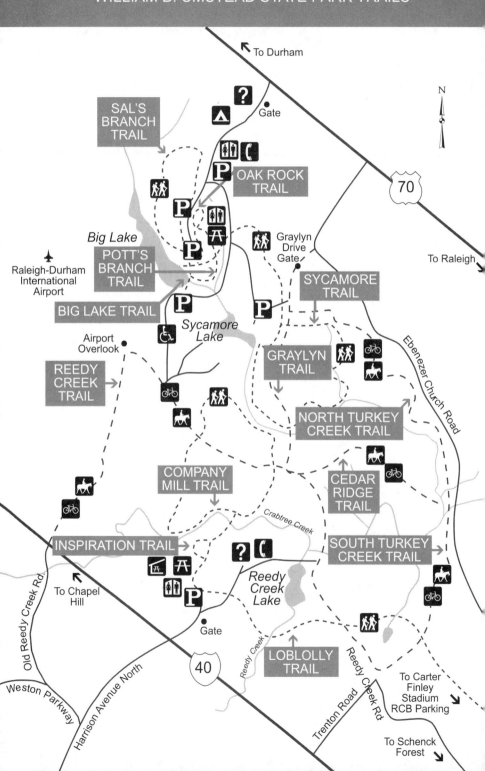

WILLIAM B. UMSTEAD STATE PARK TRAILS

To Durham

Gate

70

To Raleigh

SAL'S BRANCH TRAIL

OAK ROCK TRAIL

Big Lake

POTT'S BRANCH TRAIL

BIG LAKE TRAIL

Raleigh-Durham International Airport

Sycamore Lake

Graylyn Drive Gate

SYCAMORE TRAIL

GRAYLYN TRAIL

Airport Overlook

REEDY CREEK TRAIL

NORTH TURKEY CREEK TRAIL

Ebenezer Church Road

COMPANY MILL TRAIL

CEDAR RIDGE TRAIL

Crabtree Creek

INSPIRATION TRAIL

SOUTH TURKEY CREEK TRAIL

To Chapel Hill

Reedy Creek Lake

Gate

40

LOBLOLLY TRAIL

To Carter Finley Stadium RCB Parking

Old Reedy Creek Rd.

Weston Parkway

Harrison Avenue North

Reedy Creek

Reedy Creek Rd.

Trenton Road

To Schenck Forest

N

Sal's Branch Trail (2.6 miles; easy)

Trailhead and Description: This orange-blazed *Sal's Branch Trail* loop can be accessed from a 200-yard spur trail from the campground or from the visitor center on the north side. If hiking from the visitor center, descend at the forest edge and go counterclockwise for 110 yards to cross Sal's Branch. The trail has a natural surface. It travels through a forest, which is a mixture of hardwood and pine. At 0.3 mile is the spur trail to the park's campground. At 0.9 mile, there is a bridge over a dry ravine, followed by mounds of quartz set aside by former farmers. At 1.1 miles, cross a park maintenance road. At 1.6 miles, there are views of Big Lake. The trail's scenic highlight is viewed from a high embankment on the west side of Sal's Branch at 2.3 miles. Return right to the visitor center at 2.6 miles.

Loblolly Trail (6.0 miles, moderate)

Trailhead and Description: *Loblolly Trail* has a natural surface, which is rough at times. It offers a 6.0-mile linear hiking trek. It has 2.7 miles (one-way) of trail in William B. Umstead State Park; its other mileage is in the city of Raleigh. Access to the park's section is at the northeast corner of the Reedy Creek section parking lot. (See directions above.) A signboard shows the trail beginning at a large white oak tree. It crosses the multi-use *Reedy Creek Trail* and the multi-use *South Turkey Creek Trail* before leaving the park boundary. (These trails are described in the Reedy Creek section ahead.) To access the southeast trailhead, take Edwards Mill Road onto RBC Center Road. It is a short distance to the first left, which leads to a special parking lot where a Capital Greenway sign is located. (Capital Greenway is described in Chapter 4.)

Pott's Branch Trail (1.3 miles)
Oak Rock Trail (0.6 mile)
Sycamore Trail (7.0 miles)

Length and Difficulty: 8.9 miles combined round-trip; easy to moderate

Trailheads and Description: These trails, which are designated for hikers only, can be hiked as individual loops. *Sycamore Trail* cuts across the center of orange-blazed *Pott's Branch Trail*, making the latter a double loop of either 0.6 or 0.7 mile each, depending on where you began from the parking lot.

From the visitor center, drive 0.6 mile to the lower end of the parking area loop. Pott's Branch Trail begins on the right. Descend 120 yards and turn left at a junction. (To the right is a descent to *Big Lake Trail*, which was discussed in the park's introduction above.) At 0.2 mile, arrive at the banks of Sycamore Creek and turn left among tall sycamores. As the trail goes uphill, the forest becomes primarily oaks and pines. As the trail parallels the stream, it travels among Christmas ferns, wildflowers, and rock ledges. At 0.5 mile, there is a junction with *Sycamore Trail*, which goes left, up steps to a picnic and parking area, and right across the creek bridge. This trail is discussed in more detail below.

Continuing on the Pott's Branch Trail, pass cascades, a former dam, and go uphill to an outdoor stage at 0.8 mile. Near the upper parking lot, turn left to follow a paved path to complete the loop at 1.3 miles.

At the upper parking lot is an option for hiking the white-blazed *Oak Rock Trail*. If choosing this popular interpretive trail, enter at the parking lot corner. There are signs identifying the trees. After 30 yards, fork right and descend 0.1 mile to the Rock Tree on the right. This red oak has sealed its roots in a rock shaft and made a natural work of art. Follow the path upstream beside Pott's Branch. At 0.3 mile, cross a rock bridge and circle back to the trail's origin. (It is 0.2 mile to the lower parking lot.)

The blue-blazed Sycamore Trail is accessed at the lower parking area. Go up steps to a paved trail, which goes to a picnic area. Turn left on the pavement, then take the first right to pass picnic shelter #2 on the left and then shelter #1 on the right. Descend on wide steps to cross Pott's Branch Trail and then cross a bridge over the branch. Follow the trail upstream to cross Sycamore Lake Road at 0.5 mile. Ascend easily to pass through a forest of oak, maple, sweet gum, and pine. At 1.5 miles on the top of a ridge, enter a former homesite with a grove of huge oaks. These trees and a large honey locust are entwined with wisteria. After a few yards, cross *Sycamore Road (B&B) Trail*, right and left. (To the right, this trail descends to a circular parking area accessed at the end of Sycamore Road. To the left, it is 30 yards to *Graylyn Trail*. Graylyn Trail can be accessed to the left of the gate at Graylyn Drive.)

If continuing on Sycamore Trail, descend, then curve into a cove for an ascent. To complete the trail's loop, turn left at the junction at 2.1 miles. If going ahead, descend on two switchbacks and arrive beside Sycamore Creek at 2.2 miles. Cross under a power line, and ascend. At 2.4 miles, there is a fenced, scenic cliff overlook. Descend and pass a large bed of Christmas fern. At 3.0 miles, cross Graylyn Trail.

To the left, the multi-use route ascends to the location mentioned above at the Graylyn Drive gate. To the right, it crosses a CCC-built stone bridge, which connects this trail with Reedy Creek Trail. Also across the bridge, on the right, is the 90-yard *Company Mill Spur Trail*, which links to *Company Mill Trail*. That trail, designated for hikers only, is described ahead.

To continue on the Sycamore Trail, descend steps and parallel the creek. Large boulders and high banks make this a scenic area. The trail undulates over a few ridges before leaving the creek by turning left at a tributary. At 4.0 miles, cross a bridge over a brook. Criss-cross the rocky stream. In the spring, this area is a wildflower garden of wild orchids, crested dwarf iris, trailing arbutus, and ferns. At the last crossing, located among boulders at 4.1 miles, there is a view upstream of a bridge for *North Turkey Creek Trail*. Ascend and cross Graylyn Trail at 4.8 miles. Slightly descend to complete the loop at 4.9 miles. Turn right and backtrack 2.1 miles to the parking lot.

Company Mill Trail (5.8 miles)
Inspiration Trail (0.3 mile)

Length and Difficulty: 6.1 miles combined round-trip; easy to moderate

Trailheads and Description: From the Reedy Creek section parking lot, walk to the northwest corner and descend to a display board at the edge of the woods. At 0.1 mile, there is a large stone picnic shelter in the picnic area. The orange-blazed *Company Mill Trail* descends on steps to a junction with blue-blazed *Inspiration Trail*, left, at 0.2 mile. (This 0.3-mile loop trail has interpretive signs with names of the trees.) The Company Mill Trail continues to ascend and descend to the Crabtree Creek steel footbridge at 0.8 mile. On the way, there are piles of quartz made by pioneer farmers on the rocky slopes.

After crossing the footbridge, turn right or left for a loop. If hiking right, descend between rock ledges, on the left, and the creek, on the right. At 1.0 mile are rapids and remnants of a dam. A millstone is left of the trail. Turn left at 1.5 miles and follow a tributary, crossing it a number of times among tall trees, many of them beech. Cross the multi-use *Reedy Creek Trail* at 1.7 miles. Descend from the ridge to the south bank of Sycamore Creek and turn left at 2.1 miles. (To the right is the 90-yard *Company Mill Spur Trail*, which links to the multi-use *Graylyn Trail*. To the left, the trail goes over a bridge to a junction with *Sycamore Trail*.)

Stay near the creek side, partly on a rim of a former millrace. Maidenhair fern, buckeye, and black cohosh adorn the trail. There are rock remnants of

Equestrians on Reedy Creek Trail in William B. Umstead State Park

the George Lynn Mill Dam to the right. At 2.5 miles, leave the creek on switchbacks leading to a ridge. Then descend on switchbacks to a small stream. Ascend again to reach the top of the ridge at 3.0 miles. Cross multi-use Reedy Creek Trail at 3.6 miles, and gradually descend to the bank of Crabtree Creek at 4.6 miles. Pass right of a rock slope and complete the loop at 5.0 miles. Cross the high footbridge over the creek, ascend to the picnic shelter at 5.7 miles, and to the parking lot at 5.8 miles.

Umstead's Multi-use Trails

Since the 1990s, Umstead State Park has made remarkable progress in developing a comprehensive trail system that is in the best interest of all users. The park—a model for protection of sensitive pedestrian trails— has created a first-class network of 13.0 miles of multi-use trails. Access points have been organized and all trails are color-coded. Of the five multi-use routes, only one—*Cedar Ridge Trail*—is still wilderness without a high bridge over Sycamore Creek. To many users, it provides an appealing contrast. Although it connects with the new multi-use *North Turkey Creek* and *South Turkey Creek trails*, many are satisfied to leave it in a wild state. The engineering system for the roads, which has professional maintenance and incorporates granite screening, has made the roads ideal for multi-use. For example, it is not unusual to see equestrians, bicyclists, hikers, joggers, and mothers pushing baby carriages on the *Graylyn Trail*. The brief description below describes two options for hiking combinations of the five multi-use trails. Bicyclists have five trailheads. Pedestrians have access to all trails and trail crossings. (No battery or gasoline-powered scooters, mopeds, or ATVs are allowed on any of the park's trails.)

Graylyn Trail (1.6 miles)
Reedy Creek Trail (4.6 miles)
Cedar Ridge Trail (1.5 miles)
North Turkey Creek Trail (2.6 miles)
South Turkey Creek Trail (1.4 miles)

Length and Difficulty: 11.7 miles combined, without including backtracking; easy to moderate
Trailheads and Description:

Option #1: Graylyn Trail

The first option for hiking combined trails starts with the trailhead for *Graylyn Trail*. Equestrians can only access this trail from the park's horse-trailer parking circle near Sycamore Lake. The trailhead is located at the Crabtree Creek entrance on U.S. 70. Bicyclists may use this entry also.

Bicyclists, hikers, and other pedestrians may enter the Graylyn gate at the end of Graylyn Drive. To reach this access, travel on U.S. 70 to Ebenezer Church Road. Turn right on Ebenezer Church Road if approaching east from the park entrance and drive 0.7 mile to Graylyn Drive. Graylyn Drive ends at a parking area on the west side of the road.

From the Graylyn Drive access, enter the gate at the end of the road. The road is 20 feet wide in some places. The trail passes the King Cemetery on the left and large oaks and wisteria at the site of a former homestead on the right. At 0.3 mile, the 0.1-mile access road to the horse-trailer parking site is on the right. (Thirty yards on that access road, there is a crossing for *Sycamore Trail*, which is discussed in detail earlier in the chapter.)

Continuing on Graylyn Trail, there is a junction with the multi-use *North Turkey Creek Trail* at 0.5 mile on the left; Sycamore Trail crosses at 0.65 mile. At 0.8 mile, pass a grove of wisteria; a crossing under a power line is at 0.9 mile. To the left is a good view of the ridges ahead that users will encounter later. Begin a descent to face the power line again. Birds and butterflies frequent this area. At 1.3 miles, arrive at a scenic crossing with Sycamore Trail. The scenery includes the Sycamore Creek bridge and tall trees. Cross the bridge. (To the right is a 90-yard connector trail to *Company Mill Trail*, described earlier in the chapter.) Continue ahead and begin an ascent to end Graylyn Trail at 1.6 miles. At this point, there is a connection to *Reedy Creek Trail* on the right and left.

Traveling on Reedy Creek Trail to the right, it is 2.8 miles to the west gate (and western terminal) of the trail. Horseback riders must backtrack at this terminal, but bikers and hikers can cross the bridge over I-40 and connect with the *Black Creek Greenway* into Cary. (The greenway is discussed in Chapter 4.)

If taking the left turn onto Reedy Creek Trail, it is 0.1 mile to *Cedar Ridge Trail*, which is on the left. If staying on Reedy Creek Trail, it is 1.8 miles to the park's boundary. There, all users can turn left onto *South Turkey Creek Trail*, but only bikers and hikers may continue on *Reedy Creek Greenway* into Raleigh.

(If turning left onto the Cedar Ridge Trail at its intersection with Reedy Creek Trail, briefly ascend to the trail's highest point, then gently descend. At 0.2 mile, pass under a power line and weave along the ridge among large oak trees. At 0.7 mile, the granite screenings end, revealing the trail's former identity as a gravel road. The trail narrows and descends to cross Sycamore Creek at 1.5 miles. (All users should be prepared to backtrack if the creek is high or at flood stage. Even in safe passage, users are not likely to see a low-water concrete bridge buried in the sands from flooding on Sycamore and Turkey creeks.) Connect with North and South Turkey Creek trails after 125 yards.

Option #2: North Turkey Creek Trail

To begin the scenic multi-use *North Turkey Creek Trail*, follow *Graylyn Trail* to its intersection with this trail. North Turkey Creek Trail gently descends through a mature hardwood forest, comprised mainly of white oak, maple, sweet gum, beech, and yellow poplar. At 0.4 mile, descend steeply to cross a bridge over an unnamed tributary to Sycamore Creek. (When the leaves are off the trees you may see a *Sycamore Trail* bridge down the cove.) Ascend; the trail alternates between climbing ridges and curving into coves. At 1.0 mile, descend steeply into another cove, where the amount of pine coverage and scattered quartz increases. At 1.8 miles, descend steeply to cross a ravine, which is usually dry. At 2.1 miles, strong cribbing forces the trail to narrow at Sycamore Creek bluffs. Notice the park maintenance staff has planted many new Eastern red cedars along the trail. Exit the forest at 2.4 miles and descend to cross Turkey Creek bridge. A new bridge replaced Ebenezer Church Road bridge, which is to the left. There are attractive views

Old bridge connecting the multiuse North and South Turkey Creek trails in William B. Umstead State Park

of cascades and pools at this location. At 2.6 miles, there is a connection with *Cedar Ridge Trail*, on the right. (To access Cedar Ridge Trail, wade Sycamore Creek 125 yards from this right turn. Test the water depth before crossing.)

Instead of turning right onto Cedar Ridge Trail, continue straight to connect with multi-use *South Turkey Creek Trail*. After 125 yards, cross the high bridge over Crabtree Creek. Begin an ascent into a hardwood forest shortly after crossing the bridge. At 0.6 mile, cross under a power line. At 0.9 mile, cross *Loblolly Trail*, which was described earlier in this chapter and will also be discussed in Chapter 4. At 1.3 miles, there is a picnic table under large oak and maple trees. At 1.4 miles, there is a junction with *Reedy Creek Trail*. Here, bikers and hikers have the option of turning left onto the *Reedy Creek Greenway*, which goes into Raleigh; horse traffic must turn right. (Beyond the gate at this junction is Reedy Creek Road and Trenton Street, a former popular place for trail users to park. With a new housing development and paved road at this site, there may not be space for curbside parking.)

If making a loop, turn right on Reedy Creek Trail. At 0.35 mile, cross Loblolly Trail again. In the springtime, there is fragrant wisteria on both sides of the road. Gradually descend to pass Reedy Creek Lake at 0.9 mile. (At the lake's dam crossing is the 1.2-mile-long *Reedy Creek Lake Trail*, a trail for hikers and bikers to access the parking lot at the entrance to the Reedy Creek section near Exit 287 off I-40.) Continuing on Reedy Creek Trail, cross a high bridge over Crabtree Creek at 1.15 miles. Ascend steeply at first, then follow a more moderate approach to Cedar Ridge Trail, which is on the right at 1.8 miles. Descend 0.1 mile to connect with Graylyn Trail, on the right. Following Graylyn Trail to North Turkey Ridge Trail makes a 9.8-mile loop, the longest single multi-use loop possible in the park. Add the 0.5 mile or 1.0 mile in and out on the access routes to the loop point and the claim of a 10-mile ride seems justified.

CHAPTER 3
Trails in County Parks and Recreation Areas

Three-fourths of the state's 100 counties have parks and recreation departments. They operate as a separate public unit in each county, usually under a county board of commissioners. A few counties and cities combine their departments or resources to provide joint services or special projects. Examples of city-county recreation departments in or near the Triangle are Sanford and Lee County, Fayetteville and Cumberland County, and Henderson and Vance County. In Durham County, there is no parks and recreation department, but the county government assisted in creating the Little River Regional Park and Natural Area that straddles the county lines of both Durham and Orange counties.

Some long trails are affected by priorities and regulations from dual entities when they pass through both counties and cities. One example is the Mountains-to-Sea Trail, which passes through Orange, Durham, Wake, Franklin, and Johnston counties, as well as the cities of Hillsborough, Durham, Raleigh, and Smithfield. Another example is the American Tobacco Trail, which travels through the city of Durham and the counties of Durham, Wake, and Chatham.

In the past decade, there has been a rapid increase in the Triangle's population. Because of this increase, the counties have expanded existing parks and constructed new parks, depending on available funding. County parks vary in size, facilities, and scope, from simple day-use picnic areas to complex recreational centers. Since the first edition of this guidebook was published in 1997, the number of county parks has increased by more than 50 percent. Demographic changes indicate a trend for building more parks and trails near or in new housing developments. Some county parks and recreation departments have constructed physical-fitness trails or added paved trails for track and field events at some of the public schools.

For an annual update on the facilities at county and city parks, plus those at academic institutions, military bases, national parks, historic sites, state parks and forests, related professional organizations, and therapeutic recreation agencies, you can order the *North Carolina Directory of Parks and Recreation Agencies* from Recreation Resources Service, Box 7632, N.C. State University, Raleigh, NC 27695-7632 (919-515-7118).

Franklin County

Franklinton Area County Park

> **Franklin County Parks and Recreation**
> **62 West River Road**
> **Louisburg, NC 27549**
> **Telephone: 919-496-6624; fax: 919-496-7656**

This 25-acre park has lighted ball fields, a group picnic shelter, individual picnic facilities, a large children's playground, a lighted all-weather track and walkways, and *Running Cedar Trail*. To access the 0.4-mile nature trail, park near, but inside, the park entrance and descend to cross a footbridge. Continue uphill at the loop connection and pass through a carpet of dense club moss. On the loop's descent near a small stream among tall hardwoods are spring wildflowers and ferns.

ACCESS: On NC 56 in east Franklinton, turn north at a park sign onto Burlington Mill Street and cross the old railroad track. Turn left onto Mason Street, then immediately right onto Second Street. Travel to a stop sign at the park entrance.

Lee County

Lee County Parks and Recreation
P.O. Box 1968 (mailing)
225 South Steele Street (physical location)
Sanford, NC 27331
Telephone: 919-775-1531; telephone number for San-Lee Park is 919-776-6221;
fax: 919-775-1531
http://leecountync.gov

The county's largest park is San-Lee Park, which is located outside and east of Sanford. The county also maintains Kiwanis Family Park because the city of Sanford does not have a parks and recreation department. This family-oriented park has a children's playground, a fitness trail, picnic facilities, and a paved unnamed 0.8-mile trail between Wicker Street and Carbonton Road.

Other parks in the city have facilities for athletic sports such as baseball, softball, and basketball.

San-Lee Park & Outdoor Educational Center

This park has 125 acres of forest, lakes, old waterworks, trails, picnic areas, family (RV) and group campgrounds, and a nature center with displays of live wildlife and nature study. It also offers an amphitheater, a boat launch, boat rentals, a volleyball court, and other facilities. All the trails are well designed and maintained. The park is open all year.

ACCESS: At the junction of U.S. 1 Business and Charlotte Avenue (U.S. 421/NC 87/42), take Charlotte Avenue east for 1.2 miles to Grapevine Road (also called San-Lee Drive, SR 1509); turn right. After 2.2 miles, turn right on Pumping Station Road (SR 1510) and go 0.6 mile to the park entrance, on the right.

Muir Nature Trail (1.1 miles, easy)
Gatewood Loop Trail (0.8 mile, easy)
Hidden Glen Loop Trail (0.2 mile, easy)
Thoreau Lake Trail (0.9 mile, easy)

Trailheads and Description: From the parking lot by Miner's Creek, cross the bridge, turn right, and follow the *Muir Nature Trail* signs into

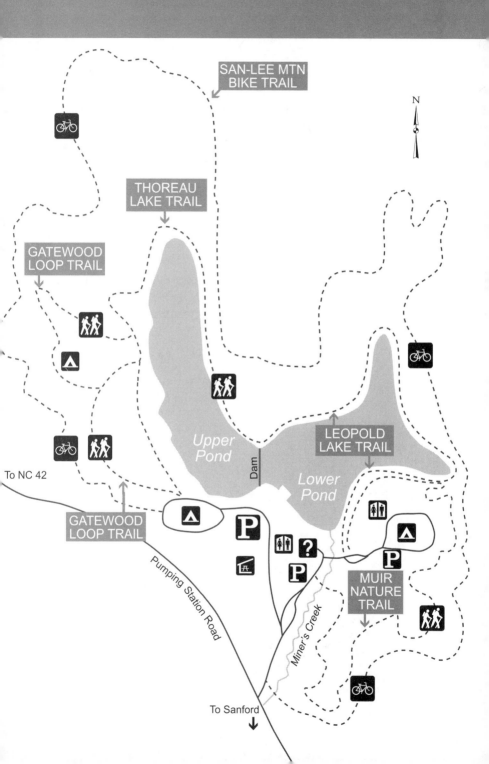

SAN-LEE PARK AND OUTDOOR EDUCATIONAL CENTER

SAN-LEE MTN BIKE TRAIL

THOREAU LAKE TRAIL

GATEWOOD LOOP TRAIL

Upper Pond

Dam

LEOPOLD LAKE TRAIL

Lower Pond

To NC 42

GATEWOOD LOOP TRAIL

Pumping Station Road

Miner's Creek

MUIR NATURE TRAIL

To Sanford

the woods; you have a choice of an upper or lower loop. At 0.5 mile, turn left at the steps at the lake's edge. You will pass through rocks, hardwoods, softwoods, and wildflowers on the return.

You may hike a few yards or park at the refreshment stand to hike the other trails. Follow the campground road to the Colter Amphitheater signs. Turn right on *Gatewood Loop Trail*. At 0.3 mile, junction with *Thoreau Lake Trail*, on the right. Turn left to reach a junction with *Hidden Glen Loop Trail* at 0.5 mile. Pass the Aldo Leopold Wilderness group campground on the return. Thoreau Trail begins at the boat launch near the bridge over Moccasin Pond. Cross the bridge and follow the shoreline to the left. Cross a bridge over Crawdad Creek and junction with *Gatewood Loop Trail* at 0.6 mile. Return either left (the shorter route) or right.

San-Lee Mountain Bike Trail (4.5 miles, easy to strenuous)

Trailhead and Description: (*Note*: Hikers using this trail should remember it is a matter of courtesy and safety to watch for bikers and quickly move completely off the trail to allow their passage.) *San-Lee Mountain Bike Trail* is located in San-Lee Park. The trail can begin at either the nature center or from a parking lot reached by bearing left at the nature center and ascending to the Upper Pond. From the parking area at Upper Pond, ascend the loop road in the RV campground to its east end. Register at the trailhead. The trail travels mainly through a hardwood forest with scattered loblolly pines.

Sign at bridge over Miner's Creek in San-Lee Park

There is also a bed of white quartz. At 0.2 mile and 0.3 mile, the trail dips into ravines. At 0.8 mile and 1.3 miles, additional dips have bridges over small streams. At 1.9 miles, cross Crawdad Creek, which is a small stream without a bridge located in a holly grove. In this grove, there are beds of partridgeberry. In the springtime, there are scattered wildflowers.

Ascend on switchbacks to a ridge top; turn right to follow an old road. Leave the old road at 2.3 miles. At 2.8 miles, cross a small stream. At 3.0 miles, cross a shallow ravine, then turn left to parallel the ravine for 0.1 mile before curving right. On a scenic hillside, there are cranefly orchids in late June. At 3.5 miles, ascend to another ridge top and briefly follow another old road. At 3.8 miles, cross a small, rocky stream; to the left is a stream tunnel that goes under the U.S. 421 Bypass, which is high overhead. From a timber cut at 3.9 miles, ascend and pass through a young forest. Along and near the trail are dense beds of trout lilies, usually on display in mid- to late March. At 4.2 miles, there is a small bridge, followed by a steep ascent. Turn right and descend into a mature forest, where there is a connection with *Muir Nature Trail* on the right at 4.4 miles. Stay straight to cross a high bridge over Miner's Creek at the park entrance at 4.5 miles. It is 0.2 mile for a return up the road to the parking lot at Upper Pond.

Orange and Durham Counties

Little River Regional Park & Natural Area

Little River Regional Park & Natural Area
301 Little River Park Way
Rougemont, NC 27572
Telephone: 919-732-5505; fax: 919-732-5574
http://www.enoriver.org/eno/parks/LittleRiverPark.html

Without the cooperative efforts of environmental and volunteer groups, this 376-acre preserve would never have existed. Some of the organizations involved include the Triangle Land Conservancy, the N.C. Parks and Recreation Trust Fund, the Land and Water Conservation Fund, the N.C. Water Management Trust, and the Eno River Association. The preserve protects historic places used by Native Americans and pioneer farmers; wildflowers seen infrequently in the area; endemic fish and mussel species,

Bicycle trail in Little River Regional Park and Natural Area

and animal species whose habitats along the Little River more closely resemble habitats found in the mountain region. Current facilities include picnic shelters, restrooms, a children's playground, and hiking and bicycling trails. There are six trails, two of which are short and located near the picnic area. The 0.25-mile, paved *Interpretive Trail* is suitable for the physically handicapped and the 0.3-mile *Bird Trail* circles the parking area. Four other trails are part of a hiking network. There is also a long unnamed mountain biking trail, which is called *Little River Mountain Bike Trail* here. These trails are described ahead.

Picnic shelters for groups can be reserved by calling 919-245-2660. Park hours are 8:00 A.M. to 5:00 P.M. November 1 to March 31; 7:00 A.M. to 8:00 P.M. June 1 to August 31; and 8:00 A.M. to 6:00 P.M. April 1 to May 31 and September 1 to October 31. Trails close one hour before the park closes. The park is closed on Thanksgiving Day, Christmas Eve, and Christmas Day.

ACCESS: From I-85 in Durham, take Exit 175 and drive north on Guess Road (NC 157) for 10.5 miles to the park entrance on the right. The entrance is about 1.0 mile after passing the Durham/Orange county line.

Ridge Trail (2.8 miles)
Homestead Trail (0.3 mile)
North River Loop Trail (0.7 mile)
South River Loop Trail (2.5 miles)

Length and Difficulty: 6.6 miles combined, overlapped, and backtracked; easy to moderate

Trailheads and Description: At the corncrib near the parking area, read the park regulations. Notice the hiking-trail blazes are color-coded green and appear every one-quarter mile. *Ridge* and *North River Loop trails* have uneven

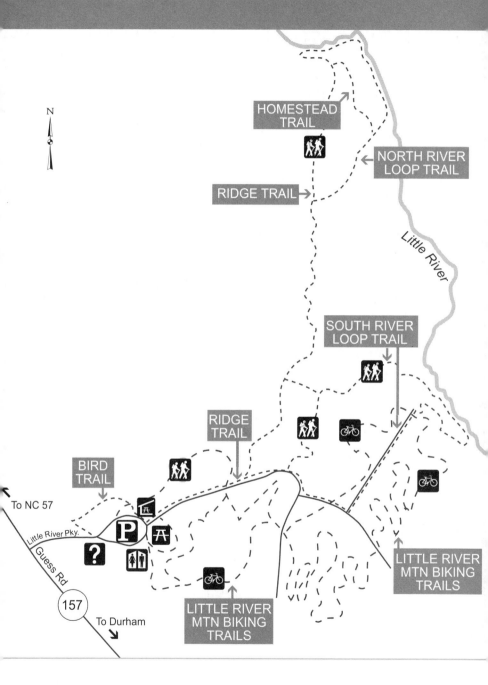

numbers; *South River Loop Trail* has even numbers.

From the park-regulations sign, take the paved *Interpretive Trail* for about 110 yards. Leave the Interpretive Trail and *Little River Mountain Bike Trail* at 0.25 mile. At 0.3 mile, arrive at the tobacco pack house, where Ridge Trail turns left and South River Loop Trail goes right. All the trails travel through forests, cross numerous small streams, and provide pleasurable vistas of the riverbanks.

Adventuring on *Ridge Trail*, pass a clear stream, with wildflowers such as May apple and atamasco lily nearby. At 0.5 mile, junction with a short connector trail on the right that goes to South River Loop Trail. At 1.0 mile, cross an old road. At 1.1 miles, pass North River Loop Trail to the right. Continuing on Ridge Trail, pass *Homestead Trail*, on the right at 1.4 miles. Homestead Trail is a 0.3-mile connector to *North River Loop Trail*. At 1.6 miles, there is a gated road where a right turn begins North River Loop Trail. North River Loop Trail parallels the river with its mossy banks, clear water, and occasional cascades. Beech and sycamore shadow the patches of trout lily, hepatica, yellow root, and wild azalea. Wildlife may be seen if your visit has some moments of quietness. Leave the banks of the river at 2.0 miles. Cross a footbridge over a small tributary and a spring, located on the left. At 2.3 miles, pass Homestead Trail on the right and return to Ridge Trail. Turn left and backtrack.

If hiking South River Loop Trail from the corncrib near the parking area, follow the directions above to the tobacco pack house. At 0.3 mile, follow the gravel road to the right. Cross a small bridge over a stream at 0.4 mile. If you stay right at the trail's loop, follow a switchback and cross another bridge. At 1.0 mile, stay left of a private road. Cross Little River Mountain Bike Trail at 1.1 miles. Within about 80 yards, keep left of another private road. At 1.4 miles, cross the mountain-bike trail again before beginning the descent to the river. Cross a boardwalk in an area of club moss. Descend, partly on steps, on the most difficult part of the trail at 1.7 miles. At 1.8 miles, a connector to Ridge Trail is on the right. At 1.9 miles, cross a bridge over a creek. To complete the loop, turn right and return to the tobacco pack house at 2.2 miles. Return to the corncrib and parking area at 2.5 miles.

Little River Mountain Bike Trail is a first-class system created by skilled members of the Durham/Orange Mountain Bike Organization (DOMBA). Special care was made during construction to avoid erosion. The blazes are color-coded blue with trail options for "easy" and "hard" venues. This single-track trail curves constantly through the forest, traveling up and down ridges. For those who enjoy drops, free-riding, stunts, and whoop-dee-doos, the most advanced challenges are deeper in the woods. The park's official policy for hikers on this trail says, "while not encouraged to use the bike trails, hikers are allowed to explore the trial system. However, biking trails are made for bikers, and hikers are advised to yield to riders." There are three places where hiking and biking sections cross; users are expected to use caution at these locations. To begin the trail, enter the forest from the north side of the parking lot. Loops range from about 1.0 mile to 6.0 miles in length. Park officials state there are between 7.0 to 7.5 miles of trails using all loops. Returns are on the south side of Interpretive Trail.

Wake County

Wake County has four major parks with pedestrian trails, plus a section of the *American Tobacco Trail (ATT)*, which is multi-use. (See Chapter 4 for information on trails in the city of Raleigh.) For information on Wake County trails, contact Wake County Parks, Recreation & Open Space, P.O. Box 550 (mailing), Suite 1000, Wake County Office Building (physical location), Raleigh, NC 27602 (919-856-6677; fax: 919-856-6181).

Blue Jay Point County Park

> Blue Jay Point County Park
> 3200 Pleasant Union Church Road
> Raleigh, NC 27614
> Telephone: 919-870-4330

Blue Jay Point County Park is located on a peninsula at Falls Lake. It offers ball fields, a playground, picnic areas, a lodge, and the Center for Environmental Education. The latter was established to educate children about the outdoors and to host training programs. Part of *Falls Lake Trail*, which is also part of the *Mountains-to-Sea Trail*, passes around the park's lake boundary. (See Chapter 1 for more about this trail.) Short connector trails (*Blue Jay Point Trail, Sandy Point Trail,* and *Laurel Loop Trail,* each 0.2 mile in length) and a paved trail for the physically disabled descend to meet the 3.1-mile segment of Falls Lake Trail.

ACCESS: Turn onto Pleasant Union Church Road, 1.5 miles south of the Six Forks Road junction with NC 98 or 1.5 miles north of its junction with Possum Track Road. Turn left at the park entrance.

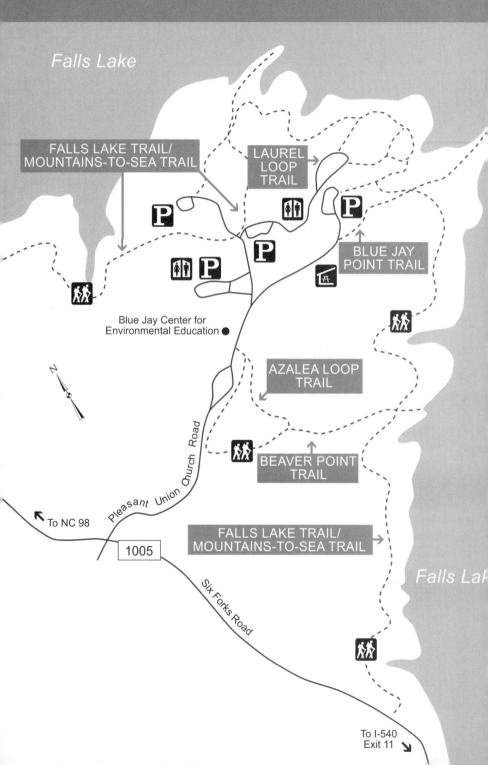

Crowder District Park

Crowder District Park
4409 Ten Ten Road
Apex, NC 27539
Telephone: 919-662-2850

Known for its environmental education program, this park has facilities that include picnic shelters, three playgrounds, an outdoor classroom amphitheater, sand volleyball courts, open-play fields, and trails, most of which are paved. In the center of the 33-acre park is a small lake with a boardwalk, which provides a scenic attraction. The park hours are 8:00 A.M. to sunset. The park is closed on Thanksgiving Day, Christmas Day, and New Year's Day.

ACCESS: From U.S. 1, south of Apex, take Exit 96. Drive east on Ten Ten Road for 4.0 miles to the park entrance on the left. From U.S. 401, south of Garner, drive west on Ten Ten Road for about 4.0 miles to the park entrance on the right.

Outer Paved Trail (0.8 mile, easy)
Inner Paved Trail (0.3 mile, easy)
Amphitheater Trail (243 yards, easy)

Trailheads and Description: If parking at the office, follow *Outer Paved Trail* clockwise. After traveling through a section in the forest, there is an exit to a wildflower garden on the right. The trail curves by a play field and parking lots as it goes to *Amphitheater Trail*, on the left at 0.4 mile. If walking Amphitheater Trail, notice the quartz rock along the path. Descend and cross a bridge before ascending to rejoin Outer Paved Trail. Turn left and follow the trail through the forest. Pass the access to *Inner Paved Trail*, as well as picnic areas, and return to the office parking area at 0.8 mile.

Inner Paved Trail can be hiked while at the lake and its boardwalk, or you can park at the lake and hike the two loops from there. The latter route provides easier access to playgrounds and restrooms.

Harris Lake County Park

Harris Lake County Park
2112 County Park Drive
New Hill, NC 27562
Telephone: 919-387-4342

Facilities at this 680-acre park include primitive group camping sites, canoe and kayak launches, a children's playground, picnic areas with shelters (that may be rented for large groups), fishing opportunities (with rental equipment), environmental education programs, disc golfing, and hiking and mountain-biking trails. (See Chapter 6 for more details about the mountain-biking trails.) Park hours are from 8 A.M. to sunset every day. The park is closed on Thanksgiving Day, Christmas Eve and Day, and New Year's Day.

ACCESS: From U.S. 1 south, take Exit 89 and travel east on New Hill-Holleman Road for 2.8 miles and turn right into entrance.

Peninsula Hiking Trail (4.4 miles)
Red Fox Trail (0.25 mile)
White Tail Run Trail (0.5 mile)
Beaver Trail (1.7 miles)

Length and Difficulty: 6.8 miles combined and overlapped; easy to moderate

Trailheads and Description: The trailhead is at the entrance to the parking lot, on the right at a kiosk. Brochures with trail maps can be found here. To hike *Peninsula Hiking Trail* clockwise, stay straight and ignore the other three trail loops. *Red Fox Trail* is the first right, *White Tail Run Trail* is the first left, and *Beaver Trail* is on the right after crossing a boardwalk.

Enter Peninsula Hiking Trail on a wide natural surface. After 35 yards, the trail turns abruptly to the right and continues on a narrow route. (If you continue straight ahead, the trail leads to a boat launch for canoers and kayakers.) After another 108 yards, Red Fox Trail makes a loop to the right around a small pond. In the summer, the pond will most likely have a green cover of watermeal. This loop also returns to the access point for Peninsula Hiking Trail. Pass White Tail Run Trail on the left. Pass under a power line where there are views of the 0.1-mile-high cooling towers of Progress Energy's Harris Nuclear Plant to the right. At 0.2 mile, there is an open area

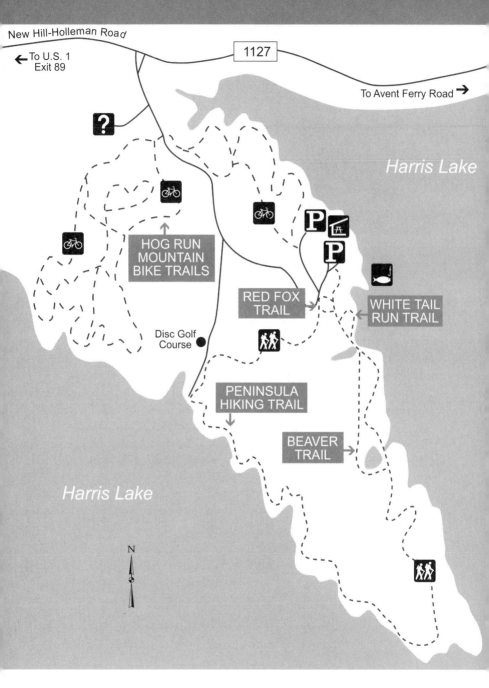

HARRIS LAKE COUNTY PARK TRAILS

New Hill-Holleman Road

← To U.S. 1
Exit 89

1127

To Avent Ferry Road →

Harris Lake

HOG RUN
MOUNTAIN
BIKE TRAILS

RED FOX
TRAIL

WHITE TAIL
RUN TRAIL

Disc Golf
Course

PENINSULA
HIKING TRAIL

BEAVER
TRAIL

Harris Lake

N

View of Progress Energy's nuclear power plant from Peninsula Hiking Trail in Harris Lake County Park

with a boardwalk and a pond on the right. Reenter the forest; after 40 yards, Beaver Trail loop is to the right. (There may not be a sign here, but there may be blazes.)

Continuing on Peninsula Hiking Trail, there is a selected restoration project for longleaf pine at 0.9 mile. The general forest has hardwoods and loblolly pines, with an understory of sparkleberry, dogwood, and sourwood. Songbirds are noticeable in the open areas. At 1.5 miles and 2.0 miles, there are good views of the Harris Nuclear Plant. On approaching the 2.5-mile point in the hike, there is an alluring hardwood forest with a lack of understory. At 3.0 miles, descend under a power line. At 3.3 miles, ascend a ridge. Arrive at an old road. A left turn leads to the lake. Turn right. At 3.8 miles, across the road to the left is a disc golf course. Pass an old homesite on the left at 3.9 miles. At 4.2 miles, cross a gravel road, after which the trail returns to the parking area.

Hog Run Beginning Loop Trail (0.6 mile)
Hog Run Intermediate Loop Trail (1.5 miles)
Hog Run Advanced Loop Trail (5.3 miles)

Trailheads and Description: The park also has a carefully designed 8.5-mile network of mountain-bike trails, accessible only to bikers. To access the designated general trailhead from the park's entrance, turn left at each road fork until reaching a parking lot. The trails are divided by degrees of difficulty, ranging from beginning to advanced. (The advanced section does not have a parking lot. As a result, users of the advanced section must first pass through

Hog Run Beginning Loop Trail in Harris Lake County Park

parts of the beginning and intermediate sections to begin the advanced loops. Another option is to bike on the entrance road back toward the park office and turn left [west] off the road.)

The blue-blazed *Hog Run Beginning Loop Trail* is 0.6 mile. This is a particularly good trail for children. At 0.2 mile, the trail reaches an amphitheater near the lake. Connected to it is the yellow-blazed, 1.5-mile *Hog Run Intermediate Loop Trail*. At 0.9 mile, there is a scenic lagoon. At 1.1 miles, there are remnants of an old homesite.

To reach the red-blazed *Hog Run Advanced Loop Trail*, cross the entrance road and turn right. At 0.6 mile, there is a short loop on the left that rejoins the trail later. (Using this connector loop and making a left turn at the next connector makes a 1.2-mile return to the entrance road.) Continuing on the main trail, there are four loops off the trail. Some of these loops have log jumps, narrow treads, and dips. At 1.2 miles, there is a loop option with both right and left turns. If taking the right turn, at the next connection you will have completed all trails next to the lake, but completing the inter-looping sections will require backtracking. If backtracking to the parking lot, the trip will travel 5.3 miles in the advanced section, plus 0.65 mile from the trailhead to the parking lot.

Historic Yates Mill County Park

Historic Yates Mill County Park
4620 Lake Wheeler Road
Raleigh, NC 27603
Telephone: 919-856-6675

This 174-acre park is the home for Wake County's last functioning gristmill. The current mill is a restoration of a water-powered mill that was originally built in the 1750s. Steep Hill Creek, which feeds a 20-acre lake, is the source of the mill's power. The mission of the park is to "celebrate its past, cherish its heritage, and nurture its resources for future generations." Facilities include a picnic area, a covered field classroom, natural-surface hiking trails, and the A. E. Finley Center for Education and Research. Among the center's major features are exhibits of the park's cultural and natural history. The park also serves as a field-research facility for N.C. State University's College of Agriculture and Life Sciences.

ACCESS: From I-440, take Exit 297. Drive south on Lake Wheeler Road for 2.8 miles to entrance on the right.

Millpond Trail (0.8 mile)
High Ridge Trail (0.7 mile)
Creekside Trail (1.0 mile)

Length and Difficulty: 2.5 miles combined and backtracked; easy to moderate

Trailheads and Description: If hiking *Millpond Trail* counterclockwise, begin at the boardwalk on the side of the lake across from the parking area. Pick up a map that shows 20 tree identification points. Using this map, notice the first number is at a sycamore before you cross the boardwalk. After crossing the boardwalk, there are trail signs for going right or left. If going left on the well-designed routing, the interpretive numbers will indicate cumulative mileage going to the mill. (If hiking *High Ridge Trail* first, the trailhead goes to the right for 125 yards and then turns left.) Continuing on Millpond Trail, pass an access to a field-classroom shelter on the right at 0.35 mile. After another 165 yards, there is a junction with High Ridge Trail on the right. Pass a canoe ramp, followed by some large white oaks near an observation deck. Cross the dam to get to the gristmill at 0.65 mile.

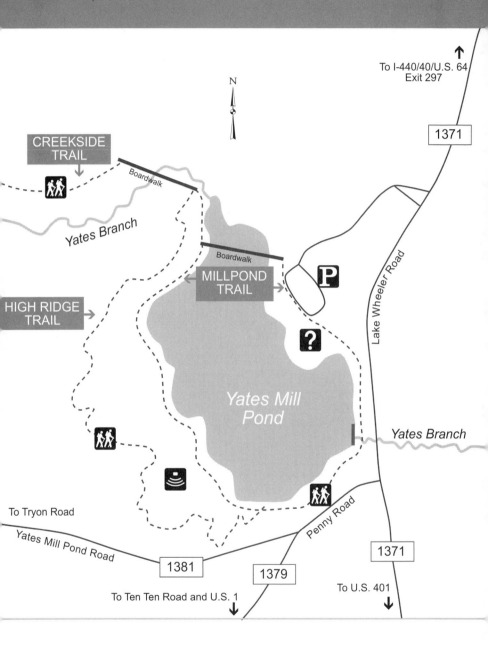

CREEKSIDE TRAIL

Boardwalk

To I-440/40/U.S. 64
Exit 297

1371

N

Yates Branch

Boardwalk

MILLPOND TRAIL

P

HIGH RIDGE TRAIL

?

Lake Wheeler Road

Yates Mill Pond

Yates Branch

To Tryon Road

Yates Mill Pond Road

Penny Road

1371

1381

1379

To U.S. 401

To Ten Ten Road and U.S. 1

Complete the circle at 0.8 mile.

If making a loop with High Ridge Trail near the mill, ascend a slope in the forest of hardwoods. Pass the outdoor classroom at 0.15 mile. Follow a path that weaves through ascents and descents. On a ridge at 0.6 mile, there are good views of the lake when the leaves are off the trees. Access *Creekside Trail* and Millpond Trail at 0.7 mile.

Creekside Trail crosses a 136-yard boardwalk over the creek and marsh. Benches provide the pleasure and opportunity to watch and listen to the waterfowl. Willow, cattails, vines, and stilt grass compete for space in the marsh. From the boardwalk, enter a forest of hardwoods and loblolly pine. The understory is generally small beech, grasses, and switch cane. Since most of the area is considered wetland there may be standing water in some places. There are ravines from agricultural fields to the right. Cross a streamlet at 0.6 mile. At 1.0 mile, arrive at Steep Hill Creek. There is a water-level gage located here. Backtrack. (There are plans to extend the trail. Request an update from the park office.)

Lake Crabtree County Park

Lake Crabtree County Park
1400 Aviation Parkway
Morrisville, NC 27560
Telephone: 919-460-3390

Bordering I-40 at the western edge of the county, this 215-acre park adjoins 500-acre Lake Crabtree. The park provides picnic areas with shelters, playgrounds, fishing piers, boat rentals, boat ramps, a long hiking trail, and a mountain-biking trail network. One short interpretive nature trail is the 0.6-mile *Old Beech Nature Trail*, which is located in a damp area. It has boardwalks among oak, loblolly pine, sweet gum, and maples (one of which has three trunk prongs and is located at 0.3 mile). Access is at the first parking lot to the right after entering the park. At this parking lot, there is also an access to *Lake Crabtree Trail*.

Across the road from this parking area is the west access to *Highland Trail*, which is popular with mountain bikers. At 0.3 mile on the entrance road into the park, the park manager's office is to the left and to the right are accesses to *Lake Trail* and Highland Trail, both described ahead. The sound of traffic from I-40 and Raleigh/Durham International Airport is prominent throughout the park. Park hours are 8:00 A.M. to sunset, seven days a week, except holidays such as Thanksgiving, Christmas Eve and Day, and New Year's Day.

ACCESS: From I-40, take Exit 285. Drive south on Aviation Parkway for 0.3 mile and turn left at the park entrance.

Lake Crabtree Trail (5.4 miles, easy to moderate)

Trailhead and Description: If parking at the trailhead for *Old Beech Nature Trail* (the closest access to the western trailhead of *Lake Crabtree Trail*), walk east on the main park road 0.3 mile to a road across from the park manager's office. The road goes to the right, leading to the boat-rental and fishing dock. At the first parking lot, notice the trailhead and signboard to the left. At 0.2 mile, cross a footbridge and turn right on the blue-blazed trail. Among the forest of young pine and oak, pass through redbud, hazelnut, sumac, and witch hazel. At 0.4 mile, there is an observation deck. Stay near the lake's edge, where mountain bikes on *Highland Trail* also use this section of trails. At 0.8 mile, parallel I-40, where cow-itch vine hugs the rocks on the lakeside. At 1.0 mile, pass through a gated fence near the top of Lake Crabtree Dam. There is a signboard with information here. To the left is a

Sailboats at Lake Crabtree in Wake County

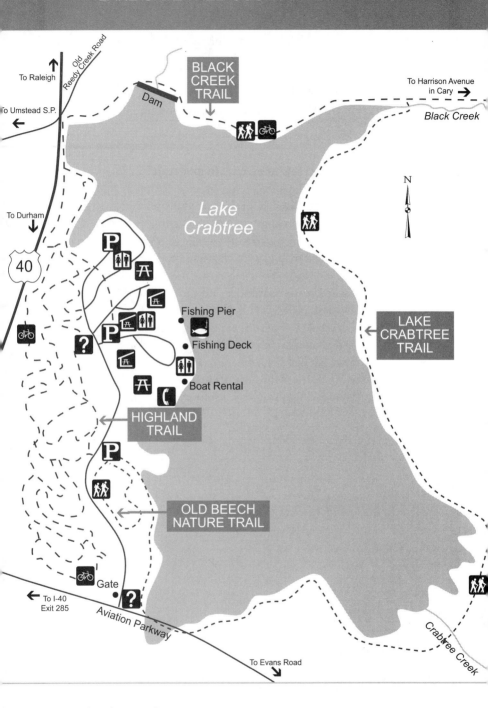

LAKE CRABTREE COUNTY PARK TRAILS

To Raleigh

Old Reedy Creek Road

To Umstead S.P.

To Durham

40

To I-40 Exit 285

Aviation Parkway

To Evans Road

Dam

BLACK CREEK TRAIL

To Harrison Avenue in Cary

Black Creek

Lake Crabtree

N

LAKE CRABTREE TRAIL

Fishing Pier

Fishing Deck

Boat Rental

HIGHLAND TRAIL

OLD BEECH NATURE TRAIL

Gate

Crabtree Creek

gate at Old Reedy Creek Road. (Access to Old Reedy Creek Road is off I-40, Exit 287; drive south on Harrison Avenue for 0.4 mile, turn right on Weston Parkway. Go 0.5 mile, turn right, and continue 0.8 mile to road-shoulder parking at the dam.)

Continue right on Lake Crabtree Trail. Cross the dam and jointly follow the asphalt-surfaced, 3.5-mile *Black Creek Trail* (part of the Cary greenway system. Construction is underway leading to Bond Park). The dam, built in 1987, is part of the Crabtree Watershed Project, which created a drainage area of 33,128 acres. The views up the lake are scenic. At 1.2 miles, descend to the lakeside. At 1.4 miles, there is a covered pavilion. Water fountains for both people and their dogs are here. Enter the woods at 1.5 miles, where an opening soon appears to the right. Here you can view turtles on old logs and waterfowl gathered around the sandbars. At 1.6 miles, cross a drainage bridge, followed by a paved access to the left. This leads to buildings located in Research Triangle Park. At 1.7 miles, turn right off *Black Creek Greenway* to cross a footbridge over Black Creek. *Note:* The bridge may be closed due to flood damage. The greenway is for hikers only. (The greenway continues upstream underneath twin bridges on Weston Parkway. See Chapter 4 for a complete description of Black Creek Greenway.)

Lake Crabtree Trail continues into the forest and begins to ascend and descend along the south edge of the lake. Follow a narrow treadway in and out of coves and pass areas close to the lake, where there are large hardwoods, with buckeye (a species found in alluvial woods and swamp forests), lavender monarda, and false foxglove. Cross a wet area at 2.6 miles. Enter an old road with a thin passage through grasses and shrubs. At 3.2 miles, there is concrete footing for a passage through a swamp. Cattail, willows, and a cacophony of frogs are found here. Reach Evans Road at 3.4 miles and walk on a narrow trail at the base of the road shoulder, then cross an arched steel footbridge over Crabtree Creek at 3.6 miles and turn right. (There may not be signs or blazes to indicate the direction.)

Stay right on an old road where you may see blue blazes near the lake. Pass through a swampy area to exit at Aviation Parkway near an undeveloped parking area at 4.6 miles. Turn right across the causeway and reenter the forest at the edge of the shoulder railing at 5.0 miles. Poison ivy is prominent in the woods. Enter a field of tall grasses and shrubs (these are wet after rains), then approach a manicured lawn of the park. Complete the loop at the Old Beech Nature Trail parking lot at 5.4 miles.

▓ Highland Trail

This trail is one of the oldest and most popular mountain-biking trails in the area. Although it is also open to joggers and walkers, "each of whom shares responsibility for the safety of the other" according to park policy, the trail is chiefly used by mountain bikers. They should be credited for reconstructing the original path and organizing to maintain it. There is a trail map at the park entrance. The loops are blazed yellow and the connectors are blazed red. The park closes the trail during rainy weather; call 919-460-3390 for trail conditions and closings.

Length and Difficulty: There are five loops and seven connector trails, which can be combined for approximately 6.5 miles. The trails vary in difficulty, but all are appropriate for beginning to intermediate riders.

Trailheads and Description: These loop trails have maps posted at nearly every intersection. Most first-time riders won't have trouble figuring out where they are in the trail network.

Access is at three trailheads. One is at the first parking lot after the entrance. Users can cross the road to a posted map, which shows that a left turn encompasses Loops #2 (0.5 mile), #3 (0.6 mile), and #4 (1.3 miles). These three loops are linked by Connector E (0.4 mile) and one unlettered connector. A turn right at the trailhead leads to Loops #1 (1.7 miles) and #5 (0.7 mile). These two loops are linked by Connector A (0.3 mile) and Connector B (0.2 mile). There is also a short, unlettered connector near the east end of the loop. Connector D (0.4 mile) is the official route to the most eastern trailhead. This trailhead is located at the dam where it connects with *Black Creek Greenway*, which goes south to Cary. It also connects, to the left, to Old Reedy Creek Road, which goes over the I-40 bridge and into the multi-use trails of Umstead State Park. (These multi-use trails are discussed in Chapter 2.) Connector C (0.5 mile), which begins at the lower east end of Loop #1 connects to Loop #5. This route can be extended at the boat-ramp crossing by going into a parking area at the fishing-pier access. This terminal is also the third trailhead for the network.

CHAPTER 4

Trails in Municipal Parks and Recreation Areas

More than 135 cities and towns in North Carolina have departments of parks and recreation. Some metropolitan areas whose boundaries join have formed joint departments, and other cities have teamed with their counties for cooperative services. A few cities are moving swiftly with long-range master plans for greenway systems that will not only serve the inner city, but also connect with other cities and into the counties. The highest concentration of connecting trails in the Triangle area occurs in the cities and towns of Raleigh, Durham, Chapel Hill, Cary, Apex, Morrisville, and Holly Springs. Other towns near the main Triangle area with either trail connections already made or in the planning stages are Dunn/Erwin; Smithfield/Selma; and Louisburg/Franklinton. Wake is the county with the largest number of county parks.

Urban trails (greenways) are usually used for walking, jogging, bicycling, birdwatching, and in-line skating. The trails frequently follow streams, city utility routes, and non-motorized roads, or travel through recreational parks and historic areas. Urban trails provide opportunities for appreciating community heritage and culture at a relaxed pace, for meeting neighbors, and for improving physical and emotional health. Urban walking clubs are growing in popularity, and books and magazines focusing on urban trails are increasing. "Trails for day use must be developed in and near urban areas," stated the National Park Service in 1986 when it was developing a national trails system plan. On the following pages are descriptive examples of diverse trails whose treadways are asphalt, concrete, brick, natural surface, and combinations of various substances. They lead into paths of history and serve as outlets for recreation and healthy exercise.

Apex (Wake County)

For an update on the town's greenway construction, contact:
Apex Parks, Recreation, and Cultural Resources
P.O. Box 250 (mailing)
53 Hunter Street (physical location)
Apex, NC 27502
Telephone: 919-249-3402; fax: 919-249-3368
www.apexnc.org

In the past decade, the Apex town government in conjunction with the town's Parks and Recreation Department has increased funding, construction, and long-range planning for its greenway system. Its oldest greenway is the Apex Reservoir Trail, which was later named *Community Park Greenway* because it was within the Community Park system.

Beaver Creek Greenway, which will be one of the longest greenways in Apex, is now partially completed. The proposed trail will extend southwest to connect with the *American Tobacco Trail*. In addition, a connector from the greenway will extend into the heart of the town, going through Apex Jaycee Park. A fork of the greenway will extend to South Salem Street. A long north-south greenway is proposed along Middle Creek. It is one of at least 20 extensions or separate sections that has been proposed. Six trails that already exist are described ahead. Trails that are located on private property in housing developments are not included.

Apex Community Park

This 160-acre park is the town's oldest and largest fully operational park. Its paved greenway is currently the longest trail in Apex. It is also the most popular. With excellent greenway engineering and adjoining facilities, it is the town's showpiece park. Other park facilities include picnic areas, athletic fields and courts, a fitness site, a children's playground, and fishing and boating areas. No swimming is allowed.

ACCESS: From the junction of U.S. 1/64, drive west 2.4 miles on U.S. 64 to Laura Duncan Road. Turn right onto Laura Duncan Road. After 0.6 mile, turn right onto Community Park Drive.

Community Park Greenway (2.0 miles, easy)
Lakeside Trail (0.4 mile, easy)

Trailheads and Description: Park in the last parking area from the entrance. Follow the paved access past a physical-fitness site; then descend to the loop trail. If going left, follow the paved *Community Park Greenway* through a forest of tall hardwoods and loblolly pine. Dogwood, tag alder, and wax myrtle are part of the understory. Ducks and geese are frequently seen. Cross a small stream at 0.6 mile. At 0.8 mile, a bench offers an excellent site for viewing the lake and sunsets. At 1.0 mile, there are views from the dam and an access to a parking lot on Lake Pine Drive. At 1.5 miles, *Lakeside Trail* joins the greenway. (If following the Lakeside Trail loop, descend to cross a bridge over a small stream in a cove. At 0.1 mile, there is a mound of sufficient size to provide views of the lake. Sparkleberry and Christmas ferns are seen along the pathway. Rejoin the greenway after 0.4 mile.)

If staying on the greenway at its junction with Lakeside Trail, continue to an access trail on the left at 1. 7 miles. (This access trail goes 135 yards to a cul-de-sac on Park Summit Boulevard.) Staying on the greenway, curve right and descend to connect with Lakeside Trail, on the right at 1.9 miles. Pass under a power line. There are two natural-surface nature trails (0.2 mile and 0.3 mile, respectively) that lead into the forest. Continuing on the greenway, you will be on a causeway. Cattails can be seen in a swamp on the left. Curve right, where a 0.2-mile nature trail turns to the left. (This nature trail goes upstream to the baseball field. The trail can be wet sometimes in the rainy season.) Complete the greenway and turn left for a return to the parking lot.

Beaver Creek Greenway Area

These greenways are described together because they all parallel Beaver Creek or one of its tributaries that flow from Jaycee Park west to a confluence with Beaver Creek. Only Charleston Village and Sutton Place greenways currently connect. There is a proposal to connect all of the trails listed above either with a greenway or sidewalk. There is also a proposal to continue the current *Beaver Creek Greenway* by adding new or existing easements downstream to connect Kelly Road and Glen parks to the undeveloped Nature Park. From there, the proposed greenway would continue west to connect with the *American Tobacco Trail* on the B. Everett Jordan Lake property.

Beaver Creek Greenway (1.5 miles, easy)

Trailhead and Description: To access *Beaver Creek Greenway*, from South Salem Street (SR 1011 or Old U.S. 1) in downtown Apex, turn right on Apex Barbecue Road (SR 1162). After 0.5 mile, turn right on Town Side Drive. Go 0.3 mile to park at Town Square, on the left, at the intersection with Village Commons Avenue. From here walk 0.1 mile (north) down the sidewalk of Town Side Drive to where Beaver Creek Greenway crosses, going

Bridge on Beaver Creek Greenway in Apex

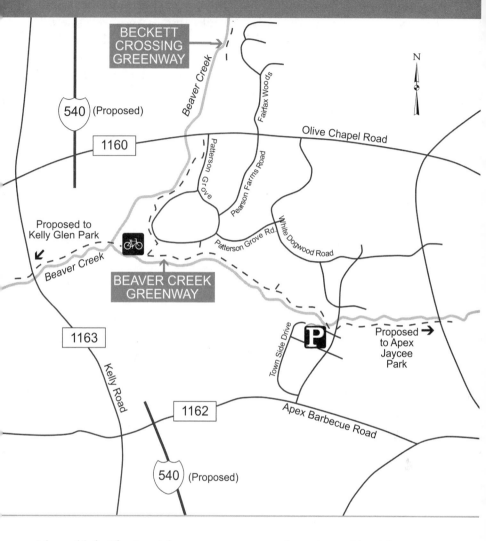

right and left. If going right, or upstream, pass through a residential area on the right and end at 0.2 mile. Backtrack. This is the route the greenway will follow in the future to reach Apex Jaycee Park and other accesses.

Going left, or downstream, on the greenway from Town Side Drive, cross a boardwalk and arched bridge on the unnamed stream at 0.1 mile. There are hardwoods and loblolly pine on both sides. Both white and blue asters grow here in autumn. This is also a desirable area for bird watchers. At 0.3 mile, there is a 45-yard access, on the right, to Patterson Grove Road. Cross another arched bridge at 0.5 mile; followed by another 50-yard access to the street. Curve right (away from the future route to Kelly Road and Glen parks) and reach Patterson Grove Road at 0.9 mile. Turn left on a wide sidewalk, but leave it by going left at 1.0 mile. The trail is now paralleling Beaver Creek. The stream the trail has followed until this location was a tributary of Beaver Creek. All too soon you leave it. Curve right, pass a children's playground, and stop at the junction of Patterson Grove Road and Chenworth Drive at 1.4 miles. Backtrack. (To the left on Patterson Grove Road, it is 0.1 mile to Olive Chapel Road. Going right [east] on Olive Chapel Road, it is 0.2 mile to Fairfax Woods Drive. Going left, Olive Chapel Road leads to Beckett Crossing Greenway.)

Beckett Crossing Greenway (0.1 to 0.3 mile, easy)

Trailhead and Description: From NC 55, drive west on Olive Chapel Road for 1.9 miles to Fairfax Woods Drive and turn right. At the fork of Fairfax Woods Drive, turn left. Watch for Beckett Crossing Residential Facility on the left (across the street from Celandine Drive). The parking lot is on the left.

Follow *Beckett Crossing Greenway* as it goes between the swimming pool and a pond with a fountain. Turn right, and then cross a bridge over a small stream. To the left is Beaver Creek. The pavement may end after 0.1 to 0.3 mile, but there is a proposed extension to Beaver Creek Commons Drive. Backtrack.

Charleston Village Greenway (0.4 mile, easy)

Trailhead and Description: From NC 55 junction with U.S. 64, drive 0.9 mile north on NC 55. At the intersection with Old Jenks Road, turn right. After 0.4 mile, turn left to park at Castleberry Park. It has a community center with a swimming pool, a children's playground, and a gazebo with picnic facilities. Follow *Charleston Village Greenway* as it goes upstream. You're paralleling Beaver Creek, which is only a streamlet at this point. On the left, there are manicured lawns of homes. Some of the hardwood trees have mistletoe. Cross over another streamlet on a culvert at 0.1 mile. Cross Castleberry Drive at 0.2 mile. In crossing Castleberry Drive, the trail shifts to the east side of the streamlet and goes into the forest. At 0.4 mile the greenway ends. Backtrack. (*Note:* About 120 feet before reaching the end of the trail, there is a 200-foot access to Sutton Place Greenway. To reach the access, hop the rocks across little Beaver Creek.)

Haddon Hall Greenway (0.6 mile or 1.2 miles if backtracked; easy)

Trailhead and Description: From the junction of U.S. 64 and NC 55, drive south on NC 55 (Williams Street) for 0.4 mile. Beaver Creek Commons Shopping Center is on the right. Turn left at the traffic light onto Haddon Hall Drive. Immediately turn right onto Haywards Heath Lane. Follow it 0.3 mile to a descent. There is a space on the left side of the street where you can park. This is the upstream access.

From the street-side parking follow *Haddon Hall Greenway* across a small stream. The main source for this stream is a lake upstream at a community center; it is a tributary of Beaver Creek. Forest growth is dense on the streamside, but new housing developments may be noticeable on the left side. At 0.2 mile, cross Haddon Hall Drive. Descend. Cross the stream again at 0.3 mile. The greenway forks where there is an unfinished passage on the left.

Turn right and follow a damp greenway. Alongside the greenway on the right is a small stream; residential houses are on the left. At 0.6 mile arrive at Blackburn Road. Either backtrack or make a loop by turning right onto Haddon Hall Drive. If making the loop, descend and then pass Colehurst Crescent. Rejoin the greenway at 0.8 mile. Turn left for a return to the trailhead at 1.0 mile.

Sutton Place Greenway (0.3 mile, easy)

Trailhead and Description: Follow the directions above for *Charleston Village Greenway*, except when turning turn off NC 55 onto Old Jenks Road, turn left immediately onto Holt Road. After 0.7 mile, turn right into Sutton Place housing development on Sutton Glen Drive. After a few yards, turn left on Hotridge Drive. Follow it for 0.2 mile to a children's playground with a picnic shelter. There is street parking along the greenway here. Walk behind the playground and by a pond on the right. Approach a T-intersection. To the left, the trail may not be finished. Going right, follow Beaver Creek downstream for 0.3 mile to the end of the greenway. The access to Charleston Village Greenway, by crossing the stream as described above, is located here.

Carrboro (Orange County)

Carrboro Parks and Recreation Department
P.O. Box 829 (mailing)
301 West Main Street (physical location)
Carrboro, NC 27510
Telephone: 919-968-7702

Carrboro Community Park

Carrboro Community Park, located on the west edge of Carrboro, is a large, modern, well-landscaped facility that would be the pride of any town this size. It offers three lighted ball fields, tennis courts, a playground, a picnic area and shelter, and a lake trimmed with the 0.4-mile *Nature Trail* in a forest of oak, beech, maple, pine, and sweet gum. The area is home to ducks, geese, squirrels, and songbirds. An easy access is located at the first parking area after entering the park.

ACCESS: From Carrboro Plaza Shopping Center (and the junction of NC 54 Bypass and West Main Street), drive 0.7 mile west on NC 54; the park is on the right.

Cary (Wake County)

Cary Parks, Recreation & Cultural Resources Department
P.O. Box 8005 (mailing)
316 North Academy Street (physical location)
Cary, NC 27512
Telephone: 919-469-4061; fax: 919-469-4344
www.townofcary.org

Begun in 1980, the Cary greenway/trail system originally confined its trails to subdivisions or city or neighborhood parks. After a couple of decades, a master plan shows an amazing expansion throughout the city with connections into adjoining cities and towns. There are an additional 18 parks and approximately 50 new trails that are either under construction or proposed for the network. At present, the city has completed more than 35 miles of its dream plan for eventually having at least 150 miles of trails. This plan will include multi-use bicycle routing on wide sidewalks or in extra

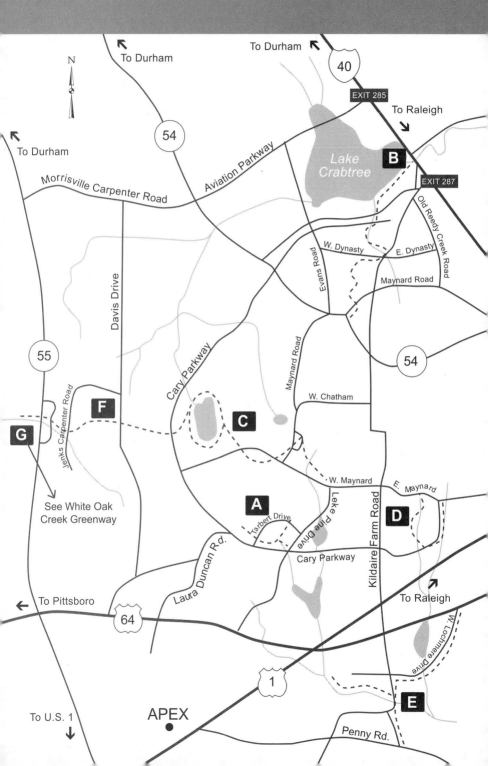

CENTRAL CARY GREENWAY SYSTEM

space along highways. Almost half of the trails are being financially supported and constructed by developers of residential or commercial locations. Other trails, such as the addition to *Hinshaw Greenway* and the pedestrian bridge over U.S. 1/64, has the state's Department of Transportation bearing half the cost.

Most of the city's trails are paved with asphalt, with occasional short sections made of concrete. They usually follow streams or city water-sanitation systems. Trails, such as those in Annie Jones Park, *Higgins Greenway*, *Hinshaw Greenway Area*, and *Pirates Cove Greenway*, originally had natural surfaces. The longest natural-surface (some sections have added wood chips) network of trails is the color-coded system in Fred G. Bond Metro Park.

Unless otherwise marked at the trailheads, all paved greenways/trails are for walking, jogging, bicycling, skateboarding, and roller-skating. Restrictions may differ on some sidewalks. Camping is not allowed on any of the trails. The trails are open only from sunrise to sunset. Dogs must be leashed. Where signs indicate, sanitary dog bags must be used to insure clean greenways.

Some of the trail projects for which there is already a commitment may be in the process of construction by the time this guidebook is published. These projects include completion of the following: *Black Creek Greenway*; a section of *Camp Branch Greenway*; *Glenkirk Greenway*; a section of *Green Level Greenway*; *Middle Creek Greenway*; *Tryon Road Park Greenway*; *Tryon Village Greenway*; a section of *Walnut Creek Greenway*; a 2.0-mile section of *White Oak Creek Greenway*; and *Yates Store Road Greenway*.

The trails described in this section are listed alphabetically by either the trail or park name. There are a few short greenway trails that are isolated or only connect to proposed routes. The following short trails are discussed here and are grouped in this order at the end of the Cary section: *Bishop's Gate Greenway*; *Camp Branch Greenway*; *Grey Hawk Landing Greenway*; *Higgins Greenway*; and *Riggsbee Farm Greenway*.

Annie Jones Park

Located in the southwest part of the city, Annie Jones Park serves a residential area. It offers a children's playground, tennis courts, a picnic area, and a lighted athletic field. The park also serves as the parking area for the Y-shaped *Annie Jones Greenway*. The greenway is a combination of four former shorter trails: McClout Court Trail, Coatridge Trail, Tarbert-Gatehouse Trail, and Lake Pine Trail. (Across the street from the park's entrance is the private Scottish Hills Recreation Club, Inc., which includes a large swimming pool.)

▨ Annie Jones Greenway (2.2 miles round-trip; easy)

Trailhead and Description: From the intersection of Southwest Cary Parkway and Lake Pine Drive, drive three blocks north on Lake Pine Drive. Turn left onto Tarbert Drive. After 0.5 mile, the park entrance is on the right at 1414 Tarbert Drive. Another access can be reached from Old Apex Road by going east on Southwest Cary Parkway for 0.5 mile. Turn left onto Tarbert Drive. Drive 0.2 mile to the park entrance, on the left.

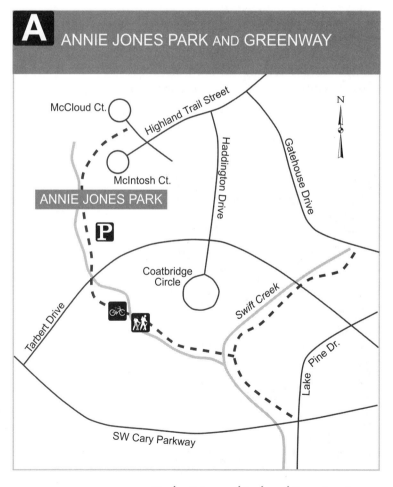

From the parking area, access the greenway by going north near the children's playground. The athletic field is on the right. After entering the hardwood and loblolly-pine forest, arrive at McCloud Court at 0.2 mile. Backtrack to Tarbert Drive, cross that street, and follow a small stream on the former *Coatbridge Trail*. Make a horseshoe curve around unseen Coatbridge Circle and arrive at a T-junction at 0.3 mile from Tarbert Drive.

To the left, the greenway goes upstream for 0.2 mile to cross Tarbert Drive. From here, it passes a picnic area and children's playground, crosses a boardwalk, and ends at Gatehouse Drive after another 0.2 mile. Backtrack to the T-junction and stay straight to parallel a stream for 0.2 mile to end at the corner of Southwest Cary Parkway and Lake Pine Road. Backtrack.

Black Creek Greenway System

Black Creek Greenway (3.9 miles one-way, easy)
Northwoods Greenway (0.8 mile one-way, easy)

Trailheads and Description: To access the northern trailhead from I-40, take Exit 287 and drive south on Harrison Avenue for 0.3 mile. Turn right

Black Creek Greenway paralleling Black Creek in Cary

onto Weston Parkway. After 0.6 mile, turn right on Old Reedy Creek Road. Go 1.3 miles to the Lake Crabtree County Park gate on the left. (Parking may be difficult here because there is not a parking lot, only narrow road shoulders. A parking lot has been proposed.) At the southern trailhead, there is a 28-car parking lot off Northwest Maynard Road. It is on the left if

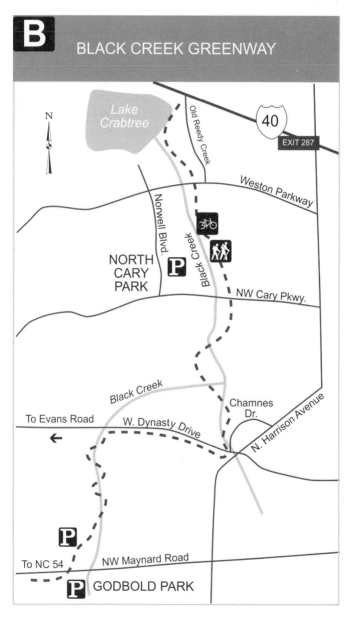

driving 0.3 mile east of Evans Road. If coming from Harrison Avenue, turn onto Northwest Maynard Road and drive 0.4 miles west to the lot on the right. Other accesses are described ahead.

Black Creek Greenway is an exceptionally scenic, popular, and unique trail. The linear asphalt route currently weaves from Lake Crabtree County Park on the north end to Chapel Hill Road (NC 54) on the south. When completed, it will end at the boat dock in Fred G. Bond Metro Park (Bond Park) for a total distance of about 7.0 miles. From Bond Park, it will join White Oak Creek Greenway for another 7.0 miles to the American Tobacco Trail.

The greenway is unique because it is the first major greenway to connect the cities of Cary and Raleigh. To the north, it connects with the trails in Umstead State Park and Reedy Creek Greenway and goes to the southeast end of Meredith College at Faircloth and Hillsborough streets in Raleigh. This multi-use routing makes a total route of 14 miles. From the Meredith location, other greenways will eventually add about 7.0 more miles in east Raleigh. Eventually the Black Creek Greenway artery will be part of a major loop, which some reports call the 100-mile Loop. This loop will connect the greenway with the Mountains-to-Sea Trail at West Point on the Eno Park in north Durham, and with Walnut Creek Greenway and Neuse River Trail in east Raleigh.

To access Black Creek Greenway's northern trailhead, the trail runs jointly with Lake Crabtree Trail as they cross the dam. At 0.25 mile, there is a descent to the lakeside. At 0.45 mile, there is a water fountain and pavilion. Enter the woods and then cross a footbridge. At an open space you may see waterfowl in the shallow water and turtles sunning on old logs. At 0.7 mile, Lake Crabtree Trail turns sharply to the right to cross a pedestrian bridge over Black Creek. After the bridge, the trail becomes a natural-surface hiking route. (The bridge was severely damaged in a 2006 flood, so it may be closed. Call Lake Crabtree County Park at 919-460-3390 for an update.)

After the split with Lake Crabtree Trail, Black Creek Greenway continues ahead, going under the twin bridges of Weston Parkway. On the right side, the creek appears innocent, with some trickling sounds coming from the rocky places while the pools are silent. This is a great contrast to what happens to the greenway during storms, when the creek waters go rushing by because of flooding. Among the trees along the way are elm, yellow poplar, oak, and black walnut. The latter is a favorite of the squirrels. Wildflowers include cardinal flower, jewelweed, and white aster. At 0.9 mile, there is a paved 76-yard access path that leads to the Tynemouth Drive cul-de-sac. At 1.1 miles, there is a 138-yard paved access on the left that goes to a cul-de-sac at Mindenhall Way. Arrive at the North Cary Park bridge over Black Creek at 1.4 miles.

To reach North Cary Park from Black Creek Greenway, you have a choice of access. To the right, the access ascends up a hill on a skillfully designed paved route for 0.3 mile to the park's parking area. To the left, the access goes to a resting place, then over a ravine, up some steps, and then crosses a high trestle before rejoining the paved area. (Also on this route, there is a paved access, on the left, that leads to Northwest Cary Parkway.) North Cary Park facilities include restrooms, an elaborate children's playground, a bouldering and rock-climbing site, a soccer field, a picnic area, basketball slabs, and sand volleyball courts. From the park, you can access Weston Greenway, which is listed ahead.

Continuing on Black Creek Greenway, pass the paved access leading to Northwest Cary Parkway, and go under the parkway bridge. At 1.5 miles, there is a rocky area in the creek and embankments along the path. A bridge crosses where there is a rock wall with mosses and lichens. After passing an access road, begin to curve away from Black Creek, following a tributary. At 2.1 miles, make the first of two crossings over the tributary before reaching West Dynasty Drive at 2.5 miles. Parking is not allowed here. (It is 0.1 mile to the left to reach North Harrison Avenue.)

Follow the greenway, which is now on the sidewalk, to the right. It ascends and then descends a ridge on West Dynasty Drive for 0.2 mile. At a bridge, where the route comes back to Black Creek, cross the street to keep on the greenway. (There is proposed rerouting of the Black Creek Greenway to connect with the current trail but avoid the West Dynasty Drive sidewalk.) Continuing upstream, cross the creek for the first of six crossings in this section. Under the forest canopy, there are patches of club moss and Pinxter. After a scenic criss-crossing of the stream, pass soccer and track fields. At 3.4 miles, there is a drinking fountain. The trail comes to a fork in the middle of the greenway system. To the right, it is 0.2 mile to Cary Middle School, traveling partially on asphalt and steps. It is another 0.2 mile to Evans Road. If staying left on Black Creek Greenway, cross a wide bridge and arrive at the south trailhead at 3.5 miles. There is a 28-car parking lot on Northwest Maynard Road (NC 54).

If continuing to Godbold Park, cross Northwest Maynard Road at a right angle to reach a parking area at 3.6 miles. (To reach this parking area by vehicle, turn left from Harrison Avenue onto Northwest Maynard Road and come 0.4 mile. From Evans Road, turn right and drive 0.3 mile.) The park facilities include basketball slabs, tennis courts, an open-play field, a picnic area, restrooms, and a children's playground. A special facility is Sk8-Cary for bicyclists, roller-skaters, and skate-boarders.

To continue on the greenway from the parking area, pass the Sk8-Cary building to a fork in the paved route. To the right, Cary Dog Park is at 0.1 mile. Stay right, pass the dog park, parallel Northwest Maynard Road to a tunnel under an access road that leads to a shopping center. Arrive at a circle with a bench at the corner of Chapel Hill Drive and Northwest Maynard Road at 0.3 mile. The total mileage for this spur is 3.9 miles. (From here, there are plans to expand the trail southwest to the boat dock in Bond Park. Along this proposed extension, two short sections have been completed already. One is a 0.3-mile loop around a small pond at Lake Hollow Circle, off Edgehill Parkway from High House Road. The other is a 0.4-mile section that begins west of Castalia Drive to connect with *Parkway Greenway* in Bond Park. (Call Cary Parks and Recreation, 919-469-4061, for an update on construction.)

Back at the fork to the Cary Dog Park, take the left fork to go on *Northwoods Greenway*. Descend into a mature forest. (Before crossing a bridge, notice an older path on the left. Steps ascend to the restroom and pavilion area of Godbold Park.) Continuing on the greenway, cross the wide bridge over Black Creek at 0.2 mile. Enter into a residential area, cross another bridge, then cross Northwoods Drive at 0.5 mile. Pass Northwoods Elementary School, which is on the right. At 0.8 mile, the greenway ends at West Boundary Street and Chapel Hill Road. There is a wide sidewalk where you can turn right to go to the corner of Chapel Hill Road and Northwest Maynard Road, the site of Black Creek Greenway mentioned above. Along the way, you pass Lowe's with its creative three-dimensional windows.

Fred G. Bond Metro Park System

Fred G. Bond Metro Park
801 High House Road
Cary, NC 27513
Telephone: 919-462-3970; boat house: 919-469-4100; fax: 919-388-1155

On the west side of Cary is Wake County's largest municipal park, the 360-acre Fred G. Bond Metro Park, named in honor of a former Cary mayor. A 42-acre lake offers fishing, boating, and boat rentals. The large community center has a gym and facilities for indoor athletic events and programs, conferences, and meetings. Swimming, wading, and camping are not allowed. Designed to preserve the environment, the park's recreation areas are separated within the forest. There are four lighted athletic fields, a playground, and two picnic shelters, one large enough to accommodate 200 people. The Sertoma Amphitheatre is arranged on a natural slope to seat an audience of more than 350. A color-coded network of trails for hikers and bikers provides multiple loops, described below. A new aspect of the trail system in the park is that the *Black Creek Greenway* now enters the park from

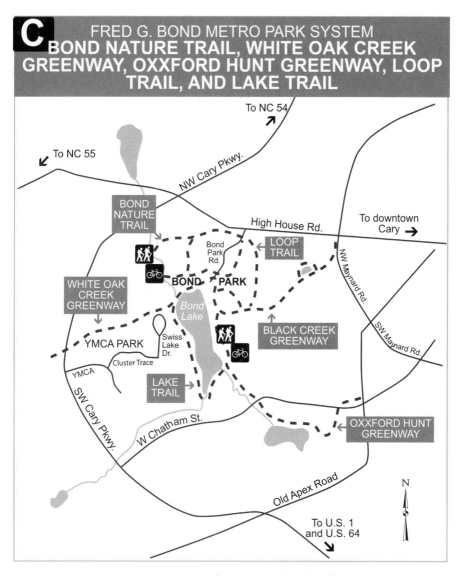

the east and travels 0.4 mile to end at the lake's boat dock. Going west from the dock, there are plans for a 0.2-mile trail to *Parkway Greenway*. Both of these trails will become *White Oak Creek Greenway*.

ACCESS: From Northwest Cary Parkway, turn on High House Road and drive 2.0 miles for a right turn to the Community Center. Ask at the center for information about the trails and access to other facilities.

Lake Trail (2.5 miles, easy)
Loop Trail (2.0 miles, easy)
Bond Nature Trail (0.5 mile, easy)
Oxxford Hunt Greenway (1.5 miles, easy)

Trailheads and Description: The trailheads are accessible from any of the parking areas in Bond Park, because they are all connected. None of the trails is paved. The trail system is designed to provide short loop walks or longer combinations. The linear trails (*Parkway Greenway* and *Oxxford Hunt Greenway*) can be backtracked, or a second vehicle may be used for shuttling.

One possible loop arrangement begins at the parking area near field #1. Enter the woods at par exercise #5 on the physical-fitness course, which may be yellow-blazed; at this point, the physical-fitness course runs right and left with the red-blazed *Loop Trail*. Turn left; after 0.2 mile, cross the park's entrance road. At 0.4 mile, join *Bond Nature Trail*, which has markers about a variety of plants, including blackjack oak whose wood is used commercially for charcoal. Cross a paved road, which leads to the right to the Parkway Athletic Complex, at 0.6 mile. At 0.8 mile, come out of the woods to a field at the base of the dam; stay left until the trail markers show a right turn. Reach a junction with the blue-blazed *Lake Trail*, which goes right and left, at 1.1 miles. (The red-blazed Loop Trail and the green-blazed Bond Nature Trail go left.) Turn right on Lake Trail to cross the dam; this is one of the most scenic views on the hike. To the right at the other end of the dam are steps that descend to the white-blazed Parkway Greenway, which will become *White Oak Creek Greenway* in the future. (At the time of publication of this guidebook, the section ended at *Southwestern Cary Greenway*.) Turn left and continue around the lake. For the next 1.2 miles, the trail dips into ravines and passes over bridges and boardwalks, sometimes close to the lakeshore. On the hillside slope, it meanders into the backyards of residents, who may watch you pass by their azalea beds and back decks. Cross a footbridge over a stream at 2.6 miles and junction with the white-blazed Oxxford Hunt Greenway near another bridge. (Oxxford Hunt Greenway leads 1.5 miles upstream and across West Chatham Street, where it becomes a private greenway open to public use.) Continue left on a service road. At 2.9 miles, rejoin the trail marked by the yellow and red markers on the right and left. Turn right; notice par exercise #17. Pass athletic fields #3 and #2 and return to par exercise #5, the point of origin (left), at 3.4 miles.

Hinshaw Greenway Area

Hinshaw Greenway (1.4 miles, easy)
Pirates Cove Greenway (0.6 mile, easy)

Trailheads and Description: Recommended parking for *Hinshaw Greenway* is at Kids Together Park. To reach that parking area, turn off U.S. 1/U.S. 64 onto Southeast Cary Parkway and drive east 0.5 mile to Thurston Road. Turn left onto Thurston Road. After 0.1 mile, turn left to the parking lot.

If you want to access Hinshaw Greenway near a mid-point, park at MacDonald Woods Park. To reach that parking area, turn off U.S. 1/64

Pirates Cove Greenway in Cary

onto Southeast Cary Parkway and drive west 0.4 mile to Seabrook Avenue. Turn right on Seabrook Avenue. After 0.35 mile, park at the street curb.

To park at the northern trailhead for Hinshaw Greenway, go to the intersection of Southeast Maynard Road and Greenwood Circle and park in the lot at the White Plains United Methodist Church annex.

From here, to access *Pirates Cove Greenway*, go east on Greenwood

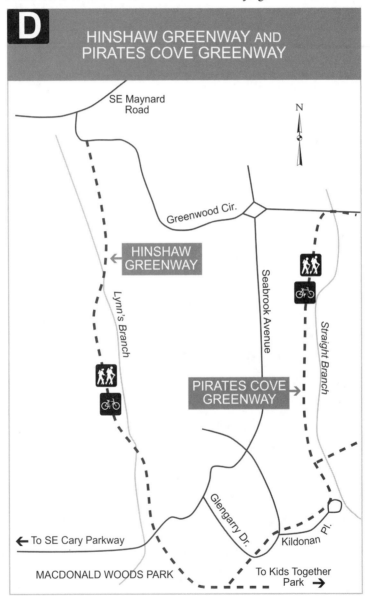

Circle for 0.45 mile to the east end of the roundabout. The greenway's south terminus is at the end of Kildonan Place.

These greenways and parks provide a showpiece of the old and the new. From the distinguished Hinshaw Greenway and its dark and deep forest, the relatively new trail extension offers sunshine on an artistic pedestrian bridge over U.S. 1/64. By combining these greenways, the route goes from curbside parking to the landscaping beauty of the parking lot at Kids Together Park. The expansion projected for the future will connect to Raleigh's *Walnut Creek Greenway* in the north, Annie Jones Park in the west, and *Piney Plains Greenway* in the east and south.

Kids Together Park is not staffed, but there are restrooms, picnic facilities, and an upscale children's playground. Facilities blend man-made art with the art of nature. From the southern trailhead for Hinshaw Greenway at this park, follow the path north to cross the 200-foot, artfully designed pedestrian bridge over U.S. 1/64 at 0.4 mile. Descend on a spiral routing to pass, on the right, an access to Pirates Cove Greenway. To access Pirates Cove Greenway's southern trailhead, walk 85 yards up to Glengarry Drive. Turn right and follow Glengarry Drive to Kildonan Place, where you turn right. Follow Kildonan Place to the end of the street after 0.2 mile. Among the city's oldest natural-surface trails, this greenway is now paved. It parallels Straight Branch. At 0.2 mile, there is a spur to the right to Bloomingdale Drive. There is another spur on the right to Vickie Drive at 0.6 mile, where the trail ends

Children with Katal the Dragon at Kids Together Park at the southern trailhead of Hinshaw Greenway in Cary

at Greenwood Circle. For the northern access to Pirates Cove Greenway, drive north on Seabrook Avenue (where Hinshaw Greenway crosses) for 0.5 mile to the Greenwood Circle roundabout. Take the first right and descend 0.1 mile to the trailhead on the right. There is curbside parking.

To continue on Hinshaw Greenway from its intersection with Pirates Cove Greenway, pass an access and a spur to the left that approaches a basketball court and children's carpeted playground at MacDonald Woods Park. Arrive at Seabrook Avenue at 0.6 mile and cross the street. Descend to parallel Lynn's Branch, which is a tributary feeding into Lochmere Lake. Among the tall trees are sycamore, oak, elm, beech, hickory, and yellow poplar, all of which harbor squirrels and songbirds. On the left at 0.8 mile, there is a proposed greenway. (The greenway will go approximately 0.3 mile to Farmington Woods Elementary School and a new park. When extended about 2.0 miles farther west, it will connect with *Annie Jones Greenway*.) Continuing on Hinshaw Greenway, cross the last bridge at 1.1 miles. Near the end of the trail is a plaque commemorating Robert C. Hinshaw, whose years of community service enabled the citizens of Cary to "enhance the quality of life."

Panther Creek Greenway (2.0 miles, easy)

Trailhead and Description: From NC 55 (between Alston Avenue and Good Hope Church Road), turn west on Cary Glen Boulevard. Cross Carpenter Fire Station Road at 1.5 miles. After 0.3 mile, cross Green Level-to-Durham Road to descend toward the lake. Hikers and bikers may need to park by the street curb, near entrance signs at both sides of the causeway.

This greenway is one of the most recently constructed. The paved trail circles a western lake in a western suburb of the city. Waterfowl is present. Shrubbery and wildflowers are part of the landscape along the easy 1.5-mile route that travels between residential sections on the west side of Cary Glen Boulevard. Until a new forest develops, this greenway provides plenty of sunshine. On the east side, there is a 0.5-mile circle around a smaller lake that uses a tunnel under Green Level-to-Durham Road. From this location, a multi-use trail is planned to go north on Green Level-to-Durham Road for a connection to trails at Research Triangle Park. A greenway is also proposed to go east to Hawes (a large undeveloped open space) that will parallel I-540 north as the *Outer Loop Trail*. Also from Hawes, there will be a route south to Thomas Brooks Park and Sears Farm Road Park.

Sears Farm Road Park

One of the most recently developed city parks, Sears Farm Road Park has distinctive engineering design that sets it apart. On the highest point of the park, there is a combination of metal sculpture and artistic benches. There is a grassy pyramid and a contrasting inversion. Nearby, there are a children's playground, restrooms, swings, and café-style picnic tables with umbrella-type covers. Special shrubbery and flowers are part of the landscaping. The park is a hub for greenways going in three different directions.

ACCESS: At the crossroads of NC 55, High House Road, and Green Level Road West, drive north on NC 55 for 0.5 mile to The Reserve residential subdivision and turn left onto Edgemore Avenue. After 1.0 mile, turn left onto Sears Farm Road, then right into the circular parking lot.

Green Hope Greenway (0.9 mile, easy)
Batchelor Branch Greenway (0.8 mile, easy)

Trailheads and Description: From the parking lot at Sears Farm Road Park, walk north to the restrooms and beyond to *Green Hope Greenway*, which goes left and right. If taking the left route, the greenway descends; to the right, it crosses Edgemont Avenue. If using the left direction first, descend on a wide greenway to cross an arched bridge at 0.1 mile. Ascend and curve left into an open area to parallel Highcroft Drive Elementary School. At 0.2 mile, the greenway goes to the right between residential homes to reach Chandler Grant Drive. After 40 yards, turn right onto Sears Farm Road. At 0.4 mile, turn left onto Green Hope Road. (A clockwise trail circle is proposed for this location.)

Backtrack to the park for a continuation on Green Hope Greenway. Cross Sears Farm Road to the south corner of Edgemont Avenue. Descend on the wide sidewalk for 0.2 mile; turn right. Cross a flat bridge over a stream into an open space. Follow a scenic boardwalk to cross Briardale Avenue (near Lindermans Drive) at 0.35 mile. At 0.5 mile, there is a T-junction with *Batchelor Branch Greenway*. (To the right, Batchelor Branch Greenway is unfinished. Proposed plans have the greenway connecting with Highcroft Drive, continuing beyond to Thomas Brooks Park and then south to cross Beaver Dam Road. It will eventually connect with *White Oak Creek Greenway*.)

Sculpture in Sears Farm Road Park in Cary

Taking a left turn at the T-junction with Batchelor Branch Greenway, the trail parallels the branch through a forest of tall trees. Near the trail are sumac, dogwood, and patches of stilt grass. Cross an arched bridge at 0.3 mile. At 0.5 mile, cross Glenmore Road. Pass a bench on the approach to Highfield Avenue in Field Stone subdivision; the trail curves left. (It is 120 yards on Highfield Avenue to NC 55.) Cross an arched bridge over the branch to reach a tunnel under NC 55 at 0.8 mile; this is the temporary end of the trail. (Proposed plans extend the trail east to *Riggsbee Farm Greenway* and the bicycle multi-use route on Davis Drive.)

At the Sears Farm Road Park, there is another greenway that will eventually connect south with Batchelor Branch Greenway. From the restroom area, the greenway descends steeply in the forest to a pond on the right. The pond features arrow arum and cattails. Continue to Highcroft Drive at 0.1 mile. (Across the road is a wide 0.5-mile sidewalk that will be used to extend the trail to the south to connect with Batchelor Branch Greenway.) Backtrack.

Speight Branch Greenway (0.6 mile, easy)

Trailhead and Description: From the intersection of Southeast Cary Parkway and Tryon Road, drive 0.7 mile east on Tryon Road. Take a left turn at The Lodge subdivision on the west side of Tryon Road Lake. From the parking space at The Lodge office, walk back to Tryon Road. Cross the road and descend 93 yards to cross a wide bridge over Speight Branch. There is a T-junction at this location. To the left, it is 55 yards to a tunnel entrance under Tryon Road. The trail becomes *Tryon Road Park Greenway* at this location. (When completed, this trail will circle the lake near The Lodge subdivision, pass a new park on the east side of the lake, and connect with the 0.7-mile *Tryon Village Greenway* to end at Walnut Street.) From the junction, go south on *Speight Branch Greenway.* Tall trees are on the right and a residential community is on the left. At 0.3 mile, pass a 60-yard access trail on the left. Cross a bridge over the branch. At 0.5 mile, cross an arched

A runner on Speight Branch Greenway in Cary

bridge, followed by a damp area with arrow arum. Ascend to Southeast Cary Parkway at 0.6 mile. There is no parking here. Backtrack. (A greenway is proposed to begin across the road and go south to Lilly Atkins Road. Another future greenway will go west to connect with Ritter Park and Hemlock Bluffs Nature Preserve.)

Swift Creek Recycled Greenway (0.8 mile to 1.2 miles, easy)

Trailhead and Description: From the intersection of Tryon and Kildaire Farm roads, drive south on Kildaire Farm Road for 0.7 mile and turn right onto West Lochmere Drive. It is 0.2 mile to Harold D. Ritter Community Park. Turn left to enter the first parking area. The trail access is straight ahead.

Unlike any other trail/greenway in the Triangle, this delightful walkway uses recycled commercial materials to form a ground covering and a recycled material called plastic lumber for the bridges. Without the multiple interpretive signs, a user may not notice the uniqueness. The trailheads do not have parking spaces, therefore it is advisable to park at Ritter Community Park. The park has an athletic field, a basketball court, picnic facilities, and restrooms.

Bridge made of recycled plastic on Swift Creek Recycled Greenway in Cary

From the parking area, walk 140 yards to a T-intersection. If turning right, cross a bridge made of plastic lumber. All four plastic-lumber bridges on this greenway have withstood severe flooding. Interpretive signs describe what ingredients are in the surface that looks like asphalt. These materials include ash from coal-powered electric-generating plants, recycled old asphalt, rubber tires, and roof shingles. At 0.5 mile, arrive at the Regency Parkway sidewalk, where the greenway ends at a bridge. Backtrack. (A user could walk across the road to a left sidewalk and hike 0.2 mile to *Symphony Lake Greenway* at Regency Business Park.)

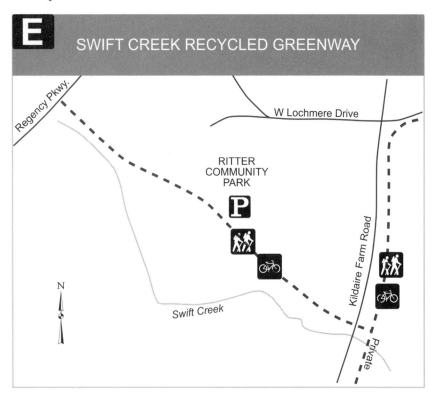

After returning to the access point, continue by going downstream. Cross other plastic-lumber bridges and pass interpretive signs. A message on one sign indicates the plaque and posts are made of recycled potato-chip bags and milk jugs. Pass under Kildaire Farm Road bridge to a T-intersection at 0.3 mile. Backtrack. A right turn crosses a footbridge over Swift Creek to connect with private hiking/biking trails in Loch Highland residential development. A turn left connects with a private trail at Lochmere Golf Club. (By going right [east], this trail parallels Kildaire Farm Road to Lochmere Drive for 2.5 miles. It is a serpentine design to Cary Parkway. The trail around Lochmere Lake has a "No Trespassing" sign; usage is for Lochmere residents only.)

Symphony Lake Greenway (1.1 miles, easy)

Trailhead and Description: From U.S. 1/64, take Exit 98 and drive east on Tyron Road. Turn right immediately onto Regency Parkway. At 0.5 mile, cross Swift Creek bridge. To the left is the west trailhead of *Swift Creek Recycled Trail.* At 0.7 mile, turn right at a traffic light. Park at the first parking lot on the left. (If it is closed for VIP parking for a performance at the amphitheater, drive ahead and search for a parking space in Regency Business Park.)

The name of this promenade reflects the musical atmosphere of the modern amphitheater on the banks of Regency Lake. Distinctively different

Symphony Lake Trail in Regency Business Park in Cary

from just another walk in the woods, users are reminded that lake reflections of human art with ivory towers and glistening glass can merge with the art of nature. The greenway is open from dawn to dusk. The gates may be locked at the amphitheater lake frontage during performances. Dogs must be on a leash.

From the parking lot, descend 115 yards to a T-junction. If hiking right on Symphony Lake Greenway, pass the esplanade of the amphitheater and the business buildings. Enter a partial forest of loblolly pine and floodplain shrubs, such as silverling. At 0.5 mile, *Regency Park Greenway* is on the right. (It goes upstream, crosses a bridge over Swift Creek, and accesses Regency Parkway at 0.2 mile.) Continuing on Symphony Lake Greenway, cross an arched wooden bridge over Swift Creek. Soon the resplendent greenway travels between tag alder on the lakeside and bluffs covered with beech, galax, ferns, and wildflowers on the right. Waterfowl are usually present. Arrive at Ederlee Drive at 1.1 miles. Turn left, follow the sidewalk along the dam, and complete the loop.

Weston Greenway
(1.8 miles, including partial backtrack; easy)

Trailhead and Description: There is public parking at North Cary Park on Norwell Boulevard, 0.2 mile north of its junction with Northwest Cary Parkway. To hike *Weston Greenway*, begin at the park's entrance and walk north on the sidewalk of Norwell Boulevard for 0.1 mile to pass the entrance of the subdivision Weston Pointe. At 0.2 mile, there is a trail sign. Although this greenway is privately owned, it is open to the public with a statement that "users assume all risks." Ascend on a paved greenway. At 0.3 mile, pass a short access spur on the right. Descend, cross a culvert, and arrive at a fork at 0.35 mile. Taking the right route, ascend and then gradually descend to arrive at Weston Parkway at 0.75 mile. (No parking here.) Backtrack to fork.

At the fork, turn right; ascend steeply. Along the way are groves of viburnum, a species related to black haw, and silverling, a shrub with snowy blossoms usually at its peak in late October and November. Ahead the forest becomes more expansive; squirrels are likely to be seen. Reach Evans Road at 0.7 mile. There is a parking area here for a few cars. (It is 0.1 mile north to Weston Parkway.) Backtrack.

White Oak Creek Greenway System

Parkway Greenway (0.8 mile, easy)
White Oak Creek Greenway (3.7 miles, easy)
Park Village Greenway (0.65 mile, easy)
Sherwood Greens Greenway (0.3 mile, easy)

Trailheads and Description: *White Oak Creek Greenway's* eastern trailhead is at Bond Park's parking area at the lake's dock. (The southwest trailhead for *Black Creek Greenway* is also in this parking lot.) To access the White Oak Creek Greenway system from the intersection of Northwest Cary Parkway and High House Road, turn right onto High House Road opposite Saint Michaels Catholic Church and drive 0.5 mile east. Coming from the opposite direction, turn left at the intersection of Northwest Maynard Road onto High House Road and drive 0.7 mile west.

There is a proposed connection from the western trailhead for White Oak Creek Greenway to *American Tobacco Trail.* The greenway is expected to be about 7.2 miles when completed. About three-fourths of the distance is either now finished or under construction. Described below, from east to west, is the greenway's route through two parks and its access to two other greenways.

From the parking area, follow the trail west, pass the Sertoma Amphitheater, and cross the dam. Descend on steps (unless a new greenway changes the routing) at 0.2 mile and connect with *Parkway Greenway* at the Bond Park boundary. (Parkway Greenway's name will change to White Oak Creek Greenway when new construction is completed.) Follow Coles Branch to the YMCA property on the left before reaching Southwest Cary Parkway at 0.8 mile. Backtrack, or continue about 0.3 mile to MacArthur Drive, if construction is underway. (From MacArthur Drive to Davis Drive Park, it is approximately another 0.3 mile, but trail construction on White Oak Creek Greenway may be delayed because of a railroad crossing.)

The next completed section of White Oak Creek Greenway is an easy 1.8 miles. It also is the section where you first meet White Oak Creek. The paved trail crosses four pedestrian bridges. It links Davis Drive Park, a connector trail to Davis Drive Middle and Elementary schools, and White Oak Park to the west. Davis Drive Park at 1610 Davis Drive has ball fields, picnic shelters, and a playground. If you want to begin the greenway at Davis Drive Park from the YMCA Park on Southwest Cary Boulevard, drive north 0.2 mile to Waldo Road Boulevard and turn left. Follow it for 0.7 mile to Davis Drive and turn left. After 0.6 mile, turn left at the entrance to the park.

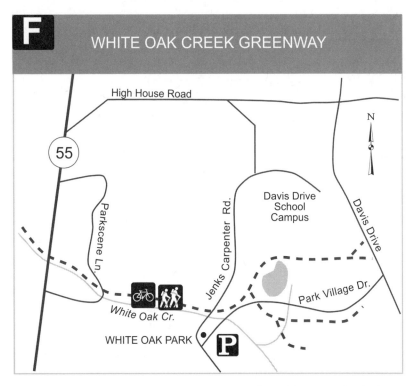

From the parking area at Davis Drive Park, walk across the highway toward the entrance of Park Valley subdivision entrance. Turn right on the Davis Drive sidewalk before the entrance. At 0.15 mile, leave the sidewalk and turn left. Here and at other places ahead are accesses to the Davis Drive schools. On the left at 0.2 mile, there is a 100-yard access to Mint Hill Drive. At 0.5 mile, leave the school boundary; pass a residential lake and dam. At 0.6 mile, cross Castle Hayne Drive. A children's playground is on the left. At 0.7 mile, there is an access and bridge going left to *Park Village Greenway*.

If following the 0.65-mile Park Village Greenway, follow White Oak Creek upstream in a forest of tall trees. Cross Park Village Drive. After 0.15 mile, there is a spur to the right with a bridge and steps leading to Old Dock Trail (a street). At 0.3 mile, the greenway forks left. The right fork continues upstream for 0.3 mile to *Sherwood Greens Greenway*. That greenway weaves through the forest and crosses bridges before turning left. It ascends and accesses Sherwood Forest Place and Halls Mill Drive. If staying on Park Village Greenway, ascend to the village swimming pool at the corner of Halls Mill and Park Village drives at 0.65 mile. (It is 0.2 mile ahead [east] on Park Village Drive to Davis Drive and Davis Drive Park.)

Continuing downstream on White Oak Creek Greenway, there is an

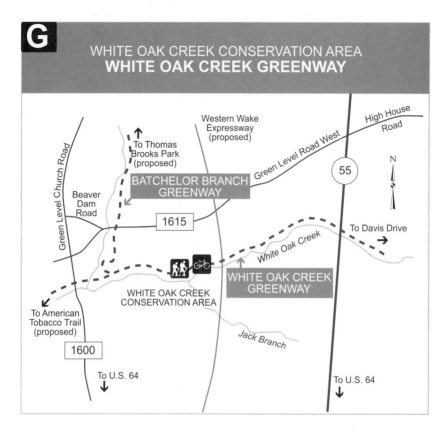

access across a bridge to White Oak Park at 0.9 mile. White Oak Park is at 9216 Jenks Carpenter Road; it has ball fields, picnic shelters, and a playground.

At 1.1 miles on White Oak Creek Greenway, cross Jenks Carpenter Road where the babbling creek and inviting greenway continue through the forest. On the right, pass a side trail, which leads to a residential area. Arrive at Parkscene Lane at 1.5 miles. Cross and pass a community-owned sand trail. At 1.8 miles, arrive at NC 55. (A gravel path to the right gives access to the NC 55 multi-use bicycle route. To the left, there is a bridge over the creek with a paved access that makes a junction with Parkscene Lane. To the right of this junction is access to NC 55.)

If continuing on White Oak Creek Greenway, go through a tunnel that goes under NC 55 to reach an open space in a hardwood forest. Wisteria is entwined among the trees to the left. At 2.1 miles, there is a curve on the right. To the left, there is a protective fence around a Cary Utility Department building. (Also to the left, there is a planned spur access to a residential area.)

At 2.4 miles, occasional scenic views of a marsh and lake in the White Oak Conservation Area begin on the left. The upstream marsh has cattails, buttonbush, and alder. The downstream area has sweet-scented water lilies. Here and in the upstream area, waterfowl can be seen in all seasons. Seeing a beaver hutch is also likely.

The proposed Western Wake Expressway is expected to pass over the greenway at 2.7 miles. At 3.3 miles, the west end of *Batchelor Branch Greenway* is on the right. (It parallels the stream north for 0.3 mile to Green Level Road West. Beyond that point, the proposed trail is scheduled to continue north to Thomas Brooks Park, then east to NC 55 to connect with a section already completed at its east end. It will also have connections to Sears Farm Park.)

Continuing on White Oak Creek Greenway, follow about 565 yards of boardwalk to end at Green Level Church Road at 3.7 miles. (There is a proposal to continue the greenway southwest for about 1.7 miles to connect with the American Tobacco Trail.)

On Green Level Church Road, turn right (north) and go 0.2 mile to Green Level Road West. Turn left (south) and go 2.2 miles on Green Level Church Road to U.S. 64. Turn east onto U.S. 64 and drive 0.3 mile to an interchange with NC 55 in Apex.

Short Trails in the Cary Greenway System

Bishops Gate Greenway (1.0 mile, easy)

Trailhead and Description: From the junction of Old Apex Road and Southwest Cary Parkway, drive 1.5 miles north on Southwest Cary Parkway to West High Street and turn left. To reach the most southwest trailhead for *Bishops Gate Greenway*, drive about 1.0 mile and look for Abbey Hall Way. Turn and drive to the cul-de-sac for parking, if there is space. (At the time of this writing the subdivision was under construction and the street may be private by the time of publication. In that case, seek another curbside space downstream.) When this greenway is completed, it will be a delightful 1.0-mile trail around or near three small lakes, which are the headwaters for a tributary that flows into Bond Lake.

Camp Branch Greenway (0.7 mile, easy)

Trailhead and Description: From the junction of Ten Ten Road and

Kildaire Farm Road, drive east on Ten Ten Road for 0.5 mile to the north side of Stanton Place subdivision's stone wall. Then go to the west end of that wall. Park on the road if space still exists. Follow *Camp Branch Greenway* between the forest and the backyards of homesites. At 0.6 mile, enter a dense forest. At 0.7 mile, ferns and switchcane survive because of the dampness found here. There is a potential future connection with *Dutchman's Branch Greenway*. Backtrack.

Grey Hawk Landing Greenway (0.4 mile, easy)

Trailhead and Description: For access, drive 1.8 miles east on Ten Ten Road from its intersection with Kildaire Farm Road. Enter the main entrance to Grey Hawk Landing on the left. After driving 0.3 mile on Grey Hawk Place, the trailhead is on the right. Look for curbside parking. Descend on *Grey Hawk Landing Greenway* to a potential fork. Turn left and come to the end of the trail at a stream bank. Backtrack. This greenway is a 0.4-mile section that when completed will connect from Ten Ten Road, on the north side, to *Camp Branch Greenway*. It will also connect with *Dutchman's Branch Greenway* east to Holly Springs Road.

Higgins Greenway (0.4 mile, easy)

Trailhead and Description: From the intersection of Southwest Maynard and West Chatham streets, drive 0.1 mile north on West Chatham Street to Danforth Drive. The north entrance to the trail is on the right. *Higgins Greenway* is a natural-surface fitness trail that goes through the woods near Swift Creek. The trail's south end is at Southwest Maynard Street between Cuscowilla Drive to the west and Pamlico Drive to the east. Backtrack.

Riggsbee Farm Greenway (0.6 mile, easy)

Trailhead and Description: *Riggsbee Farm Greenway* was constructed in 2006 as an easy 0.6-mile east-west walk on the north side of Cornerstone Village Shopping Center and the adjoining residential subdivision. For access, drive about 0.1 mile north on Davis Drive from its intersection with High House Road. Turn left into the nearest parking space of the shopping center. Begin the multi-use trail at Davis Drive and walk west. Pass a drainage retention pond and retaining wall on the right side and pass a lake with a fountain in the middle on the left side. The trail ends at Carpenter Upchurch Road. (From here a multi-use sidewalk/trail is proposed to run on Louis

Stephens Drive to Green Hope High School and elementary school parks.)
Backtrack.

Chapel Hill (Orange County)

Parks and Recreation Department
200 Plant Road
Chapel Hill, NC 27514
Telephone: 919-968-2784; fax: 919-923-2923
www.chapelhillparks.org

The Chapel Hill Parks and Recreation Department has a comprehensive master plan for its greenway system that will provide more than 38 miles of multi-use or hiking trails on paved and unpaved routes. The master plan shows corridors running mainly alongside creeks and branches; some of these new trails will extend current trails. The city maintains at least 13 parks, two of which have nature trails. The older, 0.4-mile *Tanyard Branch Trail*, is located in Umstead Park, which is unrelated to William B. Umstead State Park. To access the park, turn west off MLK, Jr., Blvd. (NC 86) at Umstead Drive, 0.9 mile north of Franklin Street in downtown Chapel Hill. From the parking lot at the park, the path travels to the right of the former recreation center. It goes along Bolin Creek to Caldwell Street. For another 0.2 mile, it goes along Mitchell Lane to Hargraves Community Center.

The trails described ahead are part of the Chapel Hill greenway system and are listed in alphabetical order.

Community Center Park

Community Center Park is the recommended parking area for *Battle Branch Trail*, its connecting trail system in Battle Park, and *Bolin Creek Greenway*. Parking here is recommended because the multiple trailheads for the Battle Park areas only have metered parking or parking areas that require university permits, except after 5 p.m. and on weekends and holidays. The western trailhead for Bolin Creek Greenway does not have a parking area or street parking at any time. The park facilities include a large children's playground, restrooms, and a picnic area.

Battle Branch Trail's eastern half is on a corridor of city property. A large

part of the western half, which includes Battle Park, was purchased by UNC in 1793. By 1975, the original land and subsequent holdings totaled 93 acres. The park was named in honor of Kemp Plummer Battle, the university's president from 1876-91. Battle created some of the original trails that lead from the forested steep ridges down to the basin of the branch, which now also bears his name. For more than 100 years, the main route went from Boundary Street and descended to the branch, which it crisscrossed to its confluence with Bolin Creek. Over the years, spur trails developed that led to upscale homes on both sides of the basin. In 2004, Battle Park and the adjacent Forest Theatre (an amphitheater established in 1919) became part of the N.C. Botanical Garden. A network of skillfully constructed short trails that connect this area with Battle Branch Trail has increased the area's educational value.

ACCESS: From the junction of I-40 at Exit 270 and U.S. 15/501, drive south on U.S. 15/501, which becomes Fordham Boulevard. Drive 2.6 miles to a traffic light at Estes Drive. Turn right and travel 0.4 mile. Turn left onto Community Center Drive and enter the parking area. (Estes Drive, which continues ahead, crosses Franklin Street East in 0.1 mile)

Battle Branch Trail (1.6 miles) Solitary Hill Trail (0.15 mile)
Sugarberry Trail (0.1 mile) Rainy Day Trail (0.3 mile)
Nature Trail (0.5 mile) Deer Track Trail (0.2 mile)
Cedar Top Trail (0.15 mile) Sourwood Loop Trail (0.3 mile)
Bent Beech Trail (0.3 mile) University Trail (0.1 mile)

Length and Difficulty: 3.7 miles one-way; easy to strenuous

Trailheads and Description: If beginning on the eastern trailhead of *Battle Branch Trail* at Community Center Park, leave the southeast corner of the parking lot at a signboard. After a short passage through the woods, follow a sidewalk to the right to travel on Shepherd Lane (it may be spelled Shepard on some maps). At 0.15 mile, turn right and go off the sidewalk into the forest. After a few yards, *Sugarberry Trail* goes left. (It is a spur that goes over a bridge of Battle Branch and onto a long boardwalk in a floodplain. Tall hardwoods rise over a dense privet understory. The trail ends at the steps leading to Sugarberry Road. Backtrack.)

At 0.25 mile, there is a fork where *Nature Trail* goes left. (For 0.5 mile, the narrow footpath parallels the branch on the left side and Battle Branch Trail on the right slope.) Both routes have tall hardwoods where wild quinine, wild ginger, spring beauty, and green and gold are among the wildflowers found. Emerge from the forest on Battle Branch Trail. The trail leads to a residential area on the corner of Glenhill Lane, which is ahead, and Weaver Road, which is to the right. Turn sharply left between a grove of wisteria on the left and crepe myrtle along the residential boundary. Immediately pass the western access to Nature Trail on the left. Cross a bridge over Battle Branch and turn right, going upstream. At 0.7 mile, pass a short access on the left that leads to Sandy Creek Trail (a street) and Greenwood Road (a residential area).

At 0.9 mile, the trail reaches the eastern boundary of Battle Park. There is a kiosk with trail maps and other information located here. After a few yards, *Cedar Top Trail* goes off to the right. (It ascends to partly follow the contour before descending on switchbacks to connect with *Bent Beech Trail*.)

Continuing on Battle Branch Trail, a few yards upstream from the access to Cedar Top Trail, Bent Beech Trail goes off to the right at 1.0 mile. (On the ridge side, Bent Beech Trail has an observation deck known as Lovers' Leap Lookout. The deck has benches and a view of the branch below. After a descent, the side trail reconnects with Battle Branch Trail.)

After reconnecting with Battle Branch Trail, there are a number of points of interest at 1.3 miles. To the right is the side trail, *Solitary Hill Trail*. Straight ahead is Anemone Spring, a natural spring flowing from a rock on the riverbank. To the left, Battle Branch Trail rock-hops the branch to reach an old brick picnic grate. (If ascending on Solitary Hill Trail, reconnect with Battle Branch Trail after 0.15 mile. Along the way, its special feature is a huge yellow poplar, which is known as "Monster of the Forest.")

If rock-hopping the branch past the old picnic spot, *Rainy Day Trail* goes to the left before reaching a small tributary of Battle Branch. To the right is a strong bridge over a rocky section of the branch. After crossing the bridge, reconnect with Solitary Hill Trail at 1.4 miles. Gradually ascend on an old road to a junction with Park Place on the right and Boundary Road on the left at 1.6 miles. This is the western end of Battle Branch Trail. (Parking at the parking area requires a university permit except for times outlined above.)

If returning to Community Center Park, a different route is available by walking left from Park Place on the sidewalk of Boundary Street for 0.1 mile to Forest Theater. On the edge of the forest, there is a kiosk with Battle Park maps as well as an access to *Sourwood Loop Trail*. Follow the loop in either direction to connect with *Deer Track Trail*. Deer Track Trail twists between boulders. Halfway along the trail, there is a connection with Rainy Day Trail. Take a right onto the ridge of Rainy Day Trail to reach an access with Country Club Road and a picnic area. (Across the road, there are parking meters.)

Backtrack and take the first right onto *University Trail* to junction with Deer Creek Trail. Turn right onto Deer Creek Trail and cross a bridge over a small stream. Ascend 70 yards to Sisters' Corner. This junction of Glandon Drive and Gimghoul Road offers benches and a plaque that honors twin sisters, Bernice Wade and Barbara Stiles. Their homesites were "radiant with flowers," much to the joy of neighbors and visitors.

Backtrack on Deer Track Trail to Rainy Day Trail and turn right. Descend among hardwoods on a trail with rocky borders and cairns for 0.15 mile. This connects with Battle Branch Trail at the bridge. Go left downstream to backtrack to Community Center Park. (Depending on how many backtracking trips were made on the network of trails, a round trip could be between 4.0 to 5.0 miles.)

Bolin Creek Greenway (1.5 miles, one-way; easy)

Trailhead and Description: The east terminus of the paved and elegantly landscaped *Bolin Creek Greenway* can be found at Community Center Park. From the parking area, begin the trail between the children's playground and a seat shaped like human hands. Pass a gazebo and floral garden, enter

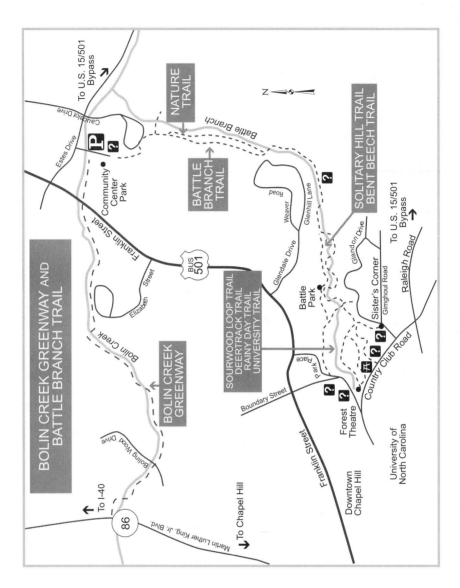

a street cul-de-sac, and pass under East Franklin Street bridge. Sycamore, beech, loblolly pine, red bud, autumn olive, and hornbeam are found near the greenway, which weaves alongside the creek. The elevated manholes are painted with green tree leaf designs and their titles lend a unique feel to the trail. At 0.7 mile, there is a paved access to Elizabeth Street on the left. Cross scenic bridges at 0.8 mile and 1.4 miles. Arrive at Martin Luther King, Jr. Boulevard (NC 86) at 1.5 miles. Backtrack, or arrange a shuttle. Of the proposed 7 phases of this greenway, only 3 are complete at this writing.

Bolin Creek Greenway in Chapel Hill

Booker Creek Greenway—Lower (0.8 mile, easy)

Trailhead and Description: The trailhead is near Eastgate Shopping Center on North Franklin Street. Parking is available at the shopping center. Cross North Franklin Street at Center Drive, where there is a traffic light near a service station. After crossing, turn right and follow a trail sign north on the sidewalk for a few yards before making a left turn. This serpentine greenway is an easy route paralleling Booker Creek from the shopping center. The route has a 10-foot-wide concrete base and grassy sides. It travels through a hardwood forest and a floodplain. In the springtime, there are wild white roses; in the summertime, jewelweed and water hemlock can be seen. At 0.6 mile, there is an arched bridge over Booker Creek. The trail ends at Booker Creek Road. Backtrack to the shopping center. From there, the greenway continues southeast at an angle between the backside of the shopping center and Village Plaza for 0.3 mile to a parking area near the junction of Elliott Road and U.S. 15/501 (Fordham Boulevard). The landscaped Linear Park is along the route near Booker Creek. There are plans for the greenway to continue southeast down Booker Creek to eventually connect with the future *Little Creek Trail.* Of the six phases on the master plan for Booker Creek, two have been completed at this writing. Call 919-968-2787 for an update.

Cedar Falls Park

Among the city's oldest parks, Cedar Falls Park has a large hardwood forest located on hills and valleys. The understory includes virburnum, crane-fly orchids, wild ginger, and muscadine grapes. The park's trail system is a maze that has increased the original number of loops with short cuts and spur trails leading to residential areas. The park has three baseball fields, a picnic area, restrooms, a children's playground, and tennis courts.

ACCESS: From I-40, take Exit 266 and drive 0.4 mile south on NC 86 (Martin Luther King, Jr. Boulevard) to Weaver Dairy Road. Turn left onto Weaver Dairy Road. After 1.5 miles, turn right into the entrance for the park. If approaching from U.S. 15/501, turn west on Erwin Road, which is 1.2 miles south of its intersection with I-40. Drive 0.5 mile to Weaver Dairy Road; turn left. After 1.2 miles, turn left at the park entrance. After entering the parking area, drive to the southside parking lot. It is left of a yellow gate at the ball fields. Follow the paved trail to a signboard.

Jo Peeler Nature Trail (0.7 mile, easy)
Blue Trail (0.9 mile, easy)

Trailheads and Description: *Note:* The original trails at Cedar Falls Park had yellow, blue, and white blazes. You may notice some blazes are faded or missing; a white-blazed path may be used as a connector.

The yellow-blazed loop is *Jo Peeler Nature Trail*, named in honor of Jo Peeler because she "encouraged the town to acquire land as an open space for others to enjoy." To access the trail from the parking lot, walk to the signboard in the forest, which is on the left close to the yellow vehicle gate that accesses the ball fields. A laminated page that explains the 26 posts identifying plant life along the trail is available in a box on the signboard.

Enter the trail on the right side of the signboard at Post #1. Follow the path past the children's playground and the fenced tennis courts, both of which are on the left. At 0.2 mile, there is a connection with *Blue Trail* (this may be white blazed). Jo Peeler Nature Trail stays to the left. At 0.4 mile, stay left at another intersection. At 0.6 mile, pass through a grove of large white pines. After passing the former homesite of Jesse Johnson, exit to the parking lot for completion of the trail.

To access *Blue Trail*, walk left of the signboard into the forest for 125 yards on a wide paved route to the fenced tennis courts. Along the way, pass the children's playground on the right. Facing the gate to the tennis courts, turn abruptly right outside the fence onto a wide, natural-surfaced trail. At 0.2 mile, cross Jo Peeler Nature Trail. (After a few feet, the white-blazed connector is on the right.) At 0.4 mile, stay right at a fork. At 0.5 mile, there

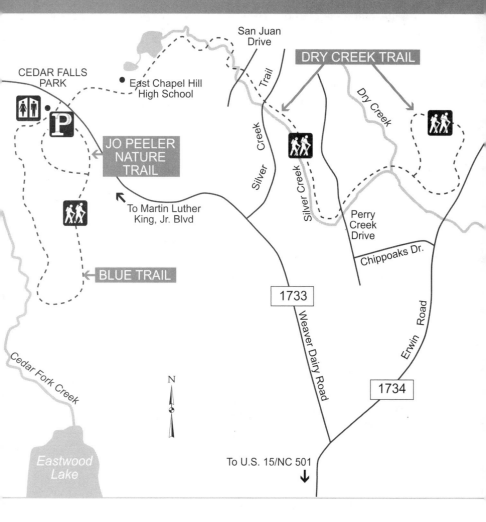

is a junction with the white-blazed connector again. Stay straight. Ascend to a ridge and another fork at 0.6 mile. (To the left, there is a side trail to a scenic rock outcropping at Cedar Creek. Wildflowers, ferns, and pink wild azaleas are seen on the descent to the cascades. From this area, it is 0.1 mile to Lakeshore Lane, but no parking is allowed there.) Continue on the right side of the loop by ascending the ridge. Stay left of red- or white-blazed loops. At 0.9 mile, exit at the ball field; keep right to pass the restroom and return to the parking area near the yellow gate.

Dry Creek Trail (2.8 miles round-trip; easy to moderate)

Trailhead and Description: The western trailhead for *Dry Creek Trail* is located at East Chapel Hill High School, across Weaver Dairy Road from Cedar Falls Park. If hiking from the park's parking area, you can follow a paved route east as it parallels Weaver Dairy Road for 0.2 mile to a traffic light. Cross to the left. Walk another 0.2 mile northeast to a school parking area at the north end of the football stadium. (If driving, go through the main entrance to the school and park in the area described above.) The trail begins from the parking area. Descend on an old road for 260 yards. The trail, which is partially asphalt, has two small lakes on the left. Continue ahead to a sharp right turn off the old road. Go up an embankment and into the forest. (If you are on the old road and go under a powerline, you have gone too far.) Through the woods, the trail crosses scenic rocky sections of Silver Creek. Crested dwarf iris, hepatica, and wild ginger grow along the stream banks.

At 0.3 mile, cross San Juan Drive, then descend on steps into the forest. At 0.5 mile, cross Silver Creek Trail (a street) and descend on steps. Parallel the creek and cross a boardwalk in a floodplain. At 0.9 mile, ascend steps to Perry Creek Drive to a trail sign. (Sidewalk parking is available here. To reach this location by vehicle, drive from Weaver Dairy Road to Erwin Road. Drive north on Erwin Road for 0.5 mile; then west on Chippoaks Drive for 0.2

Unique footbridge over Silver Creek on Dry Creek Trail

mile. Turn right onto Perry Creek Road and drive for 0.1 mile.)

Cross the street and look to the right for a gravel trail that descends to a flat area in the forest. At 1.1 miles, cross a bridge over Dry Creek at a left curve. After a few yards, stay right on a loop that parallels Erwin Road on the left to 1.3 miles. (There is no parking here.) Continue on the loop to backtrack to Perry Creek Road at 1.9 miles. To backtrack to the school, it is 2.8 miles round-trip. (The city proposes a 0.7-mile extension across Erwin Road and southeast to Eastowne Office Park.)

Fan Branch Trail (1.1 miles, easy)

Trailhead and Description: Travel south on U.S. 15/501 to the junction with Culbreth and Mount Carmel Church roads, just after crossing the Morgan Creek bridge. Parking is on the southwest corner of that junction.

Fan Branch Trail is a 10-foot-wide asphalt passage, which is professionally landscaped and exceptionally clean. As it runs through a stylish residential area, it crosses two arched bridges with scenic views of the streams. After crossing the second bridge at 0.35 mile, the trail gradually ascends to large homes and open places filled with sunshine. There is a children's playground at 0.9 mile. After 0.2 mile, there are several accesses to Mary Scroggs Elementary School. Fan Branch Trail is now completed to the elementary school. Future plans have the greenway extending another 0.7 mile through the adjoining Southern Community Park to a southern terminal at U.S. 15/501.

Southern Community Park

Southern Community Park has been on the city's greenway master plan for future development since 1997. Meanwhile, the city has given permission to local volunteers from adjoining Southern Village and other residential areas to construct and maintain a hiking and biking loop trail through the mature forest.

Southern Community Park Trail (1.5 miles, easy)

Trailhead and Description: From the intersection of Culbreth Road and U.S. 15/501, drive south on U.S. 15/501 for 0.8 mile. Turn right on Market

Street into Southern Village. Curve around Harrington Bank, pass a church and a Park-and-Ride lot, then go straight across to the far side of the parking area. There is a trail sign here.

Southern Community Park Trail enters the forest and goes to a fork. If turning left, pass through mixed hardwoods and loblolly pine where honeysuckle thrives. The trail runs parallel to U.S. 15/501. At 0.4 mile, cross Dogwood Acres Road. At 1.0 mile, return to cross the road at a lower level. At 1.1 miles, avoid the spur trail to the left near a ravine. Slightly ascend to rejoin the loop and exit.

A few yards to the west along the edge of the parking lot, there is 0.2-mile greenway. It passes between the school and athletic field, then curves left for an ascent to Polliwog Pavilion, a sheltered picnic facility. The trail dead-ends here. If you walk to the front of the school's west side, there is a trailhead for *Fan Branch Trail*.

Clayton (Wake County)

Clayton Park and Recreation
P.O. Box 879
Clayton, NC 27520
Telephone: 919-553-5777; fax: 919-553-1521

As the town's population continues to increase and its economic development expands, Clayton has a heightened awareness for the need for more recreational options and services. Two of its major parks are Legend Park and Clayton Community Park.

Legend Park

Legend Park features athletic fields and a prominent 8.0-mile network of mountain-biking trails that run through a mature forest with streams and steep hillsides. Although it has some sections for beginners, the park has developed a good reputation for having routes for advanced stunts. A reporter once described the network as the "free-ride capitol of the Triangle."

Some of the longer trails in the network are *Sam's Long and Short Loops* (1.4 miles), *Little Big Horn* (0.7 mile), and *Magnolia Run* (1.1 miles). Hikers are allowed to use the trails with the understanding that hikers will use caution and give bikers the right-of-way. Mountain-bike volunteers designed and constructed the trails. They would appreciate hikers' assistance in maintaining the trails if they frequently use the network.

ACCESS: In the heart of Clayton on U.S. 70 Business, turn north at a traffic light onto Robertson Street. After 0.6 mile, cross Main Street and a railroad crossing. When Robertson Street dead-ends, turn left onto Stallings Street. Immediately watch for City Road; turn right and drive 0.5 mile to the parking area on the right.

Clayton Community Park

Facilities include multiple soccer and softball fields, picnic shelters, tennis and volleyball courts, a children's playground, and trails. (Adjoining the park on the east side are three athletic fields for Clayton Middle School.) Among the future plans for the park is the building of a permanent amphitheater to replace the temporary one, additional playgrounds, more picnic shelters, more parking spaces, two baseball fields, and a building for concessions. Additional plans also include construction of a greenway from the park to Little Creek.

The park has three unnamed loop trails and one called *Nature Trail.* These trails are described here as a single unit of 1.1 miles. From the parking area, pass the children's playground on a paved trail that travels 0.1 mile to the dam of a small lake. The trail that enters the forest may be composed of

Nature Trail in Clayton Community Park

gravel or duff. The trail makes a loop through a mature hardwood forest with some longleaf pine. At 0.6 mile, it passes an amphitheater. On the return to the lake, the trail is scenic. Interpretive signs are located near planted trees and shrubs. At the upper end of the lake, follow the paved loop around the athletic fields for a return to the parking area.

ACCESS: From the traffic light in Clayton at the intersection of U.S. 70 Business and Amelia Church Road, drive south on Amelia Church Road for 1.3 miles and turn left into Community Park.

Dunn~Erwin (Harnett County)

A former railroad connection between the historic towns of Dunn and Erwin is now a hiking and bicycling rail-trail. The trail corridor was made possible by the North Carolina Rail-Trails Land Trust. It is supported by the local governments, chambers of commerce, and local citizens. Signs indicate usage is during daylight hours only. You should stay on the trail, not walk alone, have pets on a leash, and use caution at vehicular crossings.

Dunn Area Tourism Authority
P.O. Box 310 (mailing)
209 West Divine Street (physical location)
Dunn, NC 28335
Telephone: 910-892-3282 or 4113, fax: 910-892-4071

Dunn Parks and Recreation Department
P.O. Box 1065
Dunn, NC 28335
Telephone: 910-892-2976, fax: 910-892-2320

Erwin Parks and Recreation
P.O. Box 459
Erwin, NC 28339
Telephone: 910-897-5840, fax: 910-897-5542
North Carolina Rail-Trails: www.ncrail-trails.org

Dunn-Erwin Rail-Trail (5.3 miles, easy)

Trailheads and Description: To reach the Dunn trailhead, from I-95, take Exit 73 and drive on U.S. 421/NC 55 North into Dunn. Turn right onto Orange Avenue (next to a bank). Drive three blocks to park at Harnett

Primary School. The trailhead is behind the school.

To reach the trailhead in Erwin, continue on U.S. 421/NC 55 past Dunn. In Erwin, at the intersection of U.S. 421/NC 55 and NC 82 (North 13th Street), turn onto North 13th Street and continue downtown. Parking is available on East H Street in front of shops and restaurants.

If going east from Erwin, follow the trail between a cluster of historic and attractive shops. Pass a sign for the Centennial Walk. There are mile markers in the center of the trail. On a gravel trail, leave the town. The trail travels under U.S. 421 at 0.8 mile. At 1.0 mile, there is a pond on the right. For the next mile, the trail goes into a more open space to avoid the wye of the original railroad. There are large oaks and sweet gums along the right of the trail here. At 2.3 miles, cross busy Old Field Church Road. (Six other roads are crossed before crossing Watauga Avenue in Dunn.)

Pass under a power line at 2.9 miles. At 3.0 miles, cross a bridge over the wild Black River. This is a good place to stop and absorb the beauty of the wetland's floral displays and to observe birds and other wildlife. In the springtime, you'll usually hear a chorus of spring peepers. There also may be evidence of beavers. At 4.3 miles, a spur trail on the right leads to where John Haywood Byrd, a Confederate soldier, is buried. At 5.0 miles, arrive at Harnett Primary School near James Street. (The old railroad track used to continue east for a short distance to connect with a mainline track at Railroad Avenue.)

Durham (Durham County)

Department of Parks and Recreation
101 City Hall Plaza
Durham, NC 27701
Telephone: 919-560-4355; fax: 919-687-0896

The Durham Parks and Recreation Department maintains more than 62 developed parks and seven undeveloped parks. Two of the parks have a network of trails, which are described below. Among the parks that have trails, the West Point on the Eno Park has the largest trail network. The Durham Open Space and Trails Commission has master plans for nearly 170 miles of trails in the city and county. One plan is for the *North/South Greenway*. It begins at the parking area for the Amphitheater at West Point in West Point on the Eno Park and goes south through the heart of the city to connect with the *American Tobacco Trail* (ATT) at Durham Bulls Athletic Park. From there, the ATT completes the greenway project through the city and county. Farther south, the ATT has sections in Wake and Chatham counties before it ends near the community of Bonsal.

In addition to the North/South Greenway plans, *Eno River Greenway* now provides an east-west route from the West Point area to Penny's Bend Trail and Old Oxford Road. (East of this point, *West Falls Lake Trail* connects with *East Falls Lake Trail*, all of which is part of the *Mountains-to-Sea Trail*.) Future plans have West Point on the Eno Park's *Eagle Trail* combining with Eno River Greenway/Mountains-to-Sea Trail to extend through Eno River State Park.

Spurs and future connections along North/South Greenway are described in this section in the order they appear, going from north to south. The future connections mentioned here, plus other plans from the master plan first approved in 1985, could result in about 25 miles of additional trails. (For an update on progress, contact the sources listed ahead.)

West Point on the Eno Park

West Point on the Eno Park
5101 North Roxboro Road
Durham, NC 27704
Telephone: 919-471-1623

This 388-acre city park emphasizes the history and the recreational potential of the West Point Mill community, which existed from 1778 to 1942. The McCown-Mangum farmhouse, mill, blacksmith shop, and gardens have been restored or reconstructed. The park offers picnicking, fishing, rafting, and canoeing, as well as hiking on a network of trails described below. Camping and swimming are not allowed. The Festival of the Eno is held annually during the weekend of the 4th of July. For information call 919-477-4544. Support for the park comes from Friends of West Point, Inc. (919-477-2442) and the Eno River Association (919-620-9099).

South River Trail (0.5 mile)
Laurel Cliffs Nature Trail (0.4 mile)
Buffalo Trail (0.4 mile)

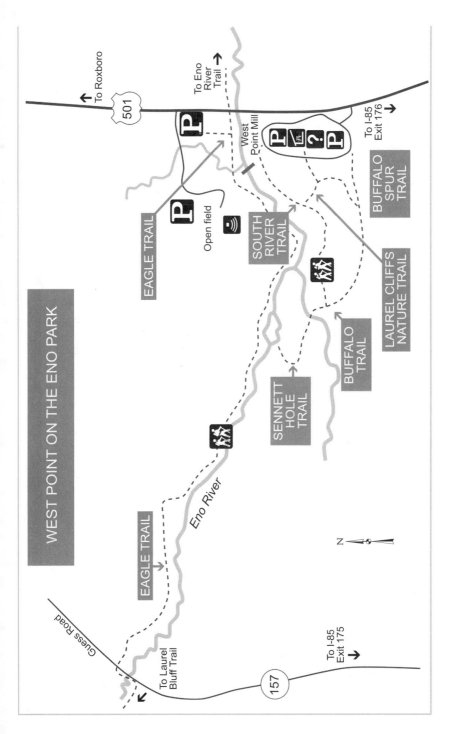

WEST POINT ON THE ENO PARK

To Roxboro

501

To Eno River Trail →

To I-85 Exit 176 →

West Point Mill

EAGLE TRAIL

Open field

SOUTH RIVER TRAIL

BUFFALO SPUR TRAIL

LAUREL CLIFFS NATURE TRAIL

BUFFALO TRAIL

SENNETT HOLE TRAIL

Eno River

EAGLE TRAIL

N

Guess Road

To Laurel Bluff Trail

157

To I-85 Exit 175 →

Buffalo Spur Trail (0.15 mile)
Sennett Hole Trail (0.15 mile)
Eagle Trail (1.8 miles)

Length and Difficulty: 3.4 miles one-way, combined; easy to moderate

Trailheads and Description: From I-85 in Durham, take U.S. 501 Bypass (North Duke Street) north for 3.5 miles and turn left into the park at a traffic light. (The turn is across the road from the Riverview Shopping Center.) Follow the park road to the right.

If parking near the West Point Mill, walk across the millrace bridge toward the dam. Ascend left to begin *South River Trail.* (Part of this trail includes *Laurel Cliffs Nature Trail,* which has interpretative markers. Maps and brochures explaining the markers are available at the park office and trail-entrance signboards.)

On a rocky bluff, there are views of the dam. The trail passes through mountain laurel, wintergreen, and galax. The route passes a connection with Laurel Cliffs Nature Trail, on the left. At 0.5 mile, there is a connection with *Buffalo Trail.* Turn right and cross a bridge over Warren Creek to begin *Sennett Hole Trail.* Stop at the riverbank—this is the site of the first gristmill on the river. Here, there are great views of the rapids, rock formations, and an island. Backtrack. If using Buffalo Trail, you can use *Buffalo Spur Trail,* or exit near the picnic shelter at the south end of the circle road.

To access *Eagle Trail,* drive 0.5 mile north of the park's main entrance on

View of Eno River from Eagle Trail in West Point on the Eno Park in Durham

U.S. 501 (Roxboro Road) to another park entrance on the left. A parking lot is immediately to the left. (The entrance road, which may be gated, continues ahead to the amphitheater.) The trailhead is near the gate on the left. Descend on steps into a grassy meadow and turn left. At 0.1 mile, pass through a cut in a low-level ridge, which was formerly a dam. After 100 yards, there is an access on the left to the proposed pedestrian bridge over the Eno River to West Point Mill. (When completed, this access will pass under the U.S. 501 bridge to Eno River Trail. Although not in the West Point on the Eno Park, this 3.0-mile part of the trail is under construction. When finished it will lead to trails in Penny's Bend Nature Preserve. Eno River and Eagle trails are part of the *Mountains-to-Sea Trail*.) Stay right, rock-hop Crooked Run Creek, and ascend to a junction with an old road near the amphitheater. At 0.2 mile, turn left. Pass through a forest of tall white oak, loblolly pine, yellow poplar, and sycamore, with spots of running cedar. At 0.5 mile, curve right in a damp area, going toward the edge of the Eno River. At 0.6 mile, pass the rapids and rocky area of Sennett Hole. On the rocky banks, there are beds of trout lily, spring beauty, and toothwort, which break through the leaves in early March. There are more scenic rapids at 0.8 mile. Turn away from the river and ascend a ridge at 1.2 miles. At 1.7 miles, pass remains of an old homesite on the left and a pond on the right. At 1.8 miles, there is a residence on the left. Access to Guess Road and the Eno River bridge is ahead. Backtrack or arrange a shuttle. (To continue on the 2.5-mile *Laurel Bluff Trail*, cross the bridge and find the trail on the right. More information about Laurel Bluff Trail is in Chapter 2 under "Eno River State Park.")

Whippoorwill Park

Part of the overall *North/South Greenway* plan is the 0.8-mile *Upper Warren Creek Trail*, whose main access is at Whippoorwill Park. To access the trail from the parking circle near the entrance to the tennis courts in the park, follow the sidewalk past the restrooms and descend 105 yards to the asphalt greenway entrance on the right. Cross an arched bridge and follow the trail downstream. The mixed forest has flowering shrubbery and wildflowers, some of which were planted by landscapers. Songbirds frequent the area. At 0.8 mile, there is a patch of wild blackberries near the end of the trail at Horton Street. Backtrack. (Call 919-560-4355 for an update on the proposed greenway that will follow Warren Creek from here to West Point on the Eno Park.)

From the southwest corner of Whippoorwill Park, between the tennis courts, another part of the North/South Greenway project continues into the forest on asphalt. Wildflowers, such as green and gold, are here. Cross a concrete bridge. At 0.2 mile, exit the forest at Stadium Drive and turn right on the wide sidewalk.

> **ACCESS:** In north Durham from the junction of NC 157 (Guess Road) and Carver Street, drive north 0.4 mile on NC 157 to Kirkwood Drive. Turn right onto Kirkwood Drive. After 0.2 mile, turn left onto Britt Street. After another 0.1 mile, turn right on Rosemont Street. The park entrance is on the left.

Rock Quarry Park, Glendale Heights Park, and Northgate Park

Trails in these parks are part of the *North/South Greenway*. Their northern trailheads connect with the planned greenway section that will run from the corner of Duke Street (U.S. 501 Bypass) and Stadium Drive on to Whippoorwill Park.

Ellerbee Creek Trail (1.3 miles)
Rock Quarry Trail (0.4 mile)
South Ellerbee Creek Trail (1.2 miles)

Length and Difficulty: 2.5 miles one-way, combined; easy
Trailheads and Description: To follow these trails from north to south, take Exit 176 off I-85 and drive 0.9 mile north on Duke Street. Turn right onto Stadium Drive. The northern trailhead for *Ellerbee Creek Trail* is at this corner. Parking is available 0.1 mile from this corner, on the right next to the National Guard Armory.

The asphalt Ellerbee Creek Trail descends through a forest of large trees and crosses a bridge. It parallels Ellerbee Creek for 0.5 mile to Murray Avenue. (The southern terminus of *Rock Quarry Trail*, which will be discussed ahead, is on the left.)

Continuing on Ellerbee Creek Trail, turn right on Murray Avenue. After 170 feet, cross the street into Glendale Heights Park. The trail continues past the lighted Jaycee ball field in scenic Northgate Park. At 1.3 miles, arrive at West Club Boulevard. This is the end of Ellerbee Creek Trail and the beginning of *South Ellerbee Creek Trail*.

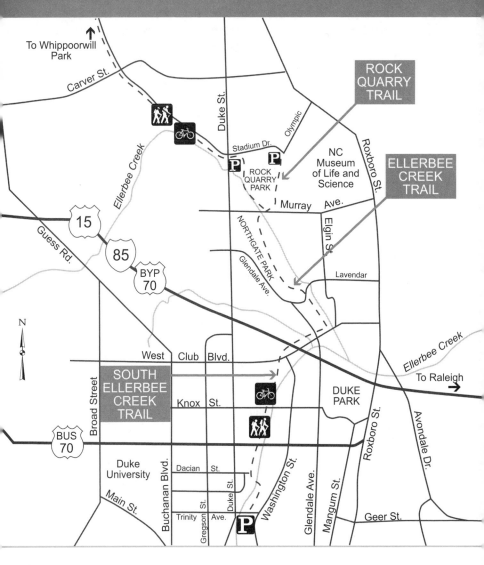

To follow South Ellerbee Creek Trail, turn right onto the sidewalk along West Club Boulevard. Cross Glendale Avenue, pass Club Boulevard Elementary School, and go under U.S. 15/70 Bypass/I-85. At the Washington Street traffic light at 1.7 miles, cross to the southwest corner. The trail follows a curvy route paralleling a tributary of Ellerbee Creek as it travels upstream. Descend on a wide, recently constructed greenway through a forest with tall trees and large, swinging grapevines. The greenway is like a golden path of opportunity for neighbors to visit each other on a tranquil street; children can walk or ride their bikes from near the crowded heart of the city north to a museum, a swimming pool, athletic fields, and acres of green grass. The disabled can use wheelchairs for a touch with nature. At 2.0 miles, cross Knox Street. Residences are nearby on the right. Wild roses grow near the trail and stream. Cross an arched bridge, then cross Green and Markham streets before going under a power line as the trail approaches Dacian Street. At 2.3 miles, cross Dacian Street. Cross a culvert bridge, turn left, then right to end at Trinity Avenue after 2.5 miles. Backtrack or arrange for a shuttle. *Rock Quarry Trail* connects into Ellerbee Creek Trail at its 0.4-mile point. To begin your hike at Rock Quarry Trail's trailhead, the parking area for Rock Quarry Park is on Stadium Drive, 0.3 mile from North Duke Street and 0.9 mile from I-85. The park has athletic fields and tennis courts.

To reach Rock Quarry Trail, follow trail signs that go beside the restrooms and into the forest on a broad asphalt bike/hike trail. At 0.2-mile, you will pass left of a Vietnam War memorial. There are meditation benches placed here. One of the statements carved in the marble reads: "For those who fought for it, freedom has a flavor the protected will never know." The trail passes the Edison Johnson Recreation Center and the North Carolina Museum of Life and Science on a sidewalk to Murray Avenue. To enter Northgate Park, cross the street, turn right, and continue over the Ellerbee Creek bridge to an immediate left at the trail sign.

Follow an asphalt trail across a meadow. After 125 yards, there is a replica of a brontosaurus. Enter a shady area of large oaks and pines. At 0.8 mile, pass around the edge of a lighted Jaycee ball field in Northgate Park. Continue on the trail through elm, maple, and evergreens. Cross Lavender Avenue. Willow, oak, ash, sycamore, and poplar tower over a peaceful lawn. Squirrels and songbirds are usually present. Cross a footbridge; on the left are a playground, a picnic shelter, and parking areas. At 1.2 miles, arrive at West Club Boulevard, which is the south end of Rock Quarry Trail and the beginning of South Ellerbee Creek Trail. Directions for South Ellerbee Creek Trail were given above.

When you reach the end of South Ellerbee Creek Trail, on the left, there is an abandoned railroad; to the right is a parking lot on the east side of Duke University Diet & Fitness Center. It is one block west to Duke Street. If you turn right (north) onto Duke Street, the Ellerbee Creek Trail where this section started, is at the corner Stadium Drive, on the right. (Future plans have the greenway system extending south from this Trinity Avenue location to the north terminus of the *American Tobacco Trail* at Durham Bulls Athletic Park.)

Westover Park and Indian Trail Park

▊ West Ellerbee Creek Trail (0.7 mile, easy)

Trailhead and Description: *West Ellerbee Creek Trail* is part of a southwest spur from the planned *North/South Greenway* that will extend from the *Ellerbee Creek Trail* terminus at Stadium Drive to Westover Park.

To access the eastern end of West Ellerbee Creek Trail, take Exit 175 off I-85. Drive south for 0.5 mile on Guess Road to Wagoner Street/Forest Road. Turn right at Westover Park, which is at this intersection. Turn right again to access the parking area.

From the parking space at the trailhead, follow the sign and start on the asphalt greenway. The open, scenic route parallels Ellerbee Creek; tall forest trees are on both sides. Along the trail, there are mulberry trees (the fruit is ripe in mid-May), jewelweed, and milkweed. At 0.3 mile, there is a garden of wildflowers off the trail on the left, which was developed from a former city trash pile by the Ellerbee Creek Watershed Association. Turn right and cross a bridge over the creek to Indian Trail Park, which has a children's playground and picnic area. The western end of the trail is here. To access this trailhead, take Exit 174 off I-85 and go south on Hillandale Road for 0.2 mile. Turn left onto the street named Indian Trail. Indian Trail Park is on the right.

Sandy Creek Park and Sandy Creek Greenway

The restored Sandy Creek Park and *New Hope Bottomland Trail*, which is described in the next entry, are separate entities, but they are both near Durham/Chapel Hill Boulevard (U.S. 15/50l) and both are north of I-40. Neither is part of the current North/South Greenway system. The Sandy Creek Park has picnic and restroom facilities near a few large willow oaks and a pond. There is a path around the pond and a 0.5-mile paved *Sandy Creek Greenway*, which runs north along Sandy Creek to Pickett Road. North of the pond on the greenway, there are wildflowers and a wetland, which has an unusually large display of white buttonbush. You can backtrack to the parking area. Sandy Creek Environmental Education Center is planned for the park.

ACCESS: At the crossroads of Pickett Road and Nello Teer Senior Highway (U.S. 15/501 Bypass), drive west a few yards on Pickett Road and suddenly turn left onto Sandy Creek Road. Drive 0.6 mile to the dead-end road at the park.

New Hope Bottomland Trail (3.4 miles, easy)

Trailheads and Description: If coming from the north to the crossroads of Old Chapel Hill Road and Watkins Road or coming from the south to Old Chapel Hill Road and Farrington Road, drive east on Old Chapel Hill Road for 0.2 mile. Turn left into the parking lot of Githens Middle School.

To access *New Hope Bottomland Trail* from the Githens Middle School parking lot, walk to the northeast corner and go around the track for 0.2 mile to descend on steps at its northeast corner. Turn left on an old road, which parallels water-treatment space. (The white-arrow blazes are for the school's running trails.) At 0.3 mile, pass the last white arrow and continue ahead. At 0.6 mile, turn right into the woods. After 130 yards, the trail divides. If going right, proceed through an outstanding example of bottomland with tall hardwoods. Some sections of the dense forest undergrowth are entangled with honeysuckle and wild grapevines. At 0.8 mile, cross the first of at least 15 footbridges or boardwalks. There are two places where the trail passes under a power line. At 1.2 miles, there are scenic views of New Hope Creek. Ahead, you can hear the sound of traffic on Durham/Chapel Hill Boulevard. Between 1.4 miles and 1.9 miles, there is a low area that is subject to flooding. This area has 11 boardwalks. (At 2.1 miles, there is a 0.1-mile side trail that goes right to Hopedale Avenue. Hopedale Avenue runs through a private

New Hope Bottomland Trail in Durham

housing development, but it leads to the public Wilkins Road.) Continue on the main trail and complete the loop at 2.8 miles; continuing to the school parking lot brings the total mileage to 3.4 miles.

Bicyclists on the multi-use American Tobacco Trail

American Tobacco Trail

Although the 22.0-mile *American Tobacco Trail* (*ATT*) runs through multiple counties, the trail description here covers where the trail begins in the north and travels through Durham and Durham County for about 12.1 miles. The trail also runs through Chatham (4.6 miles) and Wake (5.3 miles) counties, and partly through the Jordan Lake property. In the future, the trail may have connections to nearby towns and communities, such as Cary and Apex. ATT is part of the national rails-to-trails movement. It runs on the former property of the New Hope Valley Railroad and later the Durham & South Carolina Railroad. The trail project was made possible by the influence and leadership of the Triangle Rails-to-Trails Conservancy (a volunteer nonprofit organization) and the Durham Parks and Recreation Department. (When this guidebook was published, ATT was not completed for a few miles in Chatham County and for a section immediately south of the I-40 crossing in Durham County. In the planning stage is construction of a bridge across I-40 and repair to one of the old railroad bridges in Chatham County. The sections in Wake County are complete.)

For more information about ATT: contact 919-545-9104; 919-560-4355, or www.triangletrails.org.

Length and Difficulty: 22.0 miles, combined; easy

Trailheads and Description: The description that follows begins at the northern trailhead. In downtown Durham, the trail begins diagonally across from the Durham Bulls Athletic Park on the corner of Jackie Robinson Drive. Suggested parking is at the corner of Morehead Avenue and Blackwell Street. (Durham Freeway goes overhead.)

Beginning at the trail sign, travel south on the asphalt greenway, which is open to hiking and bicycling. Cross a wide steel bridge over Lakewoods Drive at 0.2 mile. Kudzu and honeysuckle may be on the sides of the trail. At 0.8 mile, go under the Roxboro Street bridge. At 1.4 miles, cross Otis Street. Sweetgum and mimosa are noticeable at the forest edge. Cross Fayetteville Street near a mini-mart across the street on the corner of Pilot Street. At 2.0 miles, there is a plaque honoring a local popular bluesman, "Blind Boy Fuller," a.k.a. Fulton Allen, who is buried nearby. (A few feet ahead, on the left, is the 0.7-mile *Rocky Creek Trail* that parallels Third Fork Rock Creek upstream to Elmira Park at the intersection of Dakota Street and NC 55. Forking off the trail after 0.15 mile is the 0.9-mile *Pearsontown Trail.* It also passes Elmira Park as it goes north. It crosses eight streets in a residential area. At 0.6 mile, Pearsontown Trail passes through Shady Oaks Park. At 0.9 mile, it stops at the Nelson Street Campus Ministry Building of N.C. Central University. A proposed greenway would follow Third Fork Rock Creek southwest to Woodcroft Parkway and New Hope Road [NC 751].)

Continuing on the ATT, cross a bridge over Third Fork Rock Creek and go into a forest for the next 0.3 mile. (Your cumulative mileage from the northern trailhead is now 10.0 miles.) At 2.9 miles, pass Hillside High School, on the right. At 3.0 miles, follow an access road on the left to Riddle Road. (If you want to begin the ATT here, there may be some roadside parking. You can also park at the nearby high school.) Cross Riddle Road. After 30 yards, there is a junction with *Riddle Road Spur Trail* on the left. (Riddle Road Spur Trail goes through a forest for 0.5 mile, then crosses Riddle Road. At 0.8 mile, it crosses NC 55; at 1.2 miles, it crosses South Alston Avenue. It ends at a parking lot on Bridges Avenue at 1.5 miles.)

Back on the ATT, cross Cornwallis Road at 3.2 miles. Along the greenway, there are wild red roses, Queen Anne's lace, and mullein. At 3.8 miles, cross Martin Luther King, Jr. Parkway. (At this junction, *MLK, Jr. Parkway Street Trail* uses sidewalks and bicycle lanes for 3.1 miles as it goes east to NC 55 and west to Hope Valley Road.) At 3.9 miles, cross United Drive; at 4.1 miles, cross Belgreen Road. The trail crosses Fayetteville Road after another 55 yards. Pass by basketball courts and a playground on the right.

At 5.0 miles, on the right, pass Southwest Elementary School in the

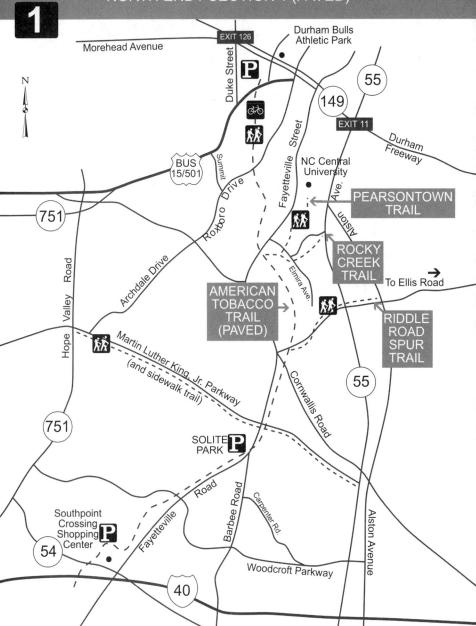

AMERICAN TOBACCO TRAIL
MIDDLE SECTIONS 2, 3, AND 4
(UNPAVED AND PARTS UNDER CONSTRUCTION)

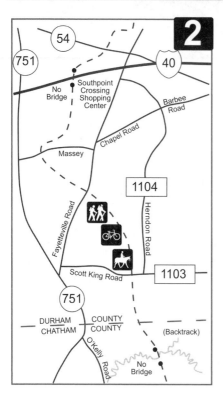

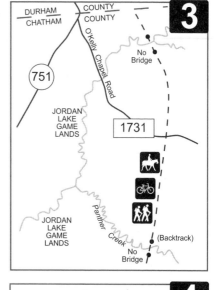

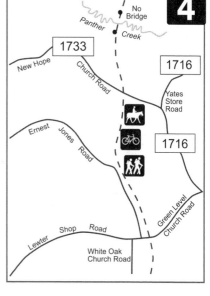

AMERICAN TOBACCO TRAIL
Middle Sections

Section 2 bridge planned over I-40

Section 3 bridge planned over
Northeast Creek

Section 4 bridge planned over
Panther Creek

N

For updated progress check
www.triangletrails.org

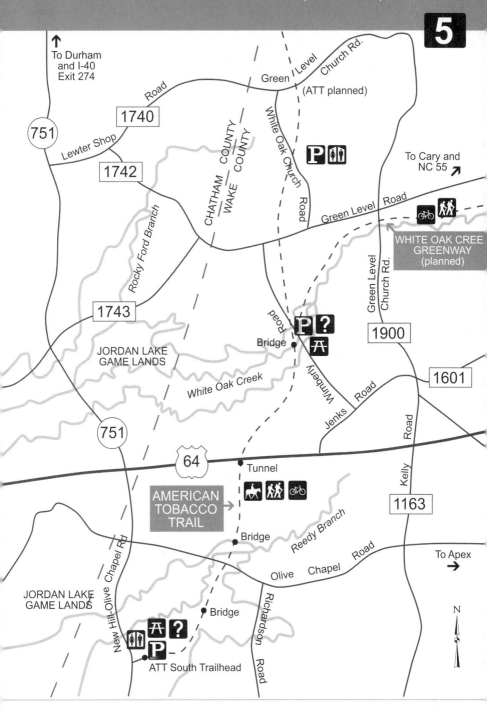

AMERICAN TOBACCO TRAIL (ATT)
SOUTH END / SECTION 5 (UNPAVED)

5

↑
To Durham
and I-40
Exit 274

Green Level Church Rd.

(ATT planned)

751

1740

Lewter Shop Road

White Oak Church Road

1742

CHATHAM COUNTY
WAKE COUNTY

To Cary and
NC 55 ↗

Green Level Road

Rocky Ford Branch

WHITE OAK CREE
GREENWAY
(planned)

1743

Green Level Church Rd.

JORDAN LAKE
GAME LANDS

Road

Bridge

Wimberly

1900

White Oak Creek

1601

751

Jenks Road

Kelly Road

64

Tunnel

AMERICAN
TOBACCO
TRAIL →

1163

Bridge

Reedy Branch

To Apex
→

New Hill-Olive Chapel Rd.

Olive Chapel Road

JORDAN LAKE
GAME LANDS

Bridge

Richardson Road

N

ATT South Trailhead

community of Arborfield. After crossing more streets and traveling through sections of forest on the old railroad bed, pass under a power line at 6.0 miles. At 6.4 miles, turn right off the old railroad track to follow the sidewalk behind The Streets at Southpoint mall, but remain on the residential-housing sidewalk. At 6.6 miles, stop at NC 54. If you want to start the ATT here, parking is available at the shopping center. (This may be a temporary access until the planned ATT bridge is constructed over I-40.)

To continue south on the ATT, you need to drive to connect the segments. The cumulative mileage count stops here. Drive south across NC 54 and I-40 on Fayetteville Road for 1.2 miles to Massey Chapel Road. (Streets at Southpoint mall and Massey Chapel are along the way.) After turning right on Massey Chapel Road, drive 0.6 mile to the trailhead on the left. You can park on the roadside. (To the right of the trailhead is the unfinished ATT, which has an uncertain future access until the I-40 bridge is constructed.) The ATT follows a gravel/grassy route among pines. At 0.3 mile, pass a housing development, followed by a water-treatment plant, on the left. At 0.7 mile, pass under the Fayetteville Road bridge. At 1.0 mile, cross a bridge over Crooked Creek. Cross under a power line at 1.6 miles. At 1.8 miles, arrive at Scott King Road. (From here, it is 0.9 mile to the right [west] to reach Fayetteville Road.)

To complete this section, cross the road where there is an informational sign. On a gravel/grassy treadway, pass under a power line and soon enter a deep forest. After 1.0 mile, arrive at the partial frame of a railroad bridge over Northeast Creek near the Durham/Chatham county line. Backtrack to Scott King Road. To continue the ATT, you will have to drive to the next section. You can either get a shuttle to pick you up at Scott King Road or backtrack to the parking spot on Massey Chapel Road.

From Scott King Road, drive west 0.9 mile to Fayetteville Road. Turn left. At 0.1 mile, turn left on NC 751. Drive 0.8 mile before staying left on O'Kelly Chapel Road. After 1.8 miles, the ATT crosses on the right and left. Park off the road.

Walk north into the forest and then through an upscale housing area. At 0.4 mile, pass a pond on the left. At 1.0 mile, stop at the railroad bridge over Northeast Creek described above. Backtrack to O'Kelly Chapel Road. If going south across O'Kelly Chapel Road from this point, enter the forest. At 0.4 mile, pass old railroad crossties with pieces of railings. At 0.8 mile, exit through a grassy section to Oakley Road. (Ahead is a damaged railroad bridge over Panther Creek.) Backtrack, or arrange a shuttle from where you parked on O'Kelly Chapel Road. Then drive east for 0.6 mile on O'Kelly Chapel Road and turn right onto Oakley Road. It is 1.1 miles to an ATT crossing. (Oakley Road deadends farther west.)

Until the damaged railroad bridge is repaired or reconstructed, it is suggested you begin at the Wake County/Wimberly access and hike south to the end of ATT or start there and hike north to Wimberly. Access is from U.S. 64 west of the junction with NC 55. Turn right on Jenks Road and drive 0.6 mile to make a left on Wimberly Road. After 1.1 miles, park right at the ATT sign. (Plans call for the ATT to go north from here for 1.5 miles to cross Green Level Road and end at a crossing of White Oak Church Road, where there is a parking area. At this point, it is 0.7 mile to the north on White Oak Church Road to Green Level Church Road. It is 0.7 mile south on White Oak Church Road to Green Level Road West.)

At the Wake County/Wimberly parking area, cross Wimberly Road and go south to enter the forest. On the wide, smooth greenway, there are benches for resting along the way. At 0.1 mile, pass a gate, followed by a bridge. At 1.4 miles, enter a tunnel, which goes under U.S. 64. At 2.2 miles, pass under a power line and travel by a scenic stream area. There may be high water in a few places in the hardwood and pine forest below the railroad grade. At 2.9 miles, cross a bridge. At 3.7 miles, turn right to access the parking area. Backtrack or arrange a shuttle to drive from the parking area. If shuttling, drive 0.2 mile out to NC 751 (New Hill-Olive Chapel Road) and turn right. After 2.2 miles, turn right onto U.S. 64. Drive 1.7 miles to a left on Jenks Road. After 0.5 mile on Jenks Road, turn left on Wimberly Road to go 1.1 mile to the Wake County/Wimberly parking area. (It is at this parking area that *White Oak Creek Greenway*, coming from Bond Park in Cary, will connect with the American Tobacco Trail.)

Fuquay-Varina (Wake County)

> **Fuquay-Varina Parks, Recreation, and Cultural Resources Department**
> **820 South Main Street**
> **Fuquay-Varina, NC 27526**
> **Telephone: 919-552-1430; fax: 919-557-3112**

Fuquay-Varina's management sets a good example by having drama and dance programs, arts and crafts exhibits, and concerts in its community center. Adjoining the center is South Park, where physical recreation is the emphasis with ball fields, a 0.6-mile paved track and walking trail, and other sports facilities. The community center also features Carroll Howard Johnson Environmental Education Park, which has a trail network described below.

Carroll Howard Johnson
Environmental Education Park

The 28-acre Johnson Environmental Education Park features educational trails, a picnic area, an amphitheater, overlooks, bridges, benches, and a restroom. The park is open daily from sunrise to sunset. Neither horses nor ATVs are allowed in the park. It is accessible by a connecting trail from South Park, or by driving south from South Park on Main Street (U.S. 40l) for 0.4 mile to Wagstaff Road. Turn right onto Wagstaff Road and drive 0.3 mile to a parking area on the left.

Honeysuckle Lane Trail (92 yards)
Holly Ridge Trail (0.3 mile)
Loblolly Loop Trail (165 yards)
Laurel Lane Trail (0.17 mile)
Creekside Trail (0.15 mile)
Heritage Trail (0.3 mile)
Persimmon Trail (90 yards)

Length and Difficulty: 1.7 miles (or more if backtracking); easy
Trailheads and Description: *Note:* There are several short connectors in this trail network, which are not detailed in the description below. They are: *Hickory Hollow Loop Trail* (0.3 mile, easy); *Hummingbird Lane Trail* (0.12 mile, easy); *Kenneth Crossing Trail* (60 yards, easy); *Whitetail Trail* (141 yards, easy); and *Willow Way Trail* (82 yards, easy).

From the crescent-shaped parking area with huge oaks, examine the park's signboard near the restroom and amphitheater. Notice a labyrinth of multiple color-blazed trails. Once on these trails, there are markers with an aggregation of information about the area's natural history and vascular plants. If going to the picnic shelter or taking a clockwise approach to the trails, choose a trailhead on the left. Going clockwise will include *Honeysuckle Lane Trail* and *Holly Ridge Trail* for the 0.2-mile walk to the picnic shelter on *Loblolly Loop Trail*. Both Holly Ridge Trail and *Laurel Lane Trail* take you along the hillside, under a power line, before reaching a meeting place beside the stream (Kenneth Branch). These trails also connect with *Creekside Trail*, which leads to bridges for *Heritage Trail* and other trails on a hillside. (The shortest trail from the parking area to the arched Kenneth Bridge and Heritage Trail is the 90-yard *Persimmon Trail*. Pick up this trail by going right of the amphitheater and trail-map board.) Heritage Trail meanders upstream beside Kenneth Branch. In the open areas under the power line, there are wildflowers, as well as such birds as cardinals, bluebirds, and towhees. The shrubbery near the stream includes sparkleberry and fragrant titi. At 0.3 mile, Heritage Trail crosses Wagstaff Road. It travels upstream for another 0.3 mile before reaching the third (lowest) baseball field at South Park.

Garner (Wake County)

Town of Garner Parks and Recreation
P.O. Box 446
Garner, NC 27529
Telephone: 919-772-8765; fax: 919-602-5135

As with other towns facing the Triangle area's urban expansion, Garner is feeling the need for a master plan for its trails. Fortunately, the town has already purchased property to be used for trails. One example of such a purchase is the 96-acre White Deer Park off Buffalo Road between downtown Garner and Lake Benson. Plans are to create a community center with educational programs and recreational facilities. In addition, there will be about 12 to 15 miles of trails, some of which will be paved. A few of Garner's other parks have short tracks at athletic fields. One of these— Garner Recreation Park—is described below.

Garner Recreation Park

Garner Recreation Park has a hiking and mountain-biking trail, which is described ahead. Other facilities at this park are an athletic field, a picnic area, restrooms, and a shuffleboard court.

Hilliard Creek Trail (3.0 miles, easy to moderate)

Trailhead and Description: From I-40, take Exit 303 and drive southeast 1.3 miles on Jones Sausage Road to a crossroad with East Garner Road. Turn right onto East Garner Road. After 0.8 mile, turn right at the park sign and park at the end of the entrance road.

Hilliard Creek Trail is named for the stream that flows north between steep slopes on each side of the trail. The route has multiple connections and loops that connect other areas of the park property and the adjoining Creech

Elementary School. Although the trail is open to both hikers and bikers, it is used primarily by mountain bikers. At the slanted parking area, a trail sign states "pedestrians have the right of way. Please be mindful of each other."

The sign also indicates the trail is color-coded with blue (1.2 miles), red (1.2 miles), and green (0.5 mile) loops. From the parking lot, descend to the edge of the woods. The red section goes to the left; the blue to the right. Both of these loops connect with the green loop. The trail features moderate dips, mounds, and log jumps. All of the trails travel through a mature forest of tall trees.

If users take the blue route, they travel briefly up a ridge, then down to a bridge across the creek at a large beech tree at 0.3 mile. At 0.6 mile, there is a connection with the green trail. There is another connection with the green loop at 0.9 mile.

The red section is mainly on the west side of the creek. Part of its loop goes up a hollow and runs to the edge of the park's athletic fields. Some spurs leading to athletic fields near the school may intersect with the color-coded sections of the main trail. One example of where confusion might occur is *Pine Ridge Trail*. At some points, users may inadvertently go onto extra spurs, which have been created but don't have blazes. As a result, users may find themselves coming to private property signs, where they will have to backtrack.

Holly Springs (Wake County)

Holly Springs Parks and Recreation
P.O. Box 8
Holly Springs, NC 27540
Telephone: 919-557-3934; fax: 919-553-5569

The town of Holly Springs was first settled in 1826 near a spring in a grove of American holly. Although the area has other springs near holly trees, it seems likely that early settlers established a community near the spring that is located downtown near the corner of West Center Street and Avent Ferry Road. It is found between a large white house and Holly Springs United Methodist Church; there is also a parking space here. From the parking space, the official sign for the spring is at the edge of the woods. Follow the *Nature Trail* into a forest of tall trees, some of which are garnished with English ivy. Descend and pass the Benton Cemetery. At 0.15 mile, turn left on an old road. At 0.2 mile, there is a small, old brick foundation near the spring. Sweet gum and yellow poplar tower above the damp area. Ascend and return to complete the loop at 0.3 mile.

Today, Holly Springs is experiencing a remarkable expansion in housing, shopping centers, and other development. As with other towns in the Triangle, the planning board is also expanding the number of greenways, parks, and other open spaces. Following the Recreation and Parks Department's master recreation plan, the town has completed more than a dozen short greenways. Another dozen are in planning stages, and at least ten more are proposed. This does not even include the subdivisions that are developing private greenways. When this guidebook was published, the longest completed greenway was *Bass Lake Greenway*, which is described ahead.

Some of the planned or proposed trails have not been named yet, but brief descriptions are provided here. There is a proposed public greenway that will run northwest from Bass Lake on Bass Lake Road. It will turn left on Earp Street (where the section is partly completed or in planning stages already). It will then cross North Main Street. At 2.2 miles, it will end at Oaks of Avent Acres on the left.

From Oaks of Avent Acres, a trail, which is in various stages of completion, planning, or proposal, will run southwest for about 3.5 miles. It will then cross NC 55 and parallel Utley Creek part of the way into Harris Game Land. At its west end, the trail may go north for approximately 3.0 miles, traveling near White Oak Creek to Woods Creek Road. (About 1.5 miles on this trail, a connection is proposed that will go south to Evergreen

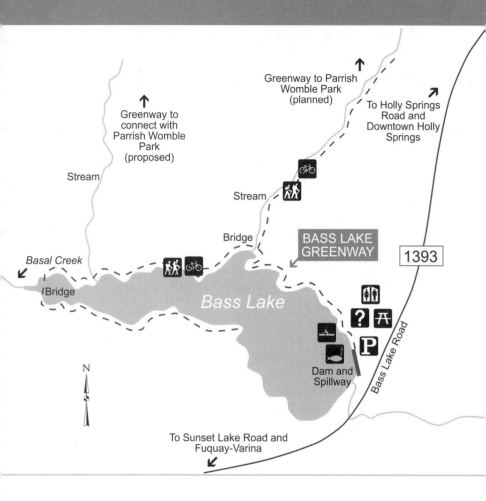

View Drive and continue to the Braxtonville subdivision.)

There are two other trails that are either being constructed or planned. One will run northwest from *Bass Lake Greenway* for 0.7 mile to Parrish Womble Park. The other will go northwest for about 1.0 mile to an existing greenway at Grigsby Avenue on the south side of Parrish Womble Park.

On the eastern side of the town, there is another trail that has sections that are either partially completed or in the planning stages. This 1.0-mile trail runs from Brackenbridge Lane on Settlecroft Lane to Moonrise Drive. It then goes right on Bibleway Court and left on Wescott Ridge Drive. (A swimming pool is planned for Wescott Ridge Drive.) From this location, an estimated 1.5-mile trail is planned and proposed that will go north to cross Optimist Farm Road. It will pass through Sunset Lake Shopping Center, cross Holly Springs Road (and probably go under proposed I-540), and connect to a completed greenway. The greenway has a fork to the right that leads to Scot's Laurel. (Another swimming pool is proposed for this site.)

There is also a trail located north of the downtown area, which is in various stages of completion. It goes from Holly Springs Road on the west side of Holly Springs Elementary School to Sunset Lake Road near a crossing over Middle Creek at proposed I-540. Along the way, the 1.75-mile trail will make three loops north of the elementary school, pass through undeveloped sections, and parallel Middle Creek to its end. About halfway on the trail route, there is another planned route, which will go 1.5 miles east to Holly Springs Road near Lassiter Road.

Bass Lake Park and Retreat Center

Bass Lake Park and Retreat Center includes facilities for conferences, business meetings, and social occasions. It has refreshment services, but does not have dining-hall facilities. At this park, visitors can rent boats, fish, or use the small sandy beach. Park regulations require that hikers and bicyclists stay on the trail and that dogs be on a leash.

ACCESS: From the North Main Street intersection, drive east on Holly Springs Road for 0.6 mile and turn right on Bass Lake Road. After 1.4 miles, turn right into the parking lot.

Bass Lake Greenway (2.4 miles round-trip; easy)

Trailhead and Description: From the parking lot, pass right of the buildings and follow the natural-surface *Bass Lake Greenway* past a small sandy beach. There are markers that identify some of the trees along the way. Most of the trail is open enough to offer scenic views of the lakeside. At 0.3 mile, there is a steel trestle, a kiosk, and a greenway. The greenway goes right to Parrish Womble Park. Continuing on the greenway, enter the forest at 0.6 mile and watch for a spur trail on the left. That spur goes to a grove of tag alder, where a pavilion-style blind allows people to watch waterfowl. Back on the greenway, before passing over another steel trestle, look for a new greenway to the right. It may still be in planning stages. (This new greenway will go to the south end of Parrish Womble Park at Grigsby Avenue.) On Bass Lake Greenway, cross the steel trestle curve on the left and follow the edge of the lake to the 1.2-mile point. The end of trail is at an information kiosk. Backtrack. (There are plans to extend the trail to Bass Lake Road for a complete loop.)

Louisburg (Franklin County)

Louisburg Parks and Recreation
110 West Nash Street
Louisburg, NC 27549
Telephone: 919-496-4145; fax: 919-396-6319

Louisburg is known for its historic district of Victorian, Georgian, and Federal houses. It is also known as the home of Louisburg College. Founded in 1787, Louisburg College is the oldest, church-related (United Methodist), two-year college in the nation.

The town also has two parks. Tar River Park, which is mainly a picnic area, is located on the east side of a cascading section of the Tar River. It is located at the end of Church Street. Joyner Park, which is in phases of development, is on the west side of the river. In addition to picnic areas and a children's playground, Joyner Park has a paved loop around an open athletic field and two named trails, which are discussed ahead.

The town has constructed a 2.2-mile greenway, which goes from downtown Louisburg to Vance-Granville Community College (Franklin County Campus). Because this trail follows the old railroad bed of a train spur that ran to Louisburg to transport cotton and other farm products from Franklinton, the Franklin County Advisory Greenway Board recommended the 2.2-mile spur, and the other 7.8 miles for the rest of the greenway, be named the *Cotton Market Rail-Trail*.

To access this rail-trail when walking or bicycling from downtown, enter near the south side of the Tar River Bridge, where you see the L.H. Dickens & Son sign on a historic warehouse. The trail passes mainly through a residential area. It crosses Bunn Road. At 0.7 mile, pass Toney's Lumber Company. At 1.1 miles, cross South Main Street. After passing through a forest, Pruitt Lumber Company is on the right. You can smell the aromatic pine odor coming from the Bark Plant. Exit to the left to reach a parking area at Vance-Granville Community College. (For information on the future phase of the greenway, call 919-496-4145.)

Joyner Park

River View Loop Trail (0.4 mile)
Cypress Scout Trail (1.0 mile)

Length and Difficulty: 2.4 miles combined and round-trip; easy

Trailheads and Description: From South Main Street, on the south side of the Tar River Bridge, turn upstream (west) on River Road. After 0.5 mile, turn right into Joyner Park. Access to the paved *River View Loop Trail* is from the lower parking area. It passes a high embankment, where there are views of the Tar River. It then circles back to the lower parking area or goes on to the upper parking area near the picnic shelter. It also connects with *Cypress Scout Trail*, which was constructed by Boy Scout Troop 555. The natural-surface path wanders through a hardwood forest for 1.0 mile. At 0.2 mile, pass under a power line. At 0.3 mile, there is a spur on the right that leads to an observation deck near a cypress grove. In a marsh, the large trees have conical knees, which are scaly and glazed like creatures from the movie *Alien*. Farther upriver on a bluff, there is a natural floral garden that includes ferns, buckeye, bloodroot, dotted horsemint, downy phlox, and hairy-jointed meadow-parsnip. Backtrack for a round-trip of 2.0 miles.

Cypress knees on Cypress Scout Trail in Louisburg

 (Granville County)

Oxford Parks and Recreation Department
P.O. Box 506
Oxford, NC 27565
Telephone: 919-603-1135; fax: 919-603-1138

Lake Devin

Lake Devin (also called City Lake) was originally constructed for Oxford's water supply. The 196.6-acre lake now serves as a recreational site for boating and fishing with permits. Swimming in the lake is not allowed. Picnicking is allowed at tables on *Spillway Trail* and at the parking area shelter. Detailed descriptions of the lake's trail network are given ahead.

Spillway Trail (1.3 miles)
Pine Grove Trail (0.7 mile)
Peninsula Trail (2.0 miles)

Length and Difficulty: 4.7 miles round-trip and backtracking; easy

Trailheads and Description: To reach Lake Devin from I-85, take Exit 204 and drive west on Linden Avenue (NC 96) to Hillsboro Street (U.S. 15). Take Hillsboro Street south. After 0.2 mile, stay straight (do not follow U.S. l5, which goes left). Cross the railroad track on Providence Street and pass Industry Road. At a traffic light, turn right on Old NC 75. After 0.3 mile, turn right on Lake Devin Road. Drive 0.4 mile slowly and watch for a small sign to Lake Devin on the right. If accessing from the north on U.S. 158, follow Industry Drive south. Turn right on Providence Street and pick up the directions above.

To reach *Spillway Trail* from the gravel parking area, walk across the pastoral dam among yellow buttercups. Cross a footbridge over the spillway at 0.3 mile. After 70 yards, cross under a power line to enter the forest. Follow the signs on a wide trail to make a loop. If following the loop to the right, pass a picnic site. At 0.6 mile, you may see Solomon's-seal and whorled loosestrife. Complete the loop and return to the parking area.

From the parking area, *Pine Grove Trail* begins north of the picnic shelter. The trail is currently unsigned and may not be maintained. The trail follows an old road as it enters the forest beside a fence covered with honeysuckle and other vines. Pass through tall grass in a damp area. Turn left under a power line and into a field to reach a large water pump on the left. Re-enter the forest through a mature stand of loblolly pine. At 0.4 mile, curve sharply left in a cove. Arrive at Hillsboro Street Extension and a trail sign at 0.5 mile. Turn left and cross a causeway. At 0.7 mile, turn left off the road at a sign. This leads to *Peninsula Trail*.

After 100 yards, Peninsula Trail bears to the right of a lakeside observation site and picnic table. Old directional signs indicate where the trail goes on a peninsula and through coves located among hardwoods and pine. Wood ducks and Canada geese are on the lake; wild turkey and raccoons in the woods. Ridges in the pathway indicate where tobacco rows used to be in a former farm field. At 0.4 mile, ascend steps to an open field. Continuing into the woods, there are tall blueberry bushes and wildflowers, such as pink lady's-slippers. At 1.0 mile, there is an open area and a view on the left of the "Red Barn," a property the town has preserved. Backtrack to the parking area.

Morrisville (Wake County)

Morrisville Parks, Recreation, & Cultural Resources
260 Town Hall Drive
Suite B, Morrisville, NC 27560
Telephone: 919-463-7110; fax: 919-388-1815

As with Cary, Apex, and Holly Springs, Morrisville has had a constant increase in urban population, commercial sites, shopping centers, and upscale residential development in the past few years. With the advancement of a higher standard of living has come the financial support for parks and recreation. Morrisville's greenway master plan shows a network of inter- and outer loops, with connections to Cary, Research Triangle Park, and Raleigh.

The 1.7-mile *Indian Creek Greenway* may be completed by the time this guidebook is published. Its southeast trailhead is planned for the corner of Town Hall Drive and Morrisville-Carpenter Road; the northwest trailhead at McCrimmon Parkway and Town Hall Drive. Its first and major section, *Hatcher Creek Greenway*, is described ahead.

Some of the other proposed greenways include *Cedar Creek, Fairway, Sawmill Creek*, and *Crabtree Creek*. (The latter is not part of the Raleigh system.) New parks, connector trails, and multi-use sidewalk paths are also being developed.

Children's playground in Community Park, the western terminus for Hatcher Creek Greenway in Morrisville

Hatcher Creek Greenway (0.4 mile one-way; easy)

Trailhead and Description: *Hatcher Creek Greenway* is located in Morrisville Community Park. As well as the greenway, this large facility has multiple athletic fields, a children's playground, and a picnic area with shelters. To reach the park from the intersection of Davis Drive and Morrisville-Carpenter Road, drive 0.4 mile south on Davis Drive to a traffic light. Turn left to Morrisville Parkway. Turn left at the first road and the sign for the park entrance. Drive 0.3 mile to the parking area.

The Hatcher Creek Greenway trailhead is near the childrens' playground. Follow a paved trail across an arched bridge over Hatcher Creek at 100 yards. To the left of the trailhead is a shopping center. Pass tall maple, elderberry, and willow trees, as well as blackberry patches. Cross another bridge and enter a thicker forested area. At 0.2 mile, there is a short access on the left, which leads to Blithe Place. Cross a bridge. At 0.3 mile, pass another access to a residential area at Claret Lane on the left. Enter an open space. On the left is a parking area at the end of Kudrow Lane. This parking area is accessible from Morrisville-Carpenter Road. To the right is an arched bridge over

Hatcher Creek and access to the two athletic fields. Backtrack. (There are plans for a continuation of the greenway downstream. That section will be named *Crabtree Creek Greenway*.)

Raleigh (Wake County)

The Raleigh Parks and Recreation Department maintains a comprehensive system of more than 150 diverse parks and recreation areas. Some are parks with major facilities. Others fall into such categories as nature parks, neighborhood parks, mini-parks, special parks, and open spaces. Part of its program is the Capital City Greenway System, a model development for municipal planning consisting of 245 parcels of land. The greenway system was begun in 1974 when the city responded to rapid urbanization that threatened its natural beauty. The master plan provides a system of wide greenways in both residential and forested areas for recreational activities such as walking, jogging, hiking, fishing, picnicking, bicycling, and nature study. The trails mainly follow floodplains or utility areas associated with the city's three major streams—the Neuse River and Crabtree and Walnut creeks—and their tributaries. The Greenway Corridor Master Plan shows a concept of multiple circles within a larger circle. In addition, the plan calls for connections to adjoining cities and communities.

Six of the major greenway systems, including the parks they run through and the trails they include, are described ahead in alphabetical order. They include: *Crabtree Creek Greenway*, Durant Nature Park, Lake Johnson, Reedy Creek, Shelly Lake/Sertoma, and *Walnut Creek/Rocky Branch Greenways*.

Single trails or trails in smaller groups follow the descriptions of the major greenway systems.

Crabtree Creek Greenway Area

The headwaters of Crabtree Creek come from locations in Cary and Morrisville. Other streams that feed into Crabtree Creek include Stirrup Iron Creek, which flows from Durham, and Briar and Little Briar creeks, which flow from northwest Raleigh and Durham County respectively. Crabtree Creek has a history of flooding rapidly. Lake Crabtree, situated close to I-40 and near Raleigh-Durham International Airport, was created as a reservoir to stop or slow the sudden rush of the creek's waters that inundated floodplains, as well as shopping centers such as Crabtree Valley Mall and Creekside Crossing Shopping Center. The reservoir has not completely solved the problem. Users of *Crabtree Creek Greenway* may see how the creek's seeming innocence can suddenly become dangerous. The creek's reputation, its scenery, and the skillful engineering of the greenway make usage of this classic route appealing. At the time of this writing, there are three restroom locations and two shopping centers with restaurants along the route.

The following description traces Crabtree Greenway upstream. Crabtree Greenway is actually broken into sub-trails, the most recent of which is *Middle Crabtree Trail*. The sub-trail names will be used in this description. (The greenway's future proposals include a downstream connection with the *Neuse River Trail* [and the *Mountains-to-Sea Trail*] at Anderson Point and an upstream connection with the network of trails in Umstead State Park. The latter would provide a connection with Cary's network of greenways and the *American Tobacco Trail*. The American Tobacco Trail's northern route through Durham would also connect with the Mountains-to-Sea Trail. A shorter circle of about 45 miles plans to use the Shelley Lake routing, which will go north to *Honeycutt Creek Greenway*, *Falls Lake Trail*, and south on Neuse River Trail to Crabtree Creek Greenway (West). Meanwhile, the new 2.2-mile *House Creek Greenway* will connect Crabtree Creek Greenway near Crabtree Valley Mall to *Reedy Creek Greenway* at Meredith College, where the route west on Reedy Creek Greenway will connect with *Black Creek and White Oak Creek greenways* for eventual access to the American Tobacco Trail.)

Buckeye Trail (2.4 miles)
Middle Crabtree Trail (2.3 miles)
Fallon Creek Trail (0.3 mile)
Alleghany Trail (3.5 miles)
Crabtree Valley Trail (1.1 miles)
Crabtree-Oak Park Trail (1.6 miles)

Length and Difficulty: 11.2 miles combined; easy to moderate

Trailheads and Description: One access to the trailhead is from I-440, Exit 13. Drive west on New Bern Avenue for 0.2 mile (or less depending on ramp access) and turn right on Milburnie Road. After another 0.2 mile, the trailhead is on the right.

The first section of *Crabtree Creek Greenway* is called *Buckeye Trail*. Beginning at the southeast end of Buckeye Trail, parking is suggested on the south side of Milburnie Road, slightly west of its junction with Peartree

Lane because curbside parking is not allowed at the trailhead. Here the street curbs are wider and not in front of private residences. From this parking location, walk or bicycle east on the sidewalk for 0.2 mile. Enter Buckeye Trail on the left. There is no parking available at the trailhead itself.

Follow the trail to the creekside and turn left. Pass through exceptionally tall oak, elm, beech, and loblolly pine. At 0.5 mile, ascend a steep scenic bluff. On the left at 1.0 mile, there is an access to Crabtree Street and a children's playground. On the right, there is a large play area on a grassy lawn. There is another access at 1.1 miles. At 1.3 miles, follow a horseshoe bend near the creek. After following a straight section along the creek, make a left curve around a mound that has a bench for resting. At 2.4 miles, arrive at Raleigh Boulevard. Turn right onto the sidewalk and cross the street at the traffic light to another sidewalk. This is the west end of Buckeye Trail. (To the left is a sidewalk that goes upstream along Crabtree Boulevard for 0.2 mile before crossing the street at a parking lot.)

Continuing on the greenway, you are now on *Middle Crabtree Trail.* Turn right, going north on the sidewalk. After 135 yards, turn left onto a skillfully constructed boardwalk that crosses a lake. This area is home to many aquatic species of flora and fauna. Most visible are the ducks, geese, herons, and other birds. Dragonflies rest on sawgrass and cattails. In warm weather, turtles sun on fallen logs. At 0.3 mile, pass a shelter, followed by a beaver hutch on the right. Leave the boardwalk at 0.4 mile; pass under a railroad track at 0.6 mile. At 0.7 mile, pass by an access to Yonkers Road to the right and go under

Hikers on Middle Crabtree Trail, one section of Crabtree Creek Greenway

Capital Boulevard (U.S. 1/401). To the right is another access route. The trail travels on a high boardwalk that descends to the floodplain. At 1.1 miles, there is an access up a hill to a residential area. Songbirds frequent this part of the greenway. At 1.4 miles, cross an arched steel bridge before going under the Atlantic Avenue bridge. Ahead is a railroad underpass, followed by an access on the right at 1.6 miles. At 1.9 miles, pass under Wake Forest Road. To the right is an access to Creekside Crossing Shopping Center. Cross an arched bridge over Big Branch to arrive at a fork at 2.2 miles. (To the right is a 0.1-mile access greenway to a residential area.) Cross Crabtree Creek at 2.3 miles to end Middle Crabtree Trail. A junction with *Fallon Creek Trail*, the next section of the Crabtree Creek Greenway, goes left and right.

The east end of Fallon Creek is 0.16 mile to the left to Noble Street. (This short segment used to be an interpretive trail to Kiwanis Park before it became a connector trail for the Crabtree Creek system.) Turning right onto Noble Street/Fallon Creek Trail, it is 0.1 mile to a junction of McNeill and Noble streets, where you'll find a parking lot, a playground, an athletic field, and restrooms in Kiwanis Park. The total mileage from the point where you left Middle Creek Trail for Fallon Creek Trail is 0.3 mile. Turn right on the sidewalk, heading upstream, and arrive at Anderson Drive at 0.45 mile. This is where Fallon Creek Trail ends and *Alleghany Trail* begins.

Alleghany Trail crosses the street to Claremont Road and immediately turns right. Enter an enchanting forest and follow a sweeping curve along the creek. Cross an arched bridge over the creek at 0.8 mile. Stay left at the fork. Cross the creek again at 1.0 mile and stay right at another fork. Cross the creek again at 1.4 miles and go into the forest of Drewry Hills Park. At 1.7 miles, arrive at Lassiter Mill Road. Turn left onto the sidewalk and cross the Crabtree Creek bridge. At the traffic light at Millstream Place, cross Lassiter Mill Road to the south corner of Albert Root Magnet Elementary School. Trail users may notice small blazes on some of the posts and trees. As the greenway leaves the creek, users should notice Lassiter Falls Circle, a 0.2-mile entrance road, which is also the route for *Lassiter's Mill Trail*. This leads to one of the most photographed points on the trail—the dam that was built over what was known as the Great Falls of Crabtree. From 1908 to 1958, Cornelius Jesse Lassiter operated a gristmill here. There are picnic tables along the entrance route.

Continuing on Alleghany Trail, enter the woods from a parking lot at the school and parallel Beaverdam Creek. English ivy shrouds some of the trees along the trail here. At 1.9 miles, ascend to turn right on Northampton Street. At 2.2 miles, turn right off the sidewalk and descend on steps to a dirt path. (Bicyclists can continue on the street and take the first access route on

CRABTREE CREEK AND SHELLEY LAKE GREENWAY CONNECTION

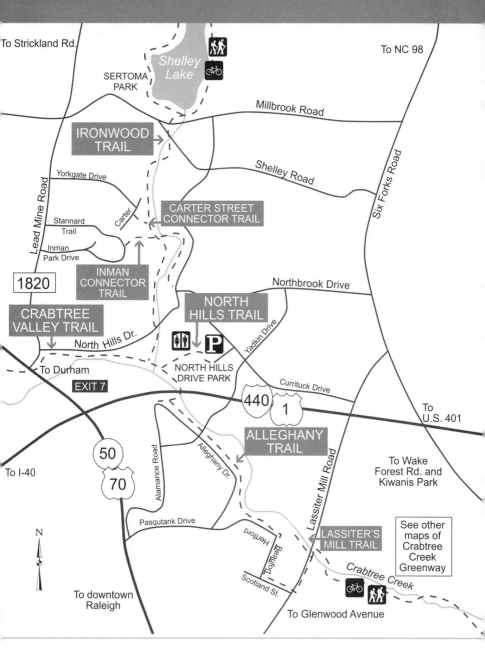

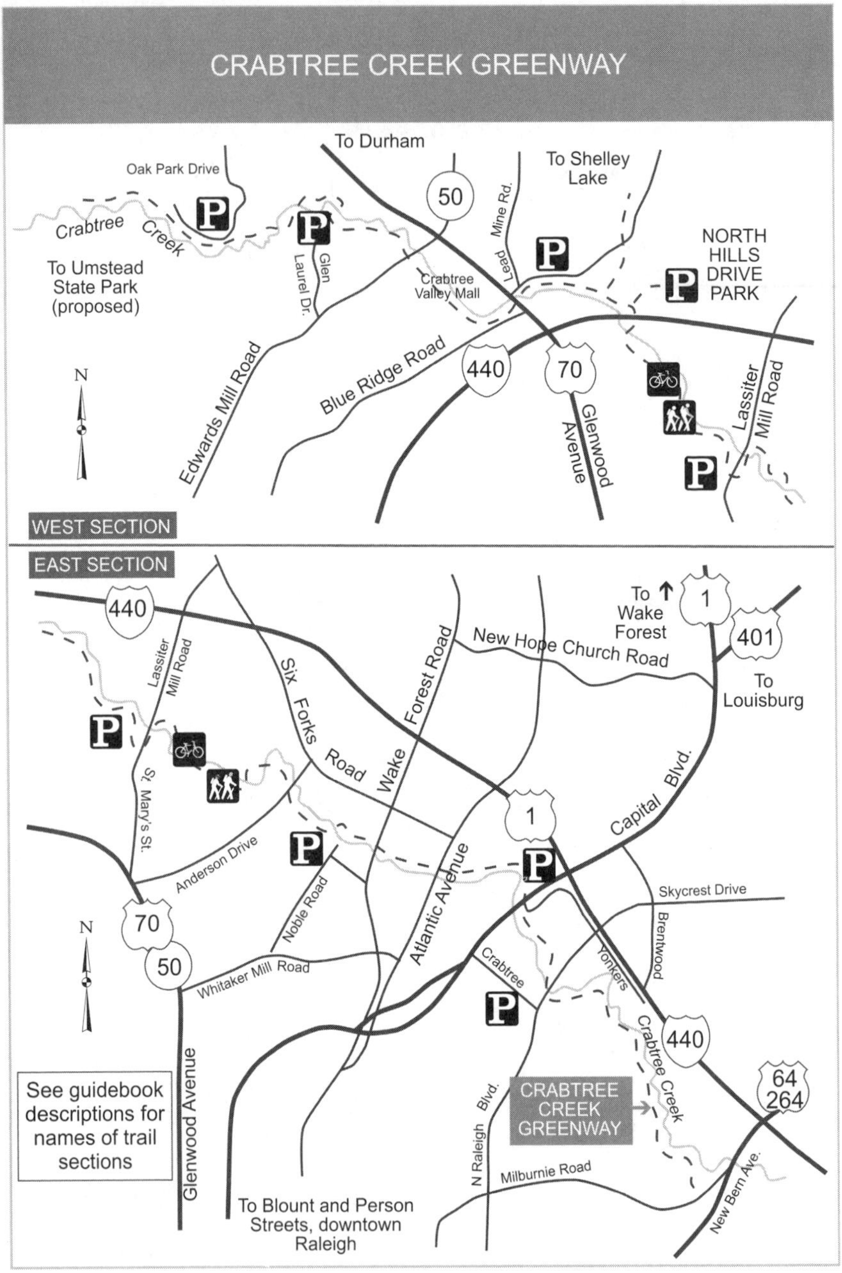

CRABTREE CREEK GREENWAY

To Durham

Oak Park Drive

50

To Shelley Lake

P

Crabtree Creek

P

Glen Laurel Dr.

Lead Mine Rd.

P

NORTH HILLS DRIVE PARK

P

To Umstead State Park (proposed)

Crabtree Valley Mall

N

Blue Ridge Road

440

70

Edwards Mill Road

Glenwood Avenue

Lassiter Mill Road

P

WEST SECTION

EAST SECTION

440

Lassiter Mill Road

Six Forks Road

Wake Forest Road

New Hope Church Road

To Wake Forest

1

401

To Louisburg

P

St. Mary's St.

Anderson Drive

Noble Road

P

Atlantic Avenue

1

P

Capital Blvd.

Skycrest Drive

Brentwood

N

70

50

Whitaker Mill Road

Crabtree

Yonkers

440

64 264

P

CRABTREE CREEK GREENWAY →

Crabtree Creek

See guidebook descriptions for names of trail sections

Glenwood Avenue

N Raleigh Blvd.

Milburnie Road

New Bern Ave.

To Blount and Person Streets, downtown Raleigh

the right to return to the paved greenway.) In this scenic area, ascend a narrow footbridge and pass rock formations sculpted by nature. Pass by a large white residence before passing under a power line at 2.5 miles. At 2.8 miles, there is a spur to the left that leads to Alleghany Drive, the route that bicyclists can use. Pass under the Yadkin Drive bridge at 2.9 miles. At 3.1 miles, curve right at a fork. (The left fork goes 110 yards to Alleghany Street and Alamance Drive.) Cross Crabtree Creek on an arched bridge. The trail curves as it goes under the I-440/ U.S. 1 bridge. The thundering sound of traffic can be heard overhead. At 3.2 miles, reach a junction with *North Hills Trail* ahead on the right. North Hills Trail and Alleghany Trail run conjunctively for 0.6 mile.

To the right (north), a steep 0.2-mile section of North Hills Trail ends at the tennis court parking area at North Hills Drive Park. Facilities here include a children's playground, a picnic shelter, restrooms, and an athletic field. To access the park by car, take Lassiter Mill Road for 0.7 mile to Currituck Drive. Turn left onto Chowan Street. A small park sign is on a light pole at the turn.

Continuing on the main trail, cross a footbridge over Mine Creek to a fork at 3.4 miles. (North Hills Trail goes right to access North Hills Drive and to connect with trails leading to Shelley Lake. Those trails are described later in this chapter.) Alleghany Trail continues left to parallel the creek. At 3.6 miles, pass through retaining walls along a rock cliff at the creekside. At 3.8 miles, Alleghany Trail ends and *Crabtree Valley Trail* begins. (To the right is a 30-yard-long access to North Hills Drive. Primary Beginnings Child Care is across that street. The access was originally created for greenway-construction contractors to have access to Alleghany Trail and other work upstream.)

Follow Crabtree Valley Trail for 0.2 mile to an access on the right. The access goes up a boardwalk to a parking lot. (To access this lot by vehicle, take Century Drive off U.S. 70 [Glenwood Avenue] or Lead Mine Road. If approaching the junction of Glenwood Avenue and Lead Mine Road from the west at Crabtree Valley Mall, turn left at the traffic light to go on Lead Mine Road. Turn right immediately onto Century Drive. If driving west from Exit 7 off of I-440/U.S. 1, turn onto U.S. 70 West. Take the right lane to access the Holiday Inn, then turn left onto Century Drive to the parking lot on the right.)

Continuing on Crabtree Valley Trail, cross an arched bridge. The concrete base on the trail is an example of outstanding engineering. To the left, there are steps up to a service station. Pass under the U.S. 70 bridges and follow the trail upstream. At 0.6 mile, the concrete ends and asphalt begins. To the left, there is a parking area and restaurant. These are located at the intersection of

Blue Ridge and Crabtree Valley roads. At 0.7 and 0.9 mile, there are accesses to a bridge, on the right, which goes over the creek to the shopping mall. At 1.1 miles, there is a greenway sign before going under Creedmoor Road. This ends Crabtree Valley Trail and begins *Crabtree-Oak Park Trail*.

To continue on Crabtree-Oak Park Trail, pass a parking area used for overflow parking from a commercial area on the right at 0.2 mile. From here the character of the greenway changes to a gorge-like atmosphere with more natural areas in a dense hardwood forest. The forest near the creek banks includes wild white roses, tag alder, spicebush, and white-flowered bladdernut. Most of the nine bridges are low constructions of concrete. At 0.6 mile, there is a 125-yard access to a business area on the right.

After crossing boardwalks, cross under a power line at 0.9 mile. At 1.1 miles, there is an outstanding display of mountain laurel on the north slope of a ridge across the creek. At present, the greenway ends at 1.6 miles when it reaches a parking area on the right by Lindsay Drive. (The proposed continuation of the greenway will go upstream about 1.3 miles to connect with Umstead State Park's trail system.) To access the parking area from Crabtree Valley Mall at the intersection of U.S. 70 and NC 50, drive 1.4 miles west on U.S. 70 to Hollingridge Drive and turn left into Oak Park Shopping Center. Immediately turn right. After less than 0.1 mile, turn left onto Oak Park Drive. Descend 1.2 miles to a junction with Lindsay Drive and turn left. Go a few yards to the parking area and trailhead.

Durant Nature Park

Durant Nature Park
8305 Camp Durant Road
Raleigh, NC 27614
Telephone: 919-870-2871

Durant Nature Park was formerly Camp Durant, established by William B. Durant in 1947 as a 237-acre retreat for Boy Scouts. It was purchased by the city in 1979. Since then, its facilities have remained much the same. It retains its mission to be a public nature preserve. The park offers nature-based and nature-compatible programs and has facilities for hiking, bicycling, fishing, boating, swimming, and group camping. The park has a children's playground and an open playing field, as well as two lodges. It is open from 8 A.M. to sunset.

Border Trail (2.2 miles, easy)
Lakeside Trail (1.1 miles, easy)
Secret Creek Trail (0.5 mile, easy)

Trailheads and Description: From U.S. 1 (Capital Boulevard), drive west 1.1 miles on Durant Road to a small sign for Camp Durant. Turn left onto Camp Durant Road and follow it to a parking area at the end of the road.

From the north parking lot, follow the paved path to the kiosk. Follow White House Road, which is marked with white blazes on the right. Follow the road for 0.1 mile to a signed intersection with the red-blazed, natural-surface *Border Trail*. Turn right onto the trail. At 0.2 mile, follow Reedy Branch upstream, then pass a rapid named Whale Rocks, and go through the wildflower-filled woodlands. At 1.0 mile, cross a footbridge over Sim's Branch. After a boggy area, enter an old homesite at 1.2 miles. Here, there is a massive display of invading wisteria whose purple grape-shaped flowers and fragrance are springtime features. Also here is an alternate trail route, the black-blazed *Beaver Pond Trail*, which offers views of the Upper Lake.

At 1.5 miles on either trail, reach the south side of the Upper Lake dam. Choose either the yellow-blazed *Lakeside Trail* (south), which offers wildflowers and views of the Lower Lake, or the less scenic Border Trail to reach the park's service road at 2.2 miles. Turn left at Campbell Lodge and follow the service road across the Lower Lake spillway and dam to the restrooms at the playing fields at 2.5 miles. Look below the restrooms for *Secret Creek Trail* with dark green blazes. Follow the trail along a scenic rocky stream, which meanders among hardwoods, pines, ferns, and wildflowers. Reach the park office at the north parking lot after another 0.5 mile.

Lake Johnson Nature Park

Lake Johnson Nature Park
4601 Avent Ferry Road
Raleigh, NC 27606
Telephone: 919-233-2121; fax: 919-233-2127
www.raleigh-nc.org/parks&rec/index.asp

One of the city's most popular parks, Lake Johnson Nature Park has about 300 acres of land and a 150-acre lake. The lake was built in 1955 to offer water-based recreation. Its activities include hiking, bicycling, boating, fishing, and picnicking. Pedal boats, canoes, rowboats, kayaks, and sunfish sailboats, as well as group picnic shelters are available for rent. Large-mouth bass, bream, shellcracker, and other varieties of fish can be found in the lake.

In addition, there are facilities for conferences, banquets, business meetings, retreats, and social events at the Waterfront Program Center. The Magnolia Cottage can be rented for private and professional functions. Special events include fishing tournaments, sailing classes, and concerts. Park restrictions prohibit swimming, dogs must be on a leash, and no alcoholic beverages or firearms are allowed. Park hours are from sunrise to sunset, every day except Thanksgiving Day, Christmas Day, and Martin Luther King, Jr. Day.

Lake Johnson Trail (3.0 miles)
Upper Walnut Creek Trail (1.2 miles)
Lakeshore Trail (1.6 miles)
Picnic Shelter Trail (0.3 mile)
North Shore Trail (2.0 miles)

Length and Difficulty: 8.1 miles, if no backtracking or overlapping, otherwise 9.6 miles; easy to moderate

Trailheads and Description: From I-440, take Exit 2 and drive east on Western Boulevard for 1.5 miles. Turn right on Avent Ferry Road. After 2.9 miles, turn left at the parking area and park office. (Parking for the trails is also across the causeway on the left.) If coming from I-40/I-440/U.S. 64, take Exit 295 and drive north on Gorman Street for 1.3 miles. Turn left onto Avent Ferry Road and drive 1.7 miles.

If parking on the north side of the lake near the park office and picnic tables, there are friendly ducks and geese. Begin the paved white-blazed *Lake Johnson Trail* along the lakeside into the forest. Pass spur trails to the left; then pass an access to Lake Dam Road, also to the left. Cross a bridge over the spillway and the rim of the dam for a scenic view upstream. At 1.0 mile, there is a fork. To the left is the *Upper Walnut Creek Trail*. It descends 0.2 mile to a parking space and crosses Lake Dam Road. Go downstream as the trail travels among an attractive display of tall hardwoods, trailside wildflowers, and squirrels. A special feature of the trail is a 100-foot boardwalk. It crosses Gorman Street at 1.0 mile. It stops at Trailwood Road at 1.2 miles. (Long

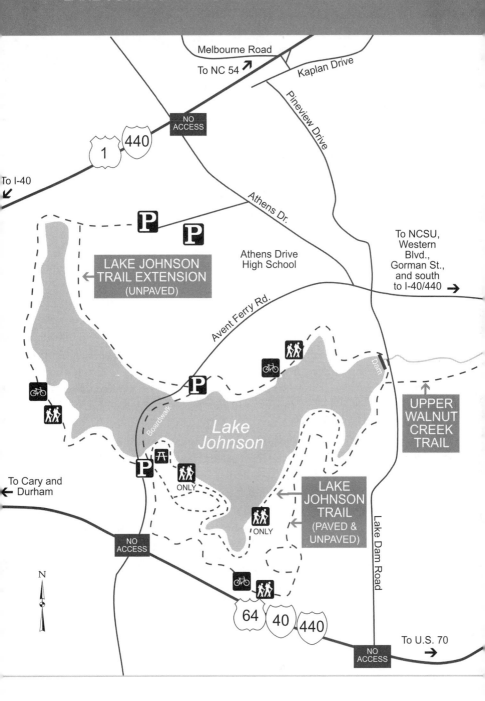

Hikers on North Shore Trail in Lake Johnson Nature Park in Raleigh

range plans are to connect Upper Walnut Creek Trail with other Walnut Creek greenways downstream.)

Continue on the paved Lake Johnson Trail to a fork at 1.3 miles. To the right is the natural-surface, green-blazed *Lakeshore Trail*. (This was the original trail around the lake before the paved route farther up the hillside was made. It winds in and out of coves for 1.6 miles. On this loop, Lakeshore Trail crosses the bridge across the lake, intersects with the 0.3-mile *Picnic Shelter Trail*, and finally returns to the parking lot on the lake's south side.)

Continuing on Lake Johnson Trail past its intersection with Lakeshore Trail, the trail connects with Lakeshore Trail again at 2.3 miles. At 2.7 miles, the trail intersects with a paved route to the bridge across the lake. From the bridge, the trail offers one of the most scenic views of the entire lake. Return to the park-office parking area at 3.0 miles.

If hiking *North Shore Trail* from the south parking lot, cross Avent Ferry Road and follow a dirt path to a floodplain area. There may be sections where users have tried to find a dry route or tried to avoid fallen logs. Try to follow the green blazes. The forest is composed mainly of hardwoods. Cross a bridge at 0.6 mile and ascend, partly on an old road. Spur routes and rocky overlooks to the right offer closer scenic views of the lake. There are also side routes to residential areas to the left. At 1.4 miles, there is a boardwalk through a marshy area. After crossing and turning right, there is a 0.2-mile access, which may be paved by this book's publication, on the left. It leads to William Stadium behind Athens Drive High School. North Shore Trail now becomes more defined and follows a wider route with a bark-chip base. Arrive at Avent Ferry Road and cross to the park's bathhouse and office area at 2.0 miles.

Reedy Creek Greenway Area

Reedy Creek Greenway is a link in the chain of trails between the American Tobacco Trail (ATT) in the west and Neuse River Trail/Mountains to-Sea Trail in the east. Other links in this chain include Black Creek and White Oak Creek greenways, which will provide links in the west, and Rocky Creek and Walnut Creek greenways in the east. Like Crabtree Creek Greenway, Rocky Creek and Walnut Creek greenways both travel through the heart of the capital city and will eventually connect with Umstead State Park and the Neuse River.

Reedy Creek Greenway will also be part of a proposed 125-mile loop that connects trails in Cary, Chapel Hill, Durham, and Raleigh. (The 2.1-mile House Creek Greenway will connect Reedy Creek Greenway at Meredith College to Crabtree Creek Greenway when it is completed. It will create a proposed inter-city loop that could include Neuse River Greenway. A master plan shows this potential loop could have interloops that resemble the ring patterns found on an endearing woolly worm.

Unlike all the other trails that have creek or river names, Reedy Creek Greenway never crosses Reedy Creek. It does, however, flirt with the creek when it passes Reedy Creek Lake and connects with Reedy Creek Lake Trail in Umstead State Park.

Reedy Creek Greenway—East (2.6 miles, easy)

Trailhead and Description: From I-440, take Exit 4 and drive west on Lake Boone Trail (a street) for 0.8 mile. Turn left onto Blue Ridge Road. After 0.4 mile, turn left at the North Carolina Museum of Art. Turn into the parking area immediately to the right. At the time of this writing, there is not an official parking lot at either end of Reedy Creek Greenway. Therefore, the parking lot at the museum is the best option.

If hiking or biking east toward the Meredith College campus, turn right from the parking-lot entrance and go to a museum sign. Follow it past a grove of trees to descend to an area with an open view of the windmill art on the right. Continue through Thomas Sayre's sculpture ellipses, titled Gyre. At 0.4 mile, stay right at a junction with Museum Green Trail. (Museum Green Trail makes a junction with Prairie Trail, on the right, before curving around the lake and ascending to the entrance of the museum. At 0.7 mile, return to the Blue Ridge Road parking lot.)

Back on Reedy Creek Greenway, at 0.45 mile Woodland Trail is on the left near Martha Jackson-Jarvis's sculpture Crossroads. (The natural-surface

Woodland Trail is a 0.5-mile loop through the forest for a visit to Chris Drury's *Cloud Chamber for the Trees and Sky*. From this location, return via Museum Green Trail mentioned above.)

As Reedy Creek Greenway continues past Woodland Trail, it ascends to a pine grove on the left at 0.6 mile. There are signs about birds and wildflowers along the way. Descend and cross a boardwalk. At 0.9 mile, cross a bridge over House Creek. To the left is Prairie Trail. (Prairie Trail goes downstream to an arched wooden bridge over House Creek for a return to Museum Green Trail after 0.4 mile. Along the way, it passes through a grassy slope with sections of blackberry bushes.)

Continuing on Reedy Creek Trail, ascend on switchbacks between stone walls, pass a dogwood grove, and arrive at the 660-foot pedestrian truss bridge over I-440 at 1.3 miles. There is a gate at the east side of the bridge as the trail approaches Meredith College property. (In the area to the left, House Creek Greenway is under construction.) College gates here and at the other end of the campus are closed from sunset to sunrise. At 1.6 miles, pass under the Wade Avenue bridge and begin the hike around the perimeter of Meredith College. At 2.2 miles, cross a bridge. At 2.4 miles, the trail reaches the main entrance to the college. The trail ends at 2.6 miles at a campus gate on the corner of Faircloth and Hillsborough streets. To the right across Hillsborough Street are restaurants and the connector to *Rocky Branch* and *Walnut Creek greenways* at Gorman Street, which is described further ahead in this chapter.

Reedy Creek Greenway—West (7.1 miles, easy to moderate)

Trailhead and Description: From the same parking area at the North Carolina Museum of Art that was used for *Reedy Creek Greenway—East*, go to the *Reedy Creek Greenway* sign at the museum's entrance corner with Blue Ridge Road. Cross the road at the traffic light to the sidewalk along Reedy Creek Road. At 0.3 mile, pass the National Guard Center, on the left, and the Agonomic Division of the Department of Agriculture at N.C. State University across the street. On the approach to Edwards Mill Road at 0.7 mile, turn left on an asphalt route to pass through a tunnel under Edwards Mill Road. Return to Reedy Creek Road at 1.1 miles. Cross the road and turn left on the greenway. At 1.2 miles, there is an access across the road that leads to Schenck Memorial Forest. (See Chapter 5 for more about Schenck Memorial Forest.) The trail gradually descends. At 1.9 miles, there is a railing to protect the greenway user. *Loblolly Trail* crosses the road at 2.1 miles. (It goes left into Schenck Memorial Forest on a route to a parking area at RBC

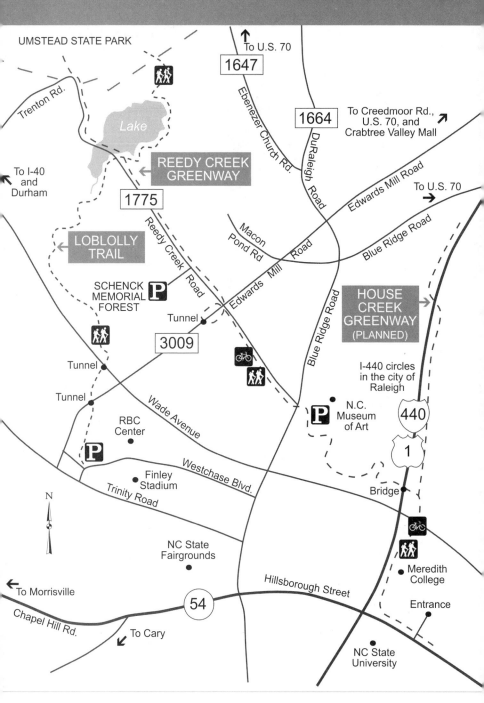

REEDY CREEK GREENWAY

UMSTEAD STATE PARK

To U.S. 70

1647

Trenton Rd.

Lake

Ebenezer Church Rd.

DuRaleigh Road

1664

To Creedmoor Rd.,
U.S. 70, and
Crabtree Valley Mall

Edwards Mill Road

To U.S. 70

REEDY CREEK
GREENWAY

To I-40
and
Durham

1775

Macon
Pond Rd

Edwards Mill Road

Blue Ridge Road

LOBLOLLY
TRAIL

Reedy Creek Road

SCHENCK
MEMORIAL
FOREST

P

Tunnel

HOUSE
CREEK
GREENWAY
(PLANNED)

Blue Ridge Road

3009

Tunnel

I-440 circles
in the city of
Raleigh

Tunnel

Wade Avenue

440

RBC
Center

P

N.C.
Museum
of Art

1

P

N

Finley
Stadium

Westchase Blvd.

Bridge

Trinity Road

NC State
Fairgrounds

Meredith
College

To Morrisville

Hillsborough Street

Entrance

Chapel Hill Rd.

54

NC State
University

To Cary

*Reedy Creek Greenway crosses
this 660-foot trestle over I-440
and Wade Avenue in Raleigh*

Center. It goes to the right around Richland Lake on its way to Umstead State Park. There is more about Loblolly Trail ahead and in Chapter 2.)

As the trail crosses a causeway over Richard Creek, there is a guardrail between the greenway and highway traffic. Waterfowl frequent this area. At 2.3 miles, the highway barrier ends. A housing development is on the left. At 2.5 miles, Reedy Creek Road ends and Trenton Road begins on the left. The asphalt greenway ends here. Firmly based granite screenings begin. The trail now becomes known as *Reedy Creek Greenway* (formerly called "B&B trail for bike and bridle"), one of five multi-use trails for hikers, cyclists, and equestrians in Umstead State Park. (See "Umstead State Park" section of Chapter 2 for more details.)

Stay straight ahead through the forested park. (To the right is *South Turkey Creek Trail*, a multi-use route that connects with multi-use *North Turkey Creek* and *Graylyn trails*. From the point where all three trails merge, turn right and go 0.3 mile to a parking area for bicyclists and hikers off Ebenezer Church Road.) At 2.8 miles, cross Loblolly Trail. Pass a grove of wisteria before gradually descending. Pass Reedy Creek Lake, which is on the left. *Reedy Creek Lake Trail* also crosses the dam to the left. (That trail is not open to horse traffic, but it is open to hikers and bikers. It ascends 1.2 miles to a parking area at the Reedy Creek entrance to Umstead State Park at Harrison Avenue, just off Exit 287 at I-40.)

Continuing on Reedy Creek Greenway, cross a bridge over Crabtree Creek at 3.6 miles. Curve left and ascend steeply among tall hardwoods to reach a junction with *Cedar Ridge Trail* on the right at 4.3 miles. (Cedar Ridge Trail, another multi-use trail, descends 1.5 miles to cross Sycamore Creek and connect with South and North Turkey Creek multi-use trails.) At 4.4 miles, there is a junction with multi-use Graylyn Trail. (Graylyn Trail descends to cross Sycamore Creek and then ascends to a junction with North Turkey Creek Trail after 0.8 mile.)

At 4.5 miles, cross *Company Mill Trail*, which goes right and left. (Company Mill Trail makes a 5.9-mile loop through the park. It is only open to pedestrians.)

Reedy Creek Trail continues through a forest primarily composed of hardwoods such as oak, maple, sweet gum, hickory, dogwood, and loblolly pine. At 5.0 miles, there is a kiosk with safety and other information about using the forest. The Warren Family Cemetery is nearby. At 5.2 miles, cross Company Mill Trail again as the trail passes among large oaks. At 5.7 miles, there is a fountain and bicycle rack where gated Group Camp Road is on the right. Most maps will show an airport (Raleigh-Durham International Airport) overlook at 6.0 miles. Curve left here, following the road to a gate at 7.1 miles, which is the end of the trail. There is not a parking area here. The road continues 0.7 mile to cross I-40. Roadside parking and access to Lake Crabtree bicycle and hiking trails are on the right. From here on Old Reedy Creek Road, it is 1.3 miles to Weston Parkway. Turn left onto Weston Parkway and travel 0.6 mile to Harrison Avenue. Turn left onto Harrison Avenue and go 0.3 mile to Exit 287 at I-40.

Shelley Lake-Sertoma Park

Shelley Lake-Sertoma Park
1400 West Millbrook Road
Raleigh, NC 27612
Telephone: 919-420-2329; Shelley Lake waterfront: 919-420-2331

The collection of trails at and near Shelley Lake-Sertoma Park have the potential to be a long city loop. The network currently has a connection south with the *Crabtree Creek Trail* system and a proposed routing northeast to Honeycutt Creek and beyond to join up with the already constructed *Falls*

Lake Trail. From Shelley Lake, the trails extend out in four prongs from a convenient parking lot. These trails are described ahead.

The activities in this area include boating, hiking, bicycling (except on the natural-surface trails), and fishing. There is no swimming. The park is open from dawn to dusk. The boathouse is open from the middle of March to the middle of October. The Sertoma Arts Center is open year-round. Its hours are: Monday through Thursday, 9 A.M. to 10 P.M.; Friday, 9 A.M. to 5 P.M.; Saturday, 9 A.M. to 3 P.M.; and Sunday, 1 to 5 P.M.

Shelley Lake Trail (2.2 miles, easy)
Snelling Branch Trail (0.6 mile, easy)
Bent Creek Trail (1.1 miles, easy)
Sawmill Trail (1.0 mile, easy)
Ironwood Trail (1.7 miles, easy)

Trailheads and Description: From the junction of U.S. 70 and NC 50 at Crabtree Valley Mall, drive north on NC 50 for 0.8 mile to Millbrook Road. Turn right onto Millbrook Road and drive 1.0 mile to a parking lot on the left. Another option is to turn west on Millbrook Road at its intersection with Six Forks Road. Drive 1.3 miles to the parking lot on the right. The lot is below the Shelley Lake dam.

From the parking area, follow the paved *Shelley Lake Trail* to the top of the dam, where the trail goes right or left. If going right, the trail enters a forest at 0.2 mile. At 0.7 mile, there is an alternate trail, on the left, that leads to a wildlife observation deck. Continuing on Shelley Lake Trail, arrive at a junction with *Snelling Branch Trail.* (Snelling Branch Trail crosses North Hills Drive after 0.3 mile. It passes a baseball field to the left and Sanderson High School to the right, before ending at the Optimist Park parking lot at 0.6 mile. Access here is off Northcliff Drive. Backtrack.)

Continuing on Shelley Lake Trail, cross a small stream with banks of yellow root and shade from river birches, yellow poplars, and sweet gums. At 0.9 mile, cross a wide bridge over Lead Mine Creek in an area of elm and ironwood. Shelley Lake Trail continues to the left; to the right *Bent Creek Trail* parallels Lead Mine Creek.

At 0.1 mile, Bent Creek Trail goes through a tunnel under North Hills Drive, after which a 0.2-mile natural-surface path veers right. (This side trail follows the rim of the stream through ironwood, dogwood, and spicebush. At the halfway mark on this side trail, there is a scenic bend in the creek at a sandbar. The side trail comes back into Bent Creek Trail in sight of the Lynn Road bridge.)

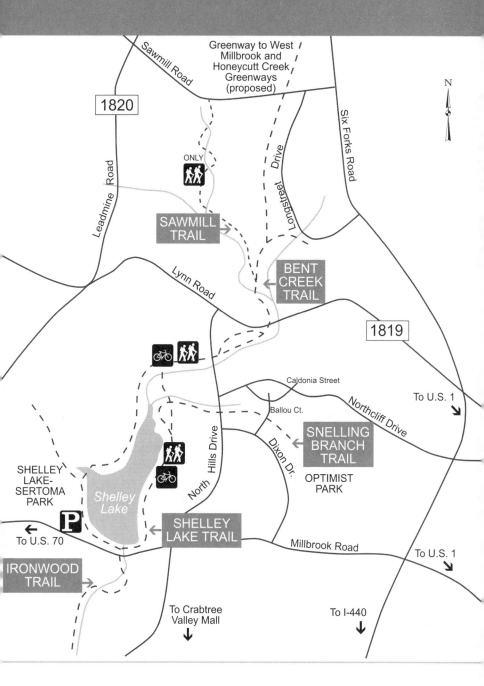

If staying on the main route of Bent Creek Trail instead of taking the side-trail loop, pass through a forest of tall yellow poplar and river birch. Go under the Lynn Road bridge, enter a forest of black walnut and yellow poplar covered with grapevines. Cross an arched steel-and-wood bridge over Lead Mine Creek. At 0.6 mile, reach a junction with *Sawmill Trail* on the left. (The scenic Sawmill Trail is a natural-surface path for foot travel only. It begins on the east side of Lead Mine Creek. At 0.4 mile, it crosses and follows a tributary of that creek. Along the way, there are rocks shaped like petrified logs. At 0.7 mile, there is a patch of cardinal flowers near a boardwalk. After crossing the last bridge, the trail enters an open area and ends at Sawmill Road. There is no parking here.)

To complete Bent Creek Trail, follow the asphalt route and cross a bridge over Bent Creek at 0.8 mile. Curve left and ascend beside the stream, which has small pools and cascades. At 1.0 mile, exit at the corner of Longstreet and Bent Creek drives. Curbside parking is available here. Backtrack to Shelley Lake Trail to complete its loop.

On returning to Shelley Lake Trail, at 1.3 miles, there is an emergency telephone and a junction with a short asphalt trail leading right to Lakeway Drive. At 1.6 miles, there are a support wall, an observation tower, and views of the lake. Cross a long and high bridge over the lake. This is a popular place to feed and watch the ducks and geese. Pass an access trail that leads right to the Arts Center and *Lake Park Trail*, a side trail for residents on Rushingbrook Drive. Restrooms are on the left. At 2.2 miles, return to the dam and descend to the parking lot.

To reach *Ironwood Trail*, go to the far end of the parking lot and descend on the paved trail to pass under the Millbrook Road bridge. This attractive trail parallels and occasionally crosses Lead Mine Creek. At 0.5 mile, there is a 0.1-mile gravel connector trail to Carter Street on the right. Along the way, this connector trail parallels a stream with cascades. On the left at 0.6 mile, there is a 0.3-mile access spur to North Hills Drive. Continuing on Ironwood Trail for a few feet, there is a 0.2-mile *Inman Connector Trail* on the right. It has a boardwalk near a wet area with willows. It ends at Stannard Trail (a street) near a park with a swimming pool. At 0.8 mile, there is a scenic rock bluff to the left of the creek. At 1.0 mile, there is a boardwalk. At 1.3 miles, cross North Hills Drive. (There is no curbside parking here.)

Turn left and travel for a few yards following the sidewalk to cross the street for a reentry into the forest. Along the way, there is an arched bridge. Tall hardwoods and loblolly pines are draped in English ivy, which covers sections of the forest floor. At 1.7 miles, there is a junction with *Alleghany Trail*, which is one of the sections of the *Crabtree Creek Greenway*. (There is a Shelley Lake sign with a directional arrow here, but there may not be signs identifying Ironwood Trail or North Hills Trail.)

Walnut Creek Greenway and Rocky Branch Greenway Area

Pullen Park
408 Ashe Avenue
Raleigh NC 27606
Telephone: Community center: 919-831-6052; aquatic center: 919-831-6197

Walnut Creek and *Rocky Branch greenways* connect to form a linear east-to-west routing that travels close to the heart of the city on its south side. The two greenways connect to *Reedy Creek Greenway* to the west. There is a proposed eastern connection with *Neuse River Trail*. The major park along the way is Pullen Park, which adjoins N. C. State University. Facilities at the park include swimming, hiking, bicycling, and picnicking. There are also facilities for athletic events, performances, and other entertainment. The community center is open year-round. Its hours are: Monday through Friday, 7:30 p.m to 9:30 p.m; Saturday, 9 to 3 p.m.

The descriptions of the trails in this section begin at Pullen Park. From Pullen Park, *Rocky Branch Greenway* continues east and connects with the lower section of the Walnut Creek Greenway system. All of the trails that connect in these systems are discussed individually in order from west to east.

Rocky Branch Greenway—West (2.0 miles, easy)

Trailhead and Description: If coming from Hillsborough Street, turn south onto Ashe Avenue; if coming from Western Boulevard, turn north onto Ashe Avenue. From the parking area at Pullen Park where signs indicate *Rocky Branch Greenway* goes west and east, park in the area closest to the Western Boulevard entrance. Go west and take Rocky Branch Greenway to cross a bridge over Rocky Branch. The trail continues on a sidewalk for 50 yards to Western Boulevard. Turn right and continue on a sidewalk. Pass a Pullen Park sign. At 0.15 mile, cross a fiber boardwalk, which protects a distinctive sycamore. On the right, there are views of the park's small-gauge railroad. At 0.25 mile, leave the sidewalk and follow alongside the branch as it goes under the Pullen Road bridge to N.C. State University.

There is an exhibit here that explains the restoration of Rocky Branch's environment. As the trail curves toward the forest, there is a paved access on the left that leads to Western Boulevard at 0.4 mile.

This paved access is *Alternate Rocky Branch Greenway*. It is explained here for those who wish to make a loop that includes Pullen Park as a parking spot. Bike or hike out to the sidewalk on Western Boulevard. Turn left and turn left again on the ramp to Pullen Road. At Pullen Road, turn right and face the traffic light to cross Western Boulevard. Enter the forest and connect with the old Rocky Branch Greenway, which goes to the right and left at 0.2 mile.

To the right, the greenway goes 0.5 mile to WRAL-TV station; 0.6 mile beyond the station, it becomes a sidewalk leading to McKimmon Education Center.

Going left on Alternate Rocky Branch Greenway, the greenway passes a spur greenway on the right after 145 yards. (This is also part of the Rocky Branch Greenway system. It goes 0.3 mile on a former paved road through an old-growth forest covered with wisteria. It exits at a traffic light on Centennial Avenue to access Centennial Campus of N.C. State University.)

Rocky Branch Greenway in Raleigh

Continue ahead on a slight descent to cross at the corner of Bilyeu and Kirby streets at 0.4 mile. Ahead is a Capital City Greenway sign for Rocky Branch Greenway. Parallel Rocky Branch through an old forest of large oaks. At 0.8 mile, arrive at Hunt Drive, the access road to Dorothea Dix Hospital. The greenway continues ahead. This is also where the other Rocky Branch Greenway connects after crossing Western Boulevard at a traffic light. If using this route for a loop, it is another 0.5 mile to Pullen Park, for a round-trip of 1.7 miles. (Rocky Branch Greenway—East is described in the next section.)

If continuing upstream on Rocky Branch Greenway from its access to Pullen Road, notice the university signs concerning the area's environment along the way. At 0.6 mile, arrive at a series of steps leading up to Morrill Drive, but turn right to enter a tunnel under the street for hikers and cyclists. Exit to a parking area for Carmichael Gym. At this point, hikers can continue upstream through the parking area, pass around the corner of a building, cross a bridge, follow a boardwalk, pass by tennis courts on the right, pass through another parking lot, and turn left on Dan Allen Drive at 0.8 mile. After crossing a bridge over the branch, pass the old football field on the left and connect with the completed greenway on the right at the corner of Dan Allen and Sullivan drives.

For cyclists using the tunnel under Morrill Drive, the route to take goes left on the Morrill Drive sidewalk to pass the old university football field. (This route is necessary until a planned greenway at the edge of the old practice field connects Morrill Drive with Dan Allen Drive.) After 0.2 mile, turn right onto Faucette Drive. Go 0.2 mile and turn right onto Dan Allen Drive. Go 0.1 mile to connect with the greenway at the corner of Dan Allen and Sullivan drives.

There are more informational signs about the environment. At 1.3 miles, cross Varsity Drive. At 1.6 miles, reach Gorman Street and turn right. There is a dense forest on both sides of the street. At 1.8 miles, cross a high bridge over a railroad track. The trail comes to a group of restaurants. At 2.0 miles, cross Gorman Street at Hillsborough Street to reach the corner of Faircloth Street at Meredith College. This is the western end of Rocky Branch Greenway and the eastern trailhead for *Reedy Creek Greenway*.

Rocky Branch Greenway—East (2.3 miles, easy)

Trailhead and Description: To continue on the eastern segment of *Rocky Branch Greenway*, which is located on the north side of Western Boulevard from Pullen Park, cross Ashe Avenue at its fork toward Western Boulevard and follow the paved sidewalk that parallels Western Boulevard. Pass the

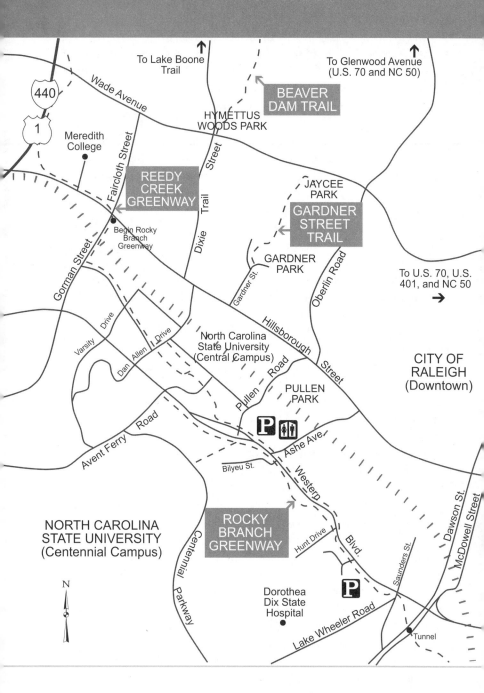

ROCKY BRANCH GREENWAY

To Lake Boone Trail

To Glenwood Avenue (U.S. 70 and NC 50)

BEAVER DAM TRAIL

440

1

Wade Avenue

HYMETTUS WOODS PARK

Meredith College

Faircloth Street

Street

REEDY CREEK GREENWAY

JAYCEE PARK

GARDNER STREET TRAIL

Dixie Trail

Begin Rocky Branch Greenway

GARDNER PARK

Gardner St.

Oberlin Road

To U.S. 70, U.S. 401, and NC 50

Gorman Street

Drive

Varsity

Dan Allen Drive

North Carolina State University (Central Campus)

Hillsborough Street

CITY OF RALEIGH (Downtown)

PULLEN PARK

Pullen Road

Avent Ferry Road

Bilyeu St.

Ashe Ave.

Western

NORTH CAROLINA STATE UNIVERSITY (Centennial Campus)

ROCKY BRANCH GREENWAY

Centennial Parkway

Hunt Drive

Blvd.

Saunders St.

Dawson St.

McDowell Street

N

Dorothea Dix State Hospital

Lake Wheeler Road

Tunnel

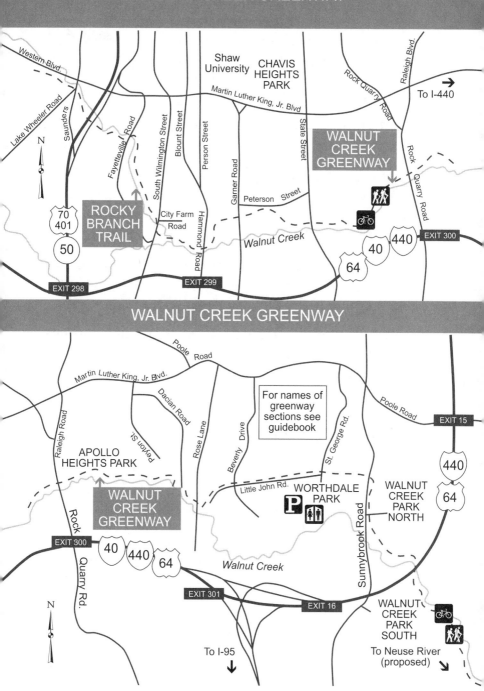

PART OF ROCKY BRANCH AND WALNUT CREEK GREENWAY

Western Blvd.

Shaw University CHAVIS HEIGHTS PARK

Lake Wheeler Road

Saunders

Fayetteville Road

South Wilmington Street

Blount Street

Person Street

Martin Luther King, Jr. Blvd

Rock Quarry Road

Raleigh Blvd.

To I-440

N

WALNUT CREEK GREENWAY

State Street

Garner Road

70 401

50

ROCKY BRANCH TRAIL

City Farm Road

Hammond Road

Peterson Street

Walnut Creek

Rock Quarry Road

40 440 EXIT 300

64

EXIT 298

EXIT 299

WALNUT CREEK GREENWAY

Poole Road

Martin Luther King, Jr. Blvd.

Dacian Road

Payton St.

Raleigh Road

APOLLO HEIGHTS PARK

Rose Lane

Beverly Drive

St. George Rd.

Poole Road

EXIT 15

For names of greenway sections see guidebook

440

64

WALNUT CREEK GREENWAY

Little John Rd.

WORTHDALE PARK

P

Sunnybrook Road

WALNUT CREEK PARK NORTH

Rock Quarry Rd.

EXIT 300

40 440

64

Walnut Creek

EXIT 301

EXIT 16

WALNUT CREEK PARK SOUTH

N

To I-95

To Neuse River (proposed)

Department of Agriculture Motor Fuel Lab at 0.35 mile, followed by an entrance road to Central Prison. At 0.5 mile, arrive at a traffic light for crossing Western Boulevard to Hunt Drive (an entrance to Dorothea Dix Hospital). At the entrance, there is a connection on the right with the Rocky Branch Greenway described in the previous section. To the left is the single greenway route. At 0.6 mile, cross under a railroad into a forest of large oaks and English ivy. The route then comes to an open space with a fence. At 0.8 mile, cross Boylan Avenue and Tate Drive, at the entrance to Dorothea Dix Hospital. There is a parking space here, which has views of an outstanding landscape with grassy slopes and large oaks. A wooden rail fence is on the right.

At 1.1 miles, cross South Saunders Street. Turn left to meet Jamaica Drive, where the trail turns right. Curve right again to be near the branch. On the left is a housing development. At 1.4 miles, enter a tunnel under Dawson and McDowell streets. At 1.5 miles, there is a large cemetery on the right. Pass through a large grove of tall trees shrouded with English ivy. At 1.65 miles, there is a rocky area of the branch. At 1.7 miles, there is a junction with Fayetteville Road and Bragg Street. Turn right to cross Fayetteville Street to reach a greenway sign. Cross an arched steel bridge over the branch, followed by two boardwalks. At 1.9 miles, there is a bridge over the branch. The route leads to *Eliza Pool Greenway*, which is now under construction. (Eliza Pool Greenway will extend south and then west to Lake Wheeler Road.) At 2.3 miles, Rocky Branch Greenway ends at the junction with South Wilmington Street and City Farm Road. *Lower Walnut Creek Greenway* begins to the right.

Lower Walnut Creek Greenway (3.1 miles, easy)

Trailhead and Description: After crossing South Wilmington Street, turn right (south) and follow the wide sidewalk for 0.1 mile to a left turn. Follow the asphalt greenway to a bridge crossing over Rocky Branch at 0.2 mile. Curve right and soon enter a 690-foot tunnel under Hammond Road. Cross a bridge over the edge of Walnut Creek, which is under a railroad bridge. Curve left, then right, and pass through a marsh of willows.

Arrive at Garner Road at 0.7 mile. Cross it and enter the woods. Go northeast. Legacy Garden is at 0.9 mile, along with an access to curbside parking on Peterson Street. At the Legacy Garden kiosk, there is information about the greenway's 24 numbered posts identifying trees and shrubs. There is a boardwalk at 1.1 miles, followed by an access to State Street on the left. Cross under a power line at 1.25 miles. There are boardwalks at 1.5 and

1.7 miles. The boardwalks cross a marsh of willow, arrow arum, and cattails. Pass under the Rock Quarry Road bridge at 1.9 miles. There is an access to a housing development at 2.0 miles. Other street accesses are at 2.3 miles (Carmen Court); 2.6 miles (Belmont Drive); and 2.9 miles (Dacian Road and a children's playground). At 3.0 miles, there is a bridge over a tributary to Walnut Creek, followed by a marsh and boardwalk. The greenway reaches Rose Lane at 3.1 miles. There is narrow roadside parking here.

Lower Walnut Creek-Worthdale Trail (0.7 mile, easy)

Trailhead and Description: If you want to begin the trail on Rose Lane, there is roadside parking on a narrow shoulder. From the end of *Lower Walnut Creek Greenway*, turn left and go 33 yards. Then, turn right onto *Lower Walnut Creek-Worthdale Trail*. After 125 yards, connect with the west end of Little John Road in a housing development. Follow the street's sidewalk or grassy shoulder for 0.7 mile to Saint George Road, where Worthdale Park and its athletic fields begins. (The park's facilities extend from here to Sunnybrook Road and the Walnut Creek Park Softball Complex. A greenway is proposed to connect these locations.)

Lower Walnut-Walnut Creek Park Trail (0.5 mile, easy)

Trailhead and Description: *Lower Walnut-Walnut Creek Park Trail* begins at the first parking area on the right for the spacious Walnut Creek Park Softball Complex. At 0.3 mile, the trail becomes paved with asphalt as it follows the rim of the parking lots to their east end. Enter the forest and descend to the banks of Walnut Creek. The route passes through a tunnel under the I-440 bridge and crosses the creek on an arched steel bridge. At 0.5 mile, there is an access to the large parking areas at Walnut Creek Amphitheatre. (A greenway is proposed that will go from this park to the Neuse River. At the river, there are proposed connections with *Neuse River Trail/Mountains-to-Sea Trail*.)

Other Raleigh Trails

The following Raleigh trails are not connected to any major greenway system. As a result, they are described alphabetically, rather than by the proximity of their locations.

Beaver Dam Trail (1.4 miles, easy)

Trailhead and Description: From I-440, drive east on Lake Boone Trail (a street) for 0.5 mile and cross Ridge Road. After driving 0.8 mile from the Ridge Road intersection, turn right on Brooks Avenue for parking. Because parking is not allowed on busy Wade Avenue (the southern trailhead), street-side parking at the northern trailhead is recommended. There is no parking on Hymettus Court, which is private.

Begin *Beaver Dam Trail* at the corner of Brooks Avenue and Lake Boone Trail. Despite its name, this trail through Hymettus Woods Nature Park no longer has a dam or a beaver. It does have an old cherished and charming natural pathway that runs from Wade Avenue to Brooks Avenue. Pedestrian bridges and picnic tables are situated along the way. The forest consists of tall, old hardwoods and loblolly pine.

To begin the trail, notice the park's green sign instructs you to begin 0.1 mile upstream where a bridge crosses Southwest Prong of Beaver Dam Creek. Follow the path to a children's playground at 0.2 mile. At 0.4 mile, Banbury Road parallels the stream. Cross Lewis Farm and Church Hill roads. At 0.8 mile, cross Leonard Road. The route then crosses a bridge and passes Saint George Anglican Church at 1.0 mile before reaching Dixie Trail (a street). Turn left onto Dixie Trail and follow the sidewalk to the Hymettus Woods Nature Park sign at the corner of Wade Avenue at 1.2 miles. Turn right for a descent to a sign and steps on the right. Follow a service road to loop back to Dixie Trail for the return.

Brentwood Trail (0.6 mile one-way; easy)

Trailhead and Description: From U.S. 1/401, located north of I-440, turn north on Brentwood Road. Travel 0.7 mile and turn right to park at the Brentwood Community Center in Brentwood Park. Park facilities include athletic fields, basketball courts, tennis courts, picnic shelters, a large children's playground, summer camp facilities, and a swimming pool, which is managed by the Home School Swim Club.

Brentwood Trail was formerly called Marsh Creek Trail. It was named for the creek it followed. It was renamed when it became a greenway. There is an access route from the parking area and athletic fields that leads to the trail in the forest. The trail also has an access upstream at Ingram Road. The trail's southern end comes after crossing a bridge over the creek to reach the west end of Glenraven Drive. (Brentwood Elementary School is located to the left or north.)

Buffaloe Greenway (1.0 mile one-way; easy)

Trailhead and Description: At the intersection of U.S. 401 and the I-540 interchange at Exit 18, drive east on I-540 for 2.0 miles to the Buffaloe Road interchange. Turn right. After 1.5 miles, turn left into Buffaloe Road Athletic Park. If coming from the U.S. 64 interchange with I-540, take Exit 24 and drive northwest 4.0 miles to Buffaloe Road and turn left (south).

Buffaloe Road Athletic Park has five lighted ball fields, a track facility, a children's playground, and restroom facilities. It also has a partially completed greenway. Access from the entrance parking area is to the right of the restrooms. After a few yards, the greenway has a spur route to the right. The greenway descends to a surprising view of a swamp from a wide boardwalk. This special place for birding is also filled with unusual plant species. Among them are arrowleaf, lizard's tail, and jewelweed. At 0.4 mile, the greenway ends where a proposed extension will connect with *Neuse River Trail*. The greenway curves left to circle around the facilities.

Durant Greenway (1.6 miles, easy)
Durant Greenway Connector (1.0 mile, easy)

Trailheads and Description: On Durant Road, 2.1 miles west of U.S. 1 (Capital Boulevard), turn left on Cub Trail (a street). After 0.1 mile, notice a greenway sign on the left. Curbside parking is available only at Cub Trail.

The asphaulted *Durant Greenway* parallels a stream. The southeast terminus is a dead-end street near Durant Nature Park and the northwest terminus is near Durant Road on Cub Trail. *Durant Greenway Connector* goes on sidewalks from Cub Trail to connect with *Falls River Greenway* described ahead.

Durant Greenway's major appeal is that it parallels Reedy Branch (unrelated to Reedy Creek), which is quite scenic with its rock formations and babbling waters. To begin the greenway, start at the trail sign on Cub Trail. At 0.3 mile, pass Durant Road Middle School on the left. Pass a swamp, then cross Hiking Trail (a street) at 0.7 mile. Along the way are young and old forests; elderberry, honeysuckle, and sumac grow along the stream. Frequently cross the branch. At 1.1 miles, the stream, now on the right side, has a rock formation known as Whale Rocks. (The formation can also be seen from *Border Trail* in Durant Nature Park.)

Cross the entrance road to Durant Nature Park at 1.4 miles. (There is a 0.1-mile access to its parking area on the right.) Descend to parallel the branch with its rocks and root formations. At the end of the trail, there is a spring nearby. Within a few yards of the end, there is a 0.1-mile paved spur to Leslieshire Drive on the left. Backtrack.

To use Durant Greenway Connector from Cub Trail, walk 0.1 mile northeast to Durant Road. Turn right (east) onto the sidewalk. At 0.4 mile, reach the traffic light. Cross the road to the Falls River Avenue sidewalk. Continue on this sidewalk to pass the Falls River Village Shopping Center, followed by a residential area with a small lake and fountain. At 1.0 mile, meet the Falls River Greenway that crosses the avenue at a bridge. (There is no curbside parking here.) Backtrack. (Directions to connect with Falls River Greenway are ahead.)

Fallon Park Trail (0.5 mile one-way; easy)

Trailhead and Description: From Anderson Drive, take Oxford Road past Our Lady of Lourdes for 0.2 mile to Overbrook Drive, which is on the right. Only streetside parking is available. The north edge of Fallon Park and the northern trailhead for *Fallon Park Trail* are located here. To reach the southern trailhead, go 0.5 mile south on Oxford Road to Kenmore Drive. Turn right there. There is streetside parking available at the Fallon Park sign.

Similar to *Beaver Dam Trail* and *Gardner Trail*, Fallon Park Trail offers natural-surface paths through the neighborhood. One difference from the other trails is that this trail has a greater elevation change and the water in Fallon Creek flows more rapidly, thus creating more splashing effects. At the northern trailhead, there is a gazebo, which was made possible by the Fallon Park Garden Club. There are bridges that cross the creek and picnic tables along the way. Fallon Creek flows through Kiwanis Park on its way to a confluence with nearby Crabtree Creek.

Falls River Greenway (1.2 miles one-way; easy)

Trailhead and Description: From the junction of U.S. 1 and Durant Road, drive west on Durant Road for 1.8 miles. Turn right onto Falls River Avenue at the Falls River Village Shopping Center. Drive north for 1.2 miles and turn right on Farmington Grove Drive. Watch for curbside parking on the right. If coming from Falls of Neuse Road, drive east on Durant Road for 0.8 mile. Turn left onto Falls River Avenue and pick up the directions given above.

This suburban asphalt *Falls River Greenway* travels through the Falls River subdivision. It meanders among tall trees behind private homes and then goes into open spaces filled with wildflowers and flowering shrubs. If hiking from north to south, Falls River Greenway passes a massive city landfill on the left. It crosses Falls River Avenue at 0.9 mile. (*Durant Greenway Connector* is on the sidewalk to the left.) Falls River Greenway curves to the right and goes under a power line to exit at Walkertown Drive.

Gardner Street Trail (0.8 mile, easy)

Trailhead and Description: To reach the southern trailhead for *Gardner Street Trail*, from Hillsborough Street turn north on Gardner Street and go 0.2 mile to the intersection with Everett Avenue. Curve right for curbside parking on Everett Avenue, which is between Gardner Park, on the left, and Rose Garden Park, on the right. To reach the northern trailhead, park at Jaycee Park on Wade Avenue and go behind the office building. (From this trailhead, it is 0.5 mile west on Wade Avenue to reach Hymettus Woods Nature Park and *Beaver Dam Trail*.)

Gardner Street Trail is another old, natural-surface footpath, which occasionally changes to gravel and travels on sidewalks. If beginning at the southern trailhead, start at a greenway sign near the corner of Gardner Street

An ancient cedar in Rose Garden Park near Gardner Street Trail

and Everett Avenue. (Opposite the corner on Everett Avenue, there are steps descending into Rose Garden Park. Raleigh Little Theatre is on the east side of the garden.) Descend into Gardner Park, where there is a basketball court, a children's playground, and a small athletic field. Cross Kilgore Street and follow the sidewalk briefly. After crossing Van Dyke Avenue, turn left on Fairall Drive, a gravel road that is shaded by tall yellow poplar, oak, and loblolly pine. At 0.6 mile, enter a forest of greater density. Leave Southeast Prong of Beaver Dam Creek with a right turn; ascend steps. Coming into Jaycee Park, pass through the Daylily Garden, which is maintained by the Raleigh Hemerocallis Club and dedicated to Charles Ben Huyett, a former aboriculturist for the city of Raleigh.

Glen Eden Trail (0.8 mile round-trip; easy)

Trailhead and Description: There are two entrances to *Glen Eden Trail*. One entrance is on Blue Ridge Road by the tennis courts; the other is on Glen Eden Drive by the community center. To reach the tennis courts' entrance, turn off U.S. 70/NC 50 onto Blue Ridge Road near Crabtree Valley Mall. Go 1.0 mile on Blue Ridge Road and turn left to reach Glen Eden Pilot Park. To reach the community center at this park, turn off Blue Ridge Road onto Glen Eden Road. After 0.3 mile on Glen Eden Road, turn left to reach the park. The name "Glen Eden" implies a secluded valley in paradise. Eden didn't have the speedway noise of I-440 to silence the songbirds, but otherwise, the name, which is used for the park and surrounding streets, seems in harmony.

Series of steps in Glen Eden Park in Raleigh

The park facilities include a community center, a children's playground, tennis courts, a fitness course, and picnic shelters.

If beginning the loop trail through Glen Eden Pilot Park at the tennis courts' parking area, follow a paved section to pass the tennis courts and the children's playground. At 0.3 mile, there is a fork. If going right, there are open green spaces and a mature forest. The route passes a small pond, followed by steps leading to the community center. To complete the loop, backtrack partially from the community center, but veer to the right. (To the left, you may notice the route could continue to parallel I-440. That may be a future connection with the 2.2-mile *House Creek Greenway* that will run north from *Reedy Creek Greenway*'s location at the east end of the pedestrian bridge across I-440 to *Crabtree Creek Greenway* at Crabtree Valley Avenue.) Continuing on Glen Eden Trail, return to the tennis courts' parking area at 0.8 mile.

Lake Lynn Trail (2.1 miles, easy)
Lake Lynn Park Trail (0.3 mile, easy)

Trailheads and Description: If coming from the east on U.S. 70/ NC 50 at Crabtree Valley Mall, drive north on NC 50 for 2.0 miles to Lynn Road. Turn left and drive 0.8 mile west to the parking lot on the right. For the north entrance to the community center, drive 0.6 mile west from NC 50 on Lynn Road and turn right on Ray Road. After l.3 miles, turn left at 7921 Ray Road.

From the parking area at the base of the dam, ascend to connect with the loop greenway. Begin *Lake Lynn Trail* to the left. The lake is fed by Hare Snip Creek and a few smaller tributaries. It is part of the Capital City Greenway system. Like the Shelley Lake facilities (1.5 miles east), the area is frequented by walkers, strollers, joggers, runners, bikers, and some in-line skaters. The lake's design gives the neighborhood residents access to the trail that loops around the lake. (The swimming pools seen from the trail on the east and west sides of the lake are not open to the public.) The main loop has six boardwalks, the longest of which leads across the marshy north end of the lake, a watery respite for turtles and waterfowl. Every 0.25 mile, there are distance markers. There are benches for resting and viewing the scenic lake area. Non-motorized boating is allowed in the lake, but swimming is not.

If walking clockwise, cross the first boardwalk in a cove at 0.4 mile. The route then passes a boat dock. At 0.5 mile, there is a sign about trail use and safety regulations. One of the longest boardwalks (238 feet) begins at 0.8 mile, where there are fewer views of residential housing. At the fourth

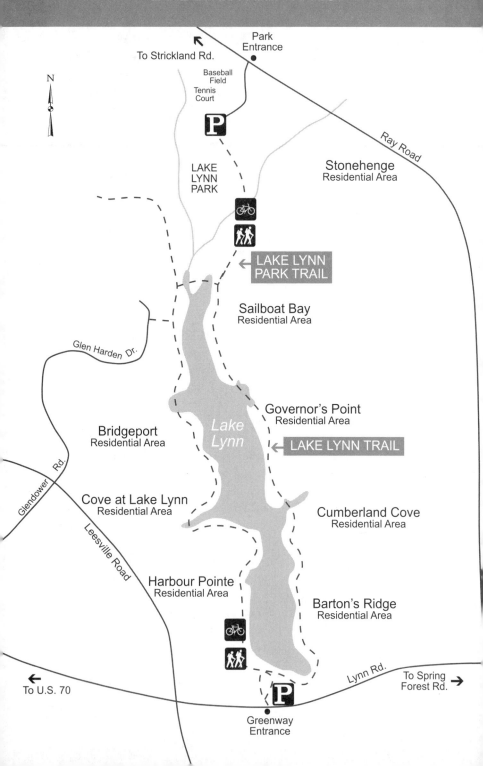

LAKE LYNN PARK TRAILS

Park Entrance

To Strickland Rd.

N

Baseball Field
Tennis Court

P

LAKE LYNN PARK

Ray Road

Stonehenge
Residential Area

LAKE LYNN PARK TRAIL

Sailboat Bay
Residential Area

Glen Harden Dr.

Lake Lynn

Governor's Point
Residential Area

LAKE LYNN TRAIL

Bridgeport
Residential Area

Glendower Rd.

Cove at Lake Lynn
Residential Area

Leesville Road

Cumberland Cove
Residential Area

Harbour Pointe
Residential Area

Barton's Ridge
Residential Area

To U.S. 70

Lynn Rd.

To Spring Forest Rd.

P

Greenway Entrance

bridge, there is an attractive marsh. Waterfowl are likely to be seen in the low waters between the willow groves. At 1.0 mile, there is a junction. (To the left, *Lake Lynn Park Trail* ascends, then dips to cross a drainage area. It junctions with an unnamed gravel trail on the right that leads to Ray Road. Remaining on the asphalt, ascend to Lake Lynn Park. The park facilities include a community center, lighted ball fields and tennis courts, and a picnic area. Backtrack to rejoin Lake Lynn Trail.)

Continuing on the main trail, arrive at the fifth boardwalk at 1.3 miles, and a sixth at 1.6 miles. At 1.8 miles, *Workout Trail* goes to the left; it offers physical-fitness stations in a residential-housing complex. Cross the grassy dam to return to the point of origin.

Little Rock Trail (0.9 mile, easy)

Trailhead and Description: There is curbside parking on Chavis Way in Chavis Heights Park, between East Lenoir and Boundary streets. If starting from the northern trailhead, park on Chavis Way and begin from the corner of East Lenoir Street and Chavis Way. This greenway is near the heart of downtown Raleigh and dear to those who dreamed and worked to make it a reality. The same can be said about Chavis Heights Park, through which *Little Rock Trail* passes.

Follow the trail through Chavis Heights Park, cross the Garner Branch footbridge, and then pass a picnic area. At 0.5 mile, cross Bragg Street. Continue among a forest of elm, ash, and sycamore to Martin Luther King, Jr. Boulevard. (Proposals are to continue the greenway to connect with *Walnut Creek Greenway*'s Legacy Garden at Peterson Street. At the northern trailhead, there is a proposal to connect to downtown Fayetteville Street by sidewalks.)

Loblolly Trail
Francis Liles Interpretive Trail

Length and Difficulty: 7.3 miles combined and one-way; easy to moderate

Trailheads and Description: The southeast trailhead is at a designated parking lot at Gate E (West) at the RBC Center. To access this parking lot from I-440, take Exit 4 west on Wade Avenue and make a right-ramp turn onto Edwards Mill Road. Turn left and go under the Wade Avenue bridge. After 0.4 mile, turn left at Gate E (west) and go 100 yards to the parking lot on the left. If coming from Blue Ridge Road on Trinity Road, turn right at

Hiker at tunnel on Loblolly Trail in Raleigh

Gate D to reach a four-way stop. Turn left and immediately turn right to the parking lot. For the northwest trailhead, drive west from Wade Avenue to join I-40. Turn off at Harrison Avenue, Exit 287. Turn right to enter Umstead State Park. The trailhead is at the northeast corner of the parking lot. (See Chapter 2 for more information about trails in Umstead State Park.)

Diverse and unique, the natural-surface *Loblolly Trail*, like *Falls Lake Trail*, provides a respite from the crowded asphalt and concrete greenways. The trail passes through two lighted tunnels; goes in and out of an experimental forest; travels past creek banks, floodplains, and lakes; and goes up and down the hills of a state park. It is even honored with its own landscaped parking lot, near one of the city's largest parking areas.

If entering from the southeast trailhead, ascend a bank to a short piece of pavement. Descend and travel left of a fence to cross a small stream. On the approach to Edwards Mill Road, descend to pass under the road. Follow an open grassy path to Richland Creek and the Wade Avenue double tunnels. There may be signs of beavers building a dam. The creek flows through the left tunnel and pedestrians use the lighted tunnel on the right. During high water periods, both tunnels may be flooded and unsafe for hiking. At the tunnel exit, ascend a bank and turn left at 0.5 mile. Follow a wide and grassy white-blazed passage downstream. At 1.3 miles, enter Schenck Memorial Forest, which is owned by N.C. State University. At 1.8 miles, connect with *Frances Liles Interpretive Trail*, on the right at a gravel road. (Francis Liles Interpretive Trail ascends through a controlled forest where there are examples of conifers being grafted for better timber quality. At 0.2 mile, the trail passes a picnic shelter to complete this part of its loop at 0.3 mile. To access this trail by car, go 0.1 mile west from Edwards Mill Road on Reedy Creek Road to State Farm Road and turn left.)

Francis Liles Interpretive Trail runs jointly with Loblolly Trail to 2.2 miles. The interpretive trail turns off to the right. (Here Frances Liles Interpretive Trail follows a hollow, crosses bridges over wet and dry ravines,

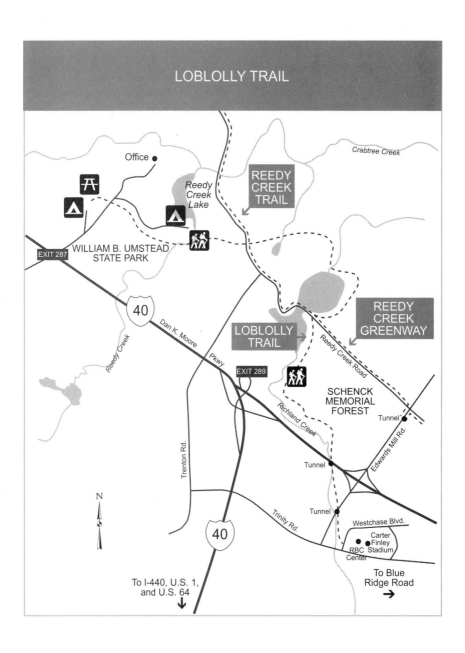

and ascends to a ridge at 0.5 mile. It completes the loop at 1.0 mile.) Continue on Loblolly Trail as it travels near the edge of Wake County Flood Control Lake. At 2.4 miles, reach Reedy Creek Road, which is a public road going right and left. (The lake is on the left; to the right, it is 0.45 mile to Edwards Mill Road.) Turn right on Reedy Creek Road. After 150 yards, turn left off the road that parallels Reedy Creek Road. Enter the forest by going down an embankment to an obscure trail entrance. Pass through a damp cove and a dry, rocky lakeside. The route travels among redbud and young hardwoods to a left turn that goes over the dam. Halfway across the dam, at 3.0 miles, turn right for a descent. At the base of the dam, enter the woods and follow the sign on the left. Enter Umstead State Park at 3.4 miles. The trail becomes blue-blazed here. Cross *South Turkey Creek* (formerly Bike & Bridal) *Trail* at 3.6 miles, descend to a damp hollow. At 3.8 miles, pass to the right of a pond, At 4.2 miles, cross a park road, which is Reedy Creek Trail (a street). After crossing two more small streams that feed Reedy Creek Lake, cross a high footbridge over Reedy Creek at 5.1 miles. At 5.7 miles, pass under a power line. Cross Camp Whispering Pines Road and arrive at the Reedy Creek parking area of William B. Umstead State Park at 6.0 miles.

Neuse River Trail (4 miles, easy)

Trailheads and Description: To reach the northern trailhead from U.S. 64/264 Business, take New Hope Road north for 0.9 mile and turn right on Southall Road. After 0.8 mile, turn right onto Castlebrook Drive. Go 0.5 mile and turn right on Abington Lane. The trailhead and parking space are at the end of Abington Lane.

To reach the trailhead at Anderson Point Park, take Exit 14 (the New Bern Avenue interchange) off I-440 and drive east on U.S. 64 for 2.0 miles. Turn right onto Rogers Lane. (Edgewater Place Shopping Center is at the corner ahead.) If coming from I-540, take Exit 24 and drive west on U.S. 64. Go 2.1 miles and turn left onto Rogers Lane.

After 0.3 mile, make a sharp right. Drive 0.9 mile and take a left onto Robbins Drive. Make an immediate right turn onto Anderson Point Drive. After 0.2 mile, turn left into a large parking lot at Anderson Point Park. At the east side of the lot, there is an access to *Neuse River Trail*.

(Although the well-designed walkways are not named, walkers and runners will be delighted as they drive or walk across the bridge from the parking lot to the southern part of Anderson Point Park. The bridge that crosses over the railroad and wide U.S. 64/264 Expressway [the Knightdale

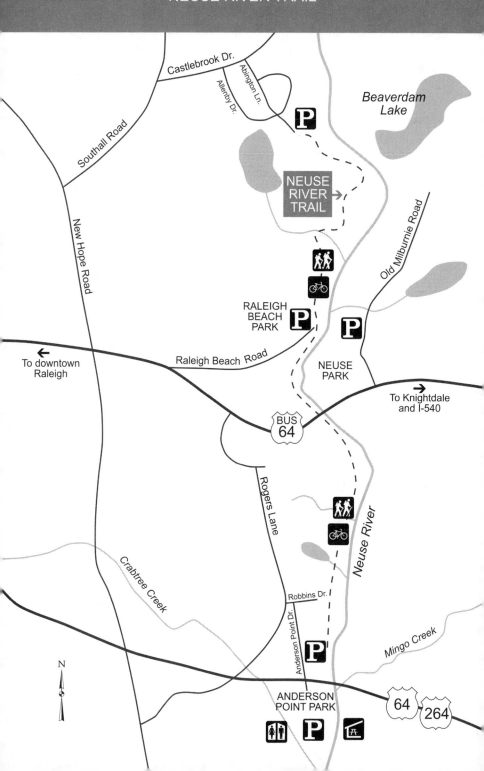

NEUSE RIVER TRAIL

Bypass] is quite a showpiece. Once on the peninsula, there are parking areas, picnic shelters, a children's playground, restrooms, and a meeting facility that can be rented. As the trail winds among the grassy hills and passes by benches, the shade provided by a grove of oaks may be most inviting. There are also old-fashioned swings, where hikers can experience a rare moment of rest. Strangely, the hum of heavy traffic off in the distance adds to the peaceful nature of the park.)

The linear north-south *Neuse River Trail* parallels the Neuse River and goes under U.S. 64/264 Business on the east side of the city. If entering from the south, the trail follows a wide road made from a city-waste line. Tall hickory, beech, and loblolly pine are prominent. Birds and butterflies are found among the willow, wax myrtle, and wildflowers.

Constructed as a greenway, this trail follows the Neuse River from the Anderson Point Park area north to near Abington Lane. A continuation is planned that will go north to Falls Lake Dam. To the south, the proposed greenway would continue as the *Mountains-to-Sea Trail* into Johnston County. Near Anderson Point Park, the greenway would also make a connection northwest along Crabtree Creek to *Buckeye Trail* on Milburnie Road.

Currently, hike or bike 1.1 miles on the trail to a long boardwalk in a wet area inhabited by frogs and some other amphibians. At 1.5 miles, pass under U.S. 64/264 Business. Turn left at a trail post. At 2.1 miles, turn right on Raleigh Beach Road. At 2.2 miles, turn left. Go up a hill for 130 yards and make a right turn. At 2.7 miles, there is a bridge near a wet area with water hyacinths. Pass left of a swamp at 3.3 miles. Leave the river, ascend and exit at the parking lot after 4.0 miles.

Wakefield Greenway (1.25 miles one-way; easy)

Trailhead and Description: If accessing the northern trailhead for *Wakefield Greenway* from NC 98, which is located on the western edge of the town of Wake Forest, turn south on Old NC 98 Road. Go 0.5 mile to a junction and turn left onto Falls of Neuse Road. After 1.0 mile, turn left onto Wakefield Plantation Drive. After 0.6 mile, park at the curbside on the right in a wide section of the street, near the Capital Area Greenways sign. The actual trailhead is at the Falls of Neuse Road sidewalk, but there is no parking here.

Wakefield Greenway is in the center of Wakefield Plantation development, where two large electric power lines cross the upscale subdivisions and expansive golf course. The shadeless trail travels among a variety of fields covered with grasses and wildflowers. The route weaves and undulates under the power lines. Patches of blackberries ripen along the path in late June. Golf carts have the right-of-way at trail crossings.

If walking south, follow the greenway for 0.35 mile to its end at London Bell Street. Backtrack to Wakefield Plantation Drive and start over for a turn east (to the right) on the sidewalk past the Wakefield Golf Course Maintenance Center. Ascend to a left turn at a greenway sign. Cross Village Springs Road at 0.5 mile. A few large homes can be seen on the left. There is a view of the golf course on the right. Arrive at the northern trailhead at Falls of Neuse Road at 0.9 mile. (A loop can be made by turning left on the road's sidewalk and entering Wakefield Plantation Drive for a return to the curbside parking after another 1.4 miles.)

Rolesville (Wake County)

Rolesville Main Street Park

Rolesville Parks and Recreation
P.O. Box 250 (mailing)
200 East Young Street (physical location)
Rolesville, NC 27571
Telephone: 919-554-6582; fax: 919-556-6852

The expanding development of the Triangle, particularly around Raleigh, has caused the rapid growth of Rolesville on the northern edge of Wake County. To meet the expectations of the residents of Rolesville, the parks and recreation department has developed an official plan for community parks. Rolesville Main Street Park is the first to be completed. The park has a meticulously manicured area extending from the entrance to an inviting pavilion. The park has three sheltered picnic sections, restrooms, and a modern children's playground.

Nature Trail (0.3 mile, easy)
Old Towne Greenway (1.0 mile, easy)

Trailheads and Description: Rolesville Main Street Park is located on the west side of U.S. 401 (South Main Street), between the traffic lights at Rogers Road and Young Street. At the park, *Nature Trail* is a loop with interpretive markers placed along the route. It leads to an arboretum in the center of the loop. (There are plans to extend the park's boundary and facilities.)

From the park, *Old Towne Greenway* connects the park with Olde Towne subdivision by going north on a sidewalk on Main Street. The route crosses Young Street. At 0.7 mile, it enters the woods, crosses a boardwalk, and exits at the entrance of the subdivision on the left on Waterstone Lane.

Smithfield (Johnston County)

Parks and Recreation Department
P.O. Box 2344 (mailing)
200 South Front Street (physical location)
Smithfield, NC 27577
Telephone: 919-934-2148; fax: 919-934-6554

The Neuse River flows on the west side of the historic city of Smithfield. In the future, the *Mountains-to-Sea Trail* will pass through or near its city limits. Until then, Smithfield will maintain the scenic *Neuse River Nature Trail* on the river's east bank and *Long Haul Trail* upriver at Smithfield Community Park. Both of these trails are described ahead. There is also a proposal to construct 3.0-mile *Buffalo Creek Greenway* to connect the two trails.

Neuse River Nature Trail (0.4 mile one-way; easy)

Trailhead and Description: The upriver access to *Neuse River Nature Trail* is off downtown Market Street (U.S. 70 Business) on Front Street. The parking area is to the north of this intersection on Front Street. Descend to the paved trail to reach the site of Smith's Ferry (1759-86), which was located on the riverbank. Turn left. The trail passes mulberry trees, which ripen in mid-May. Cross a footbridge and pass under the U.S. 70 Business bridge at 0.1 mile. Underground spring water seeps across the trail here. Pass Neuse Little Theater and an outdoor stage area on the left. Enter a pristine forest of large sweet gum, sycamore, oak, and green ash. At 0.4 mile, the trail turns left to end at Bob Wallace Jaycee Kiddie Park on Second Street. Backtrack. To drive to Kiddie Park, go south two blocks from Market Street on Second Street to reach the trailhead at the park.

Long Haul Trail (1.1 miles, easy)

Trailhead and Description: From the junction of U.S. 70 and U.S. 301/ NC 96, turn south on U.S. 301/NC 96. Pass under a bridge and drive past Center Pointe Shopping Center. Drive 1.1 miles to a service station on the right at Booker Dairy Road. After 1.3 miles, pass the high school. It is 0.2 mile to the parking entrance on the left.

The 43-acre Smithfield Community Park is a major example of how urban government can create an effective combination of educational, sports, and aesthetic facilities. The park includes *Long Haul Trail*, which circles part of the athletic facilities near Smithfield-Selma High School.

Begin Long Haul Trail on the west side of the park entrance. Follow a concrete route as it travels along the edge of the forest. At night, there is lighting along the trail's border. Along the route, there are interpretive signs. At 0.2 mile, pass a pavilion, followed by a soccer field on the left. At 0.4 mile, enter a forest and wetlands for a short distance. There are color-coded connector trails at 0.5 and 0.6 mile. At 0.7 mile in the loop, there is an access to the high school on the right. Pass a tennis court to complete the loop at 1.1 miles.

Sign for Long Haul Trail in Smithfield

Wake Forest (Wake County)

Wake Forest Parks and Recreation Department
401 Elm Avenue
Wake Forest, NC 27587
Telephone: 919-554-6180; fax: 919-554-6195

Miller Park Nature Trail (0.3 mile, easy)

Trailhead and Description: To access H. L. Miller Park from NC 98 Business, turn south on Franklin Street and go one block. Then turn right on East Elm Street. After 0.1 mile, turn right to enter the Town Hall parking area. The entrance to the park is behind the building.

One of the downtown attractions of historic Wake Forest is the H. L. Miller Park. *Miller Park Nature Trail*, which is easily accessible to users with physical disabilities, is inside the park. The asphalt trail loops among loblolly pine and hardwoods, with an understory of dogwood and mulberry. Along the route, there are three bridges, which cross over a stream. There are also picnic tables and benches for relaxation.

Kiwanis Park Greenway (0.2 mile, easy)

Trailhead and Description: The trailhead for *Kiwanis Park Greenway* is one block further south of the Miller Park access on Franklin Street. It is located near the EMS Building.

The wide greenway slightly ascends west to White Street behind the post office. The trail weaves through a forest of tall trees and is bordered with fragrant white wild roses that bloom in the month of May.

Smith Creek Trail (0.7 mile, easy)

Trailhead and Description: To access *Smith Creek Trail* from the junction of U.S. 1 and U.S. 1 Alternate, drive south on U.S. 1 for 1.9 miles. Turn left on Burlington Mills Road. Drive east for 0.7 mile and park immediately after crossing the Smith Creek bridge. The greenway sign is a few yards ahead with the trail access on the right. As the trail parallels Smith Creek, most of the trees are sweet gum, sycamore, river birch, and loblolly pine, all of which may have wild grapevines growing on them. There is a view of the creek at 0.6 mile. The asphalt ends near the Wake Forest Waste Water Treatment

Plant at 0.7 mile. Toward the right is access to the creek near its confluence with the Neuse River. Backtrack. (There is a proposed plan to extend the greenway upstream from Burlington Mill Road to a tunnel under NC 98 and on to an access at Wake Forest Dam.)

Zebulon (Wake County)

> **Zebulon Parks and Recreation Department**
> **202 East Vance Street**
> **Zebulon, NC 27597**
> **Telephone: 919-269-8265; fax: 919-269-6200**

Little Creek Trail (1.8 miles round-trip; easy)

Trailhead and Description: *Little Creek Trail* is located in Zebulon Community Park. To reach the park, turn southeast onto NC 96 (Arendell Avenue South) at its intersection with NC 97 in downtown Zebulon. Go 0.5 mile to the park on the left.

In addition to the trail, the park has a children's playground, athletic fields, a sheltered picnic area, and a 19-station fitness course. There is a trail sign at the parking area. Near fitness-trail sign #1, enter a grove of maples, followed by an open athletic field. At 0.3 mile, the fitness trail ends. Pass a water-pipeline sign. Cross a culvert and stay right. At 0.7 mile, cross East Horton Street. Turn left toward a railroad track, but turn right before crossing the road to follow the trail paralleling the railroad. At 0.9 mile, the trail reaches Little Creek and ends at a terminus sign. Backtrack.

Duke Memorial Gardens

CHAPTER 5

Trails on Private and University or College Properties

This chapter describes some of the trails in the Triangle that are on privately owned property—whether owned by individuals, colleges, or universities. The one requirement is that they be open to the public.

Some of the trails have information about user limitations at their trailheads. One example of this would be the trails in the sections of Duke Forest.

The trails may also have information about liability. Some landowners are reluctant to open their properties because of liability and trail abuse. For example, Methodist University closed its network of botanical trails to the public. Isolated from the campus, the scenic paths were located between an active railroad and the deep ravines between bluffs at the Cape Fear River.

As population increases so does the need for security. Today, *Al Beuhler Cross Country Trail* is open only in the daytime. Years ago, emergency telephones were installed at intervals along the trail.

Problems with illegal hunting, fires, and theft on private forest properties may eventually mean a loss to all. The first edition of this guidebook described the various sections of the 45-mile Buckhorn Trail in Lee County. Unfortunately, all of those sections are now closed to public access.

In 1987, the state legislature passed a bill (the Act to Limit the Liability of Landowners to Persons Using Their Land in Connection with the Trails System) to protect private landowners. That bill encouraged some landowners to open private lands to the public.

One way to see some of nature's rare places that are closed to the public is to be active in outdoors organizations. In the 50-mile radius of the Triangle, there are at least 50 private resorts, camps, preserves, hunting grounds, and equestrian and mountain-biking groups that have land that can be used only by members and their associates.

Regardless of the problems, corporate and individual landowners have a long history of cooperation with Scout teams, churches, schools, nature groups, and hunting and fishing clubs that wish to use their property. Most private trails are not publicized. If all the pathways through farm woodlands, all those favorite fishing and hunting routes, and all those walks to points of meditation were counted in the Triangle's inventory of trails, they would number in the hundreds. Frequently, private owners will give an individual or a small group permission to walk a path or roadway if the purpose is for education or aesthetics.

The private properties are listed first in this chapter, followed by the properties under the control of universities and colleges. Within each section, the properties are listed in alphabetical order.

Private Properties

De Hart Botanical Gardens (Franklin County—Louisburg)

De Hart Botanical Gardens
3585 U.S. 401 South
Louisburg, NC 27549
Telephone: 919-496-4771

De Hart Botanical Gardens is an 83-acre nature preserve. It has a developed arboretum as well as a trail for the physically handicapped that leads from the parking area to the lake. Hiking trails wind through an area of rocky bluffs and a low area located in a bamboo grove. The major blooming season is from early April through May. For hiking through the woods, there are two loops with old growth trees, some more than 200 years of age. More than 300 species of vascular plants have been identified. One species found here is wild pink, which is only found in about two dozen counties in North and South Carolina. The garden is open and free to the public on weekends. A tour guide can be arranged. Hiking and picnicking are allowed. Camping, fishing, swimming, smoking, and firearms are forbidden. Visitors must register and dogs must be on a leash.

Rock Trail (0.3 mile)
Trail for Physically Handicapped (0.1 mile)
Children's Bamboo Trail (75 yards)
Lake Loop Trail (0.3 mile)
Crane-fly Orchid Trail (0.5 mile)
Waterfall Trail (1.8 miles)

Length and Difficulty: 3.0 miles combined; easy to moderate

Trailheads and Description: From the juncture of U.S. 401 and NC 56 in Louisburg, drive south 5.3 miles on U.S. 401 to the gardens' sign and parking area on the left. Coming from Raleigh on U.S. 401 drive north to a junction with NC 98. From that intersection, stay on U.S. 401 for 4.5 miles to the gardens' sign on the right.

Waterfall at De Hart Botanical Gardens

From the parking area, visitors must register at the gazebo and use a map to decide which section of the preserve to hike. If choosing the lake area, leave the parking area to cross a bridge over a ravine. At the edge of the forest, there is a fork among azaleas. To the left, there is a short cut to the lake for hikers and those who are physically disabled. To the right is *Rock Trail*. It ascends and weaves through more azaleas to rock outcroppings and views of the lake. It rejoins the short trail to the lake and another fork at 0.3 mile. To the left is *Children's Bamboo Trail*, and to the right is *Lake Loop Trail* with more azaleas, wildflowers, and picnic tables. If going right on Lake Loop Trail, cross the pedestrian bridge across the lake for another fork. Ahead and slightly to the right begin *Crane-fly Orchid Trail*. It makes a loop in a forest of hardwoods and loblolly pine. Rock-hop a small stream, cross a footbridge, and follow the stream among wildflowers. After the loop, return to the lake where there are picnic tables at 0.8 mile.

Return to the parking area and follow the *Waterfall Trail* sign. Cross a pedestrian bridge over a stream and ascend under a power line. Reenter the hardwood forest, pass old beech trees, and arrive at a small waterfall at 0.6 mile.

Travel upstream to cross another bridge and then ascend. At 0.7 mile, turn right for a loop to a former plantation site with huge oaks. Pass a pond and arrive at a power line. To the right is a shortcut. Ahead is a longer trail that rejoins the shorter route at 1.4 miles for a return to the parking area.

Historic Occoneechee Speedway
(Orange County—Hillsborough)

Preservation North Carolina (PNC)
P.O. Box 27644
Hillsborough, NC 27278
Telephone: 919-832-3652
www. presnc.org.

Also,
CAHPT
376 Saint Mary's Road
Hillsborough, NC 27278

Historic Occoneechee Speedway is a 44-acre preserve at the former NASCAR Speedway. From 1948-68, this was a place for the noise of car racing and cheering crowds. Today, it is now a peaceful place to walk through the woods and stroll alongside the Eno River. It has also been used for football games and other community events. Placed on the National Register of Historic Places in 2002, the site may eventually be part of the *Mountains-to-Sea Trail*. Regulations for trail use include daylight use only; no bicycles or motorized vehicles; and dogs must be on leashes. Smoking, illegal drugs, hunting, and fishing are not allowed.

Speedway Trail (0.6 mile)
Big Bend Trail (0.6 mile)
Beech Bluff Trail (0.2 mile)
Wolf Tree Trail (0.5 mile)
Terrance Trail (0.2 mile)
Spectator Trail (0.25 mile)

Length and Difficulty: 2.3 miles to 2.7 miles combined and backtracked; easy to moderate

Trailheads and Description: From I-85, take Exit 165 and drive north on NC 86 for 0.5 mile to the junction with U.S. 70 Business. Cross U.S. 70 Business to Elizabeth Brady Road. After 0.3 mile, look for the parking area on the right.

From the parking area, follow the signs through a forest of cedar and hawthorn to an open space filled with wild roses. The route then goes into a pine forest. There is a kiosk at 0.15 mile. Ahead is a fork with the option to go right or left on *Speedway Trail*. If choosing the far right, pass side trails on the right. One of these side trails is *Big Bend Trail*, which makes a loop to a scenic view of the Eno River at 0.9 mile. Another side trail is *Beech Bluff Trail*. It ascends to a bluff with tall trees by the riverside at 1.2 miles. From the bluff, ascend to the top of a ridge on *Wolf Tree Trail*. To the left of the ridge, *Terrance Trail* goes 1.7 miles to concrete seating that was formerly used by spectators. Some of the seating may be covered with mosses and vines. *Spectator Trail* begins at the end of Wolf Tree Trail and descends to complete the circle.

Harris Energy and Environmental Center (Wake County)

Harris Visitor Center
3932 New Hill-Hollaman Road
New Hill, NC 27562
Telephone: 919-362-3261 or 1-800-452-2777

Progress Energy, formerly Carolina Power and Light Company, operates the Triangle's only nuclear-power system. Views of its cooling towers can be seen from U.S. 1 in the southwest corner of Wake County and the southeast corner of Chatham County. The *Peninsula Trail*, which is described in the "Harris Lake County Park" section of Chapter 3, provides a closer view under a mega power line. At Harris Energy and Environmental Center, visitors can gather information and arrange for tours. Near the center's parking area is a nature trail, which is described below, on which you can see tall trees instead of cooling towers.

▍White Oak Nature Trail (1.5 miles combined loops; easy to moderate)

Trailhead and Description: From U.S. 1, south of Apex, take Exit 89 and drive east on New Hill-Hollaman Road (SR 1127) for 1.5 miles. The center is to the right.

At the parking area, which is near the sign for the center and a picnic shelter, enter the wide natural-surface trail. Follow the yellow and red blazes along the skillfully designed trail through a mature forest. Along the way are interpretive markers about wildlife, trees, ferns, and flowers. At 0.2 mile, the trail forks with yellow routing going left. If following the yellow blazes, the trail will rejoin the red-blazed trail at 0.4 mile. The two trails, traveling conjunctively, return to the parking area at 0.5 mile. If following the red blazes, continue past the parking area to make a longer loop, which crosses boardwalks on the approach to a scenic wetland called Big Branch. At 0.7 mile, begin the return to the parking area.

Triangle Land Conservancy

Triangle Land Conservancy
1101 Haynes Street, Suite 205
Raleigh, NC 27604
Telephone: 919-833-3662
www.tlc-nc.org

The nonprofit Triangle Land Conservancy was founded in 1983 with the mission to preserve natural areas that have biological, historical, scenic, and water-quality value. In 2004, the non-profit land trust covered six counties: Chatham, Durham, Johnston, Lee, Orange, and Wake. It has nearly 25 properties, which cover 4,539 acres. It holds conservation easements on at least 20 other properties. The conservancy is governed by a board of directors and accepts membership. Among the preserves that have trails that are open to the public are the four preserves described ahead. They are open daily from sunrise to sunset.

Flower Hill Preserve (Johnston County)

Purchased in 1989, the 10-acre Flower Hill Preserve sits on a high bluff bordered by NC 231 on the north and Moccasin Creek on the east. Situated among the preserve's shrubbery and wildflowers is a grove of Catawba rhododendron (also called purple laurel), a species whose presence here may be the farthest east of the mountains.

Flower Hill Trail (0.6 mile backtracked; easy)

Trailhead and Description: From the junction of U.S. 264 and NC 39 (east of Zebulon), drive south on NC 39 for 6.0 miles and turn left (east) on NC 231. If coming from Selma, drive north on NC 39 for 14 miles and turn right (east). After 3.0 miles on NC 231, turn right onto Flower Hill Road. It is 0.1 mile up the hill to the trailhead on the left. The road's shoulder is narrow for parking. There is more space on the shoulder of NC 231, 90 yards east of the junction with Flower Hill Road.

Flower Hill Trail is for hikers only. It stays on the rim of the bluff for 0.3 mile. From there, it descends 145 yards to a spring near Moccasin Creek. Backtrack to the trailhead.

Johnson Mill Nature Preserve (Orange County)

The 296-acre Johnson Mill Nature Preserve protects a section of New Hope Creek and its tributaries. The area, which includes floodplains and steep hillsides, is a habitat for the rare four-toed salamander, the green violet, and Thorey's grayback dragonfly. The preserve has markers to honor those who made the preserve possible. Only hikers are allowed on the trails.

Johnson Mill Nature Trail (1.8 miles one-way; easy)

Trailheads and Description: There are two access points to *Johnson Mill Nature Trail*—one on Mount Sinai Road, the other on Turkey Farm Road south of Hillsborough. To access the trailhead at Mount Sinai Road from I-85, take Exit 165 and drive 5.3 miles south on NC 86 to a left turn on Mount Sinai Road (SR 1718). Go 1.0 mile to a parking space on the right, near New Hope Creek bridge. To access from Turkey Farm Road, follow the directions above to the intersection with Mount Sinai Road but continue straight ahead for 0.9 mile. Turn right on Turkey Farm Road. After 0.8 mile, there is parking space on the right.

If coming from the Mount Sinai Road access, follow the trail downstream, traveling among tall hardwoods. The trail soon ascends over a bluff. Along the way, there are spicebushes and sugar hackberry plants. At 0.3 mile, the trail comes to rapids in the stream near a former mill site. Pass under a power line and into a wide floodplain. At 0.6 mile, cross a footbridge over Old Field Creek near its confluence with New Hope Creek. On the creek bank are gnarled sycamore roots that resemble sculpture. At a trail loop turn right to complete the circle at 1.3 miles. Continue downstream along New Hope Creek. Cross a footbridge over Booth's Branch and pass evidence of the former Johnson Mill on New Hope Creek. Along the way, there are benches, some close to the scenic streamside. At 1.8 miles, arrive at the Turkey Farm Road parking space. Backtrack or arrange a shuttle.

Swift Creek Bluffs Preserve (Wake County)

Swift Creek Bluffs Trail (1.4 miles or 2.0 miles round-trip; easy to strenuous)

Trailhead and Description: From the intersection of U.S. 1/64 and Southeast Cary Parkway in south Cary, drive 2.0 miles east on the parkway to Holly Springs Drive and turn right. After 1.6 miles (across Swift Creek bridge), make an immediate right to a parking area for about six cars.

Swift Creek Bluffs Trail has numbered posts along the trail that correspond to identification information found on a brochure that may be available at the trailhead. This preserve, with its bluffs and bottomlands, is noted for the wildflowers found in the woods in the spring. Hikers pass through a grove of pink wild geraniums after beginning the hike. On the right as the trail begins, there is a plaque expressing appreciation to donors who made the preserve possible. After 75 yards, there is a fork in the trail. If turning right, the route makes a short side-trip as it turns upstream along the banks of the creek. It ends at a huge beech tree near a rocky bluff. Backtrack to pick up the main trail at Post #6. The cumulative mileage count to this location is 0.4 if not taking the side trip or 0.7 if including it. Ascend 74 steps to the summit of the bluffs. There are benches placed along this part of the trail. In the wintertime, views from Posts #7 and #8 are spectacular. The creek can be seen below, and the hardwood forest has a silver sheen. Begin a descent from the bluff to arrive at 0.7 mile (or 1.0 mile with alternates) at Lochmere Golf Course, on the right. (To the left, a 0.2-mile asphalt greenway ascends to a residential area.) Backtrack.

White Pines Preserve (Chatham County)

Like Flower Hill and Swift Creek Bluffs preserves, the 258-acre White Pines Preserve has high bluffs facing north that sometimes rise to 100 feet. The shady slopes of these bluffs keep moisture from the confluence of Deep and Rocky creeks constant, thus insuring the botanical diversity of the preserve. In the hardwood forest, there are scattered Eastern white pines. This is thought to be the easternmost stand of this species in the Southeast.

River Trail (1.6 miles)
Overlook Trail (0.1 mile)
Comet Trail (0.2 mile)

Length and Difficulty: 1.9 miles, easy to moderate

Trailheads and Description: From Courthouse Circle in Pittsboro, drive south on U.S. 15/501/NC 87 for 8.2 miles to River Forks Road and turn left. Immediately turn right. After 1.7 miles, turn right at the stop sign. After another 0.5 mile, turn left. There is a preserve property sign and parking space 0.4 mile later. Coming from the juncture of U.S. 1 and U.S. 15/501/NC 87 north of Sanford, it is 6.2 miles to River Forks Road on the right. Follow the directions above from that point.

From the parking space, begin a descent on *River Trail* at the sign on an old road. Pass under a power line and enter a gate at 0.1 mile. Pass an old chimney to the right and meet a fork at 0.2 mile. If going right, there is a bench at 0.3 mile. At 0.4 mile, there may be a River Trail sign. (To the left, it is 80 yards to *Overlook Trail*, where a plaque honors the memory of David H.

Howells (1920-95), professor emeritus of N.C. State University.)

At 0.6 mile, curve left along the banks of Deep River, a river rich in folklore. Through this floodplain area, there are sycamore, elm, and buckeye. On the slope is solid-white mountain laurel. At 0.9 mile, *Comet Trail* goes left. (It ascends 0.2 mile to connect with Overlook Trail.) At 1.1 miles, turn left, going away from the river. (Upstream are the boulders of Rocky Creek, which seems even more mysterious and ghostly than Deep Creek.) Ascend on an old road among tall white pine. To the right is a cove where you can see a mixture of white pine and hardwoods. Continue the ascent to complete the River Trail loop at 1.7 miles. Turn right to return to the parking space.

Private and Public Colleges and Universities

Degree programs in parks and recreation management are offered at 21 colleges and universities in the state. Eleven two-year colleges offer preliminary degree programs in that same field. Some of the larger institutions offer degrees in forestry and a variety of environmental fields. Two university medical centers—those at the University of North Carolina at Chapel Hill and Duke University—offer departments in recreation therapy. Although few institutions of higher education have adequate property for a trail system, all of them have courses in physical education, and 60 percent have organizations or clubs that promote or sponsor hiking on student outings or in outdoor-sports programs.

Central Carolina Community College
(Chatham County—Pittsboro)

Central Carolina Community College
Pittsboro Campus
764 West Street
Pittsboro, NC 27312
Telephone: 919-542-6495

Thanks Trail (1.0 mile, easy)

Trailhead and Description: From the downtown courthouse in Pittsboro, drive 0.8 mile west on West Street (U.S. 64 Alt) to the college entrance on the right. (On the way, you pass a junction with NC 902 on the left.)

The campus of Central Carolina Community College is distinctive in that it used an original design to couple the lawn ellipse with a scenic trail. The trail's name, *Thanks Trail*, is also distinctive. The acronym comes from "Trail for Health, Art, and Nature for Kids to Seniors." From the parking lot, travel clockwise to a picnic table under a large sweet gum. There are floral displays along the circle. At 0.4 mile, pass a physical-fitness stop. On a hilltop, a grove of walnut trees hovers over dense burdock. At 0.5 mile, a shortcut trail leads to campus buildings. Pass a picnic table at a historic bridge built in 1921. Complete the circle at 1.0 mile with views of the agriculture nursery.

Trails in Sarah P. Duke Memorial Gardens on Duke University campus in Durham

Duke University

Duke University has two major private natural-resource areas open to the public: the 55-acre Sarah P. Duke Memorial Gardens and the 7,700-acre Duke Forest, which is composed of six main divisions in four counties. To protect these remarkable properties, the university has provided guidelines and regulations, which are listed in the following descriptions. These areas offer some of the Triangle's largest, most varied, and most educationally rewarding networks of nature walks.

Sarah P. Duke Memorial Gardens
(Durham County)

Sarah P. Duke Memorial Gardens
P.O. Box 90341
Duke University
Durham, NC 27708
Telephone: 919-484-3698

The Sarah P. Duke Memorial Gardens have at least 2,000 species of vascular plants. The gardens have three main areas, each emphasizing a variety of local, national, and foreign collections. The Terraces, a memorial gift to Sarah P. Duke given by her daughter Frances Biddle Duke, have a wide range of cultivated flowering plants. The H. L. Blomquist Garden of Native Plants is a splendid presentation of 900 species of wildflowers. The Culberson Asiatic Arboretum has 550 species of Oriental plants. These special gardens and other sections are blended with manicured allées and paths that grace formal and natural woodland settings. Ponds, lawns, bogs, and forests are part of an artful landscape.

Named in honor of the wife of Benjamin N. Duke, a university founder, the gardens were begun in the early 1930s. They are open daily from 8 A.M. to dusk. Admission is free, but fees may be charged for parking. For information about reserving space for weddings, special botanical tours, educational programs, or tours for the physically handicapped, call the number above. Garden guidelines are as follows: visitors must not do any damage to the plants, dogs must be on a leash and are not allowed at all in some parts of the gardens, and biking and team sports are not permitted. With the interconnecting pathways throughout the gardens, it is difficult to give a trail length. However, if you see everything, your feet will suggest you have walked miles.

ACCESS: To reach the main entrance to the gardens, follow Anderson Street between Campus Drive and Erwin Road to a parking area. Parking is not allowed on Flowers Drive (on the northwest border of the gardens).

Al Buehler Cross Country Trail (Durham County)

Length and Difficulty: 2.9 miles (4 miles including physical-fitness and spur trails; easy)

Trailhead and Description: From U.S. 15/501 Bypass, take Exit 107 and drive east on Cameron Boulevard for 0.4 mile to a parking lot on the right at Gate #1.

Although the *Al Buehler Cross Country Trail* is technically not part of Duke Forest, it is maintained by the Office of Duke Forest. The posted trail guidelines for the trail indicate it should be used with a partner, that no motorized vehicles are allowed, that hikers must stay off the golf course, and that the trail closes at sunset; the Duke Public Safety telephone number is 919-684-2444. The wide asphalt trail is almost completely in a wooded area.

If walking counterclockwise, pass under a power line at 130 yards, then over the Sandy Creek bridge. Turn left to begin walking parallel to the stream; at the turn, there is an emergency telephone. Pass through a grove of river birch and oak with sparkleberry and dogwood as an understory. After a gentle ascent among pines at 0.5 mile, note the sound of traffic from U.S. 15/501 Bypass. Another emergency telephone is located at 0.8 mile. To the left are views of the golf course and lakes. At 1.1 miles, cross a bridge over Sandy Creek. To the right are a bog and large sycamore trees. Reach a junction and an emergency telephone at 1.3 miles. (To the right is a 0.1-mile paved spur trail that exits to Cornwallis Road and roadside parking.)

After this junction, ascend to views of the golf course, pass an emergency telephone at 1.8 miles, and enter a forest of oak, poplar, and sycamore. The understory has black cohosh, mandrake, and buckeye. There is a junction at 2.0 miles with a paved spur that goes to the right leading to *Fitness Trail*. (If using Fitness Trail, walk 0.1 mile to where it begins. The trail has 32 stations in its loop and passes through a loblolly-pine forest for 0.6 mile. It offers parking at nearby Cameron Boulevard and an emergency telephone.) Continuing on Al Buehler Cross Country Trail, cross a wooden bridge in a forest of large white oak. At 2.3 miles are another emergency telephone, a water fountain, and a junction with a paved spur leading right. (The spur goes 130 yards to a locked gate at a soccer field.) Pass the open gates to a large parking field, to the right. At 2.5 miles, cross the entrance road to the Washington Duke Inn and Golf Club, on the left. Also cross an entrance road to the Duke Faculty Club, on the left. Back on the trail, you will begin a slight descent through the forest and complete the trail at 2.9 miles.

Duke Forest

Duke Forest Resource Manager, Office of Duke Forest
P.O. Box 90332 (mailing)
Room 412 North Building (physical location)
Durham, NC 27708-0332
Telephone: 919-613-8013; fax: 919-684-8741
www.dukeforest.duke.edu/

Duke Forest is private property owned and managed by Duke University as an outdoor laboratory for teaching and research. The forest is composed of six main divisions and several smaller tracts. Though access to certain areas is

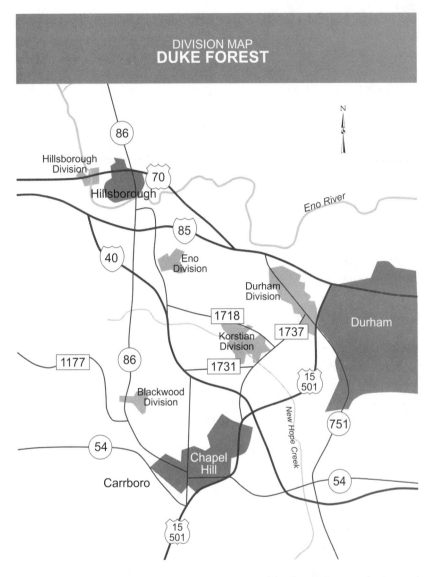

restricted for research purposes, the majority of the forest is open for limited public recreation. Permissible recreational activities are hiking, bicycling (on roads only), horseback riding (on roads only), picnicking, and fishing. Group activities must be approved in advance by the forest resource manager.

All roads are gated. Some of them are posted for foot travel only. The regulations for use (also posted at the entrance gates) are as follows: enter only at gated roads; enter at your own risk; walk with a partner; no access is permitted after sunset except at approved picnic sites; do not block gates;

unauthorized motor vehicles are prohibited; horses and bicycle traffic must stay on graded and mowed roads; no fires of any kind are allowed; no hunting or shooting of firearms is permitted; no camping is allowed; no vegetation (trees, shrubs, flowers, brush, or grasses) may be cut, picked, scarred, or damaged in any way; dogs must be kept under control as defined by local ordinance.

There are three group picnic locations in Duke Forest, all in the Durham Division at Gates C, D, and F on NC 751, west of West Campus. These picnic sites have tables and grills and must be reserved in advance; a fee is charged. There is no running water, and only site F has a pit toilet and electricity. Gates C and F have shelters. The descriptions and maps that follow should provide adequate directional options for the Duke Forest recreational areas.

Durham Division (Durham/Orange counties)

The Durham Division of Duke Forest has 24 gated roads, nine fire trails, and an interpretive trail. Some are closed for research projects or because the entrance goes through other private property. Described below are the roads and fire trails currently open. All are accessible on NC 751 with the exception of Gate #14 Road on Kerley Road, which is only 0.1 mile off NC 751. The gates are numbered 2 through 13; some are on each side of NC 751. It is 2.85 miles west from Gate #2 to U.S. 70. If going west on NC 751 from the junction with U.S. 15/501 Bypass, take Exit 107 and drive 0.3 mile. Park near Gate #2, on the right; this site is 0.7 mile west of the parking area for *Al Buehler Cross Country Trail* described above.

> Gate #2 to Gate #4 Road (3.2 miles round-trip; easy)
> Old Oxford Road (0.6 mile round-trip; easy)
> Cotton Mill Fire Trail (0.6 mile round-trip; easy)
> Mud Creek Fire Trail (0.4 mile round-trip; easy)

Trailheads and Description: Enter Gate #2 and walk under a power line. After 0.1 mile, follow a foot trail straight through woods to avoid the front lawn of a residence. Return to the road at 0.4 mile and enter a longleaf-pine forest planted in 1933 and thinned in 1988.

If including fire trails on your walk, turn right at 0.6 mile on historic *Old Oxford Road*, with its compact cobblestones; a young forest to the left allows sunlight. After 295 yards, junction with *Cotton Mill Fire Trail*, on the right. There is a beautiful path on a grassy road under large oak, shagbark hickory, and red cedar; flowers are scattered along the trail. Reach a cul-de-sac and note the sound of traffic from U.S. 15/501 Bypass at 1.1 miles, then return to Old Oxford Road. Turn right. At 1.5 miles, reach a dead-end at an apartment complex.

Backtrack to *Gate #2 to Gate #4 Road* and turn right on a gravel road at 1.8 miles. Pass through a forest where a timber harvest has been made of loblolly pine planted in 1932. Make a right turn at 2.0 miles to follow *Mud Creek Fire Trail*. It descends through a rocky area to cross a small stream in a forest of oak, poplar, and hickory. At 2.2 miles, reach the end of the trail near a housing development. Return to Gate #2 to Gate #4 Road, turn right, and follow the road through tall loblolly pine to Gate #4 at NC 751 at 2.6 miles. On the highway, it is 0.6 mile east to Gate #2.

Gate #3 Road to Gate #7 Road (2.6 miles round-trip; easy)
Pine Thicket Fire Trail (1.0 mile round-trip; easy)

Trailheads and Description: Park on the roadside at Gate #3, located 0.3 mile west of Gate #2. Enter a combined hardwood and pine forest and arrive at *Pine Thicket Fire Trail* at 0.1 mile. (Pine Thicket Fire Trail is a 1.0-mile round-trip side trail. Turn left. Reach a boundary sign after 0.3 mile. Return to Gate #3 Road and turn left at 0.7 mile.) Back on the main road, cross a wooden bridge over Mud Creek at 0.9 mile. Here are tall poplar, oak, and loblolly pine; on the forest floor are wild ginger, fire pink, New Jersey tea, wild quinine, and coreopsis. Ascend gradually through tall trees and pass a seed forest first planted in 1926. Over the years, the area has been thinned six times; some prescribed burns for timber harvesting were made in the 1980s. Descend slightly and cross a small tributary of Mud Creek at 1.3 miles. At 1.5 miles, junction with Gate #6 Road on the right and Gate #7 Road on the left. (Gate #6 Road descends on a duff-covered road and through a shady forest with buckeye in damp areas; it reaches NC 751 after 0.3 mile. It is 0.4 mile on NC 751 to Gate #3 Road for a total loop of 2.2 miles.) If continuing left on Gate #7 Road, at 1.6 miles the road passes a forest salvage cut made in 1987 because of pine-beetle infestation. Reach Gate #7 at NC 751 at 2.1 miles. It is 0.5 mile east on NC 751 to Gate #3, for a total of 2.6 miles.

Gate C Road and Shepherd Nature Trail (1.0 mile, easy)

Trailhead and Description: Gate C Road is across NC 751, a few yards east of Gate #7 Road. After entering the gate, go 250 yards to *Shepherd Nature Trail*, on the left. This 0.8-mile interpretive trail loops around the Gate C picnic area. (Ahead on the road, it is 350 feet to the Bobby Ross, Jr. Memorial Shelter, which has tables and a grill but no water or restrooms.) If hiking the nature trail, enter at the sign that credits the trail to Eagle Scout Troop 440, Duke Forest, and the National Civilian Communities Corporation. Descend on switchbacks and cross a footbridge over a tributary of Mud Creek. Then ascend and pass a number of interpretive markers at such trees as Eastern red cedar, white oak, sweet gum, and pine. At 0.5 mile, cross the stream again on a footbridge; to the right is an old farm spring. After that ascend to Gate #5 Road. (To the left, the road goes 240 yards to end at a housing development. To the right is a forest path to the picnic shelter.) Shepherd Nature Trail goes ahead on Gate #5 Road for 280 feet before turning right off the road. (Gate #5 Road goes 0.2 mile to NC 751.) Continuing on the nature trail, exit at the south side of the picnic shelter at 0.7 mile. Turn left on the gravel road to reach the point of origin at 0.8 mile and make your way back to NC 751 at 1.0 mile.

Gate #9 Road (0.4 mile round-trip; easy)

Trailhead and Description: This is an infrequently used, level, 960-foot path through a mixed young forest. It goes 0.2 mile to the forest property line; backtrack. From here, it is 0.2 mile west to Kerley Road (SR 1309) and 0.05 mile east to Gate #8.

Gate #14 and Kinsman Fire Trail (0.4 mile round-trip; easy)

Trailhead and Description: From the junction of Kerley Road and NC 751, go south 0.1 mile to Gate #14, on the right, to enter *Kinsman Fire Trail*. This is a pleasant, grassy trail among oak and pine with an understory of sourwood and dogwood dappled with sunlight. Two large oak trees form a centerpiece at the cul-de-sac at 0.2 mile. Backtrack.

Gate D Road and Picnic Area (0.2 mile round-trip; easy)

Trailhead and Description: Gate D is on the north side of NC 751; it is located 290 feet east of Gate #10 at the junction of Kerley Road. This gravel road leads 0.1 mile to a picnic table and grill under a large, spreading white oak. The impressive tree is typical of many in Duke Forest, where white oak predominates. Backtrack.

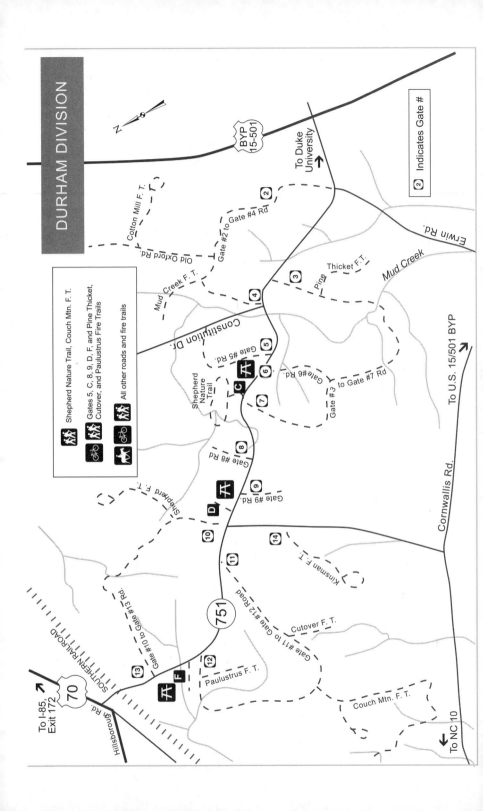

Gate #10 Road to Gate #13 Road (1.9 miles, easy)

Trailhead and Description: Using a second vehicle at either end of this hike is an advantage.

If beginning at *Gate #10 Road*, follow a gravel road used frequently by staff to reach Global Climate Research, a restricted research site off the south side of the road. At 0.1 mile, turn right on *Shepherd Fire Trail*, a route covered in duff and grass. After another 0.1 mile, turn onto an unnamed fire trail that leads 0.2 mile in and back; the scenic road boasts huge oak and hickory. Continuing on Shepherd Fire Trail, pass under a large power line to reach a cul-de-sac at 0.7 mile; wildflowers such as stone clover, yarrow, goldenrod, sneezeweed, and aster grow under the power line. Along the road banks are dogwood, deciduous holly, and downy arrowwood. Return to Gate #10 Road and turn right. On the right is a loblolly pine plantation planted in 1933 and thinned in 1954 and 1988, an example of the skillful silviculture throughout Duke Forest. On the left is another pine grove, planted in 1971 and thinned in 1991. Arrive at a power line at 1.0 mile, then pass a restricted gravel road, to the left. Wildflowers are along the road and under the power line. Cross a small stream and pass the main entrance to Global Climate Research. After passing the entrance, curve left at 1.4 miles to parallel a Southern Railroad line for the next 0.3 mile; the grassy road is bordered with willow in a wide forest space. Turn left at 1.8 miles. Arrive at Gate #13 Road on NC 751 at 1.9 miles. Backtrack or follow the highway to the left for 0.8 mile to return to Gate #10 Road. To the right on NC 751 and across the railroad bridge, it is 0.3 mile to the junction with U.S. 70.

Gate #11 Road to Gate #12 Road (3.2 miles or 5.4 miles round-trip; moderate)
Cutover Fire Trail (0.45 mile, easy)
Couch Mountain Fire Trail (2.1 miles round-trip; moderate)
Paulustrus Fire Trail (0.4 mile round-trip; moderate)

Trailheads and Description: Making these roads and fire trails into a loop and backtracking offers the longest hiking experience in the Durham Division. A main feature is the ascent of Couch Mountain, 640 feet in elevation.

Enter *Gate #11 Road*; pass a timber restoration of 1993 and 1996, to the left. At 0.1 mile, pass an unnamed restricted road, to the left; on the right is a forest-management demonstration area. At 0.3 mile, cross a small stream in a mixed forest of hardwoods and pine. Junction with *Cutover Fire Trail* at 0.45 mile; turn left. (Regardless of the fire trail's name, this is a thriving and maturing hardwood and loblolly pine forest.) After crossing a level area, descend to the forest property line. Backtrack to Gate #11 Road at 0.9 mile and turn left. Follow an undulation through an all-pine forest and reach a major triangle junction at 1.4 miles. To the right is part of the return loop; to the left is an ascent of Couch Mountain.

If hiking left, ascend 325 feet to *Couch Mountain Fire Trail*, on the left. To the right is a spur trail to Couch Mountain. If ascending the spur trail, it reaches the summit at 1.6 miles and circles the cul-de-sac in a high forest of oak, hickory, and pine enlivened by a showy display of dogwood in springtime. Return to Couch Mountain Fire Trail at 1.8 miles. The choices here are to turn right and include an additional 2.1 miles in your hike or to turn left to descend to the triangle and complete the loop. (Couch Mountain Fire Trail soon begins a 1.0-mile descent before reaching a ridge climb near the trail's end. At a few steep sections, there is road erosion. The sound of traffic from I-85 can be heard. Along the way are downy arrowwood and dogwood among a mixed forest. At 0.2 mile are large shagbark hickory. At 0.6 mile in a hollow are crested dwarf iris. At 0.7 mile, the forest hillside has a spectacular grove of large white oak. After two switchbacks, descend into an open area among blackberry bushes, and reach Gate #20 at private property. Backtrack for a round-trip of 2.1 miles.)

Continuing on the loop, descend to the triangle junction mentioned above. Turn left at 1.85 miles (4.0 miles if including Couch Mountain Fire Trail). Gradually descend on a well-graded road among hardwoods to a junction with a power line at 2.2 miles in an open area. Turn right (east) to junction with *Paulustrus Fire Trail*, located on the right at 2.3 miles. (Follow it to a dead end for a 0.4-mile round-trip through a pine forest with a ground cover of club moss.) Exit at Gate #12 Road to NC 751 at 2.7 miles (4.8 miles if including Couch Mountain Fire Trail).

To the right on NC 751, it is 0.5 mile to Gate #11 Road, for a total distance of 3.2 miles (5.3 miles if including Couch Mountain Fire Trail). To the left (west) on NC 751, it is 0.1 mile to the entrance to Picnic Area F and 280 yards on the entrance road to the R. L. Rigsbee Picnic Shelter, which offers tables, a grill, a pit toilet, and electricity; reservations and a fee are necessary for usage. Farther northwest on NC 751, it is 0.1 mile to Gate #13, on the right, described above. It is another 0.3 mile to U.S. 70 Business (also Hillsborough Road). A left turn on U.S. 70 Business leads 1.5 miles to Exit 170 at I-85; a right turn leads 2.5 miles to another junction with U.S. 15/501 Bypass.

Korstian Division (Orange County)

The 1,950-acre Korstian Division of Duke Forest is located southwest of the Durham Division between Mount Sinai Road (SR 1718) on the north and Whitfield Road (SR 1731) on the south. A distinctive feature is New Hope Creek, which originates in the hills west of the division and flows through the forest. The creek then flows between Durham and Chapel Hill and on south to Jordan Lake. Snaking through the New Hope Creek gorge, the stream is usually silted with its upstream soils. Seventeen gated roads and fire trails are in the division. Cement Bridge Road (Gates #25 and #23) and Wooden Bridge Road (Gate #24) are frequently used by walkers, joggers, runners, bikers, equestrians, and families with children and pets. Visitors must not go beyond the turnarounds at the ends of roads; trailblazing and footpath shortcuts to New Hope Creek result in severe erosion.

Using the two main gated forest roads, both of which cross New Hope Creek, visitors can enjoy an 11-mile loop hike, the longest option in the forest divisions; a second vehicle may be used for convenience by those hiking only half the distance.

From U.S. 15/501 Bypass, take Exit 107 and drive west 0.3 mile on Cameron Boulevard, then turn left on Erwin Road at the Duke Forest sign. Follow Erwin Road for 3.1 miles (pass a junction with Mount Sinai Road at 1.75 miles) and turn right on Whitfield Road. Drive 0.85 mile to Gate #25 at Cement Bridge Road, on the right. To access the other end of the loop, drive 0.5 mile farther on Whitfield Road to a narrow entrance on the right and Gate #24 at Wooden Bridge Road. (From that point on Whitfield Road, it is 2.05 miles to a junction with NC 86 and Exit 266 at I-40. To reach the northern access of Cement Bridge Road go 2.05 miles west on Mount Sinai Road from Erwin Road, or 3.0 miles east on Mount Sinai Road from NC 86.)

> **Gate #25 at Cement Bridge Road to Gate #24 at Wooden Bridge Road (10.3 miles combined; moderate)**
> **Hard Climb Road (1.2 miles round-trip; moderate)**
> **Midway Fire Trail (0.6 mile round-trip; easy)**
> **Thrift Fire Trail (0.4 mile round-trip; easy)**
> **Echinata Fire Trail (0.5 mile round-trip; easy)**
> **Big Bend Fire Trail (0.2 mile round-trip; easy)**
> **Wooden Bridge Road (1.9 miles; easy to moderate)**
> **Dead End Fire Trail (0.4 mile round-trip; easy)**
> **Bluff's End Fire Trail (0.5 mile round-trip; easy)**

Land's End Road (0.4 mile round-trip; easy)
West Road (0.6 mile round-trip; easy)
Unnamed Fire Trail (0.4 mile round-trip; easy)

Trailheads and Description: Enter Gate #25 at *Cement Bridge Road*, a gravel road, among tall hardwoods and pine. Gradually descend to cross New Hope Creek on a low-water cement bridge at 0.6 mile. After 315 feet, there is a junction with *Hard Climb Road*, to the right. Ascend steeply; at 1.1 miles, there is a junction with *Midway Fire Trail*, on the right. Turn right on a grassy route to descend to a junction with *Thrift Fire Trail*, on the left. Continue on Midway Fire Trail to a cemetery on the right at 1.3 miles. Reach the rim of the New Hope Creek gorge at 1.4 miles. Backtrack to Thrift Fire Trail at 1.6 miles. Turn right and follow it to a timber harvest at 1.8 miles, where patches of wild quinine and aster flourish in a sunny area. Return to Midway Fire Trail, turn right, and return to Hard Climb Road at 2.15 miles. Turn right. Cross a small drain and junction with *Echinata Fire Trail*, on the right at 2.3 miles. Turn right. Enter a timber cut prompted by a pine-beetle infestation, then descend to a cul-de-sac near the rim of the New Hope Creek gorge. After a return to the junction with Hard Climb Road at 2.8 miles, turn left. (The road to the north is not maintained and goes to private property.) Backtrack to Cement Bridge Road at 3.4 miles.

Turn right on Cement Bridge Road. At 3.5 miles, pass a timber cut prompted by a pine-beetle infestation in 1994. At 3.7 miles, reach the top of the hill. Turn left on *Big Bend Fire Trail*, which ends at the rim of a bend in New Hope Creek at 3.8 miles. Backtrack to Cement Bridge Road and turn left. At 4.1 miles, a development of private homes is noticeable through the forest to the right. Follow a generally straight road to a junction with *Wooden Bridge Road* at 4.5 miles. The options here are to turn left and make a loop back to Whitfield Road at 8.2 miles or to continue to Gate #23 on Mount Sinai Road at 4.8 miles.

If continuing to Gate #23, find roadside space for parking near the gate, but do not block the gate. On Mount Sinai Road, it is 1.9 miles east to Kerley Road and 3.0 miles west to NC 86. If backtracking, turn right at Wooden Bridge Road; pass through a large area of reforestation and reach a T junction at 5.3 miles. A right turn leads 200 feet to *Dead End Fire Trail*, on the left. (Straight ahead, it is 0.2 mile to the forest property line; backtrack.) On Dead End Fire Trail, cross a small stream and reach a cul-de-sac at 5.6 miles. Backtrack to Wooden Bridge Road and turn right at 5.8 miles. It is 0.4 mile through tall oak, maple, and pine to the New Hope Creek wooden bridge; the creek has a rocky streambed and occasional pools

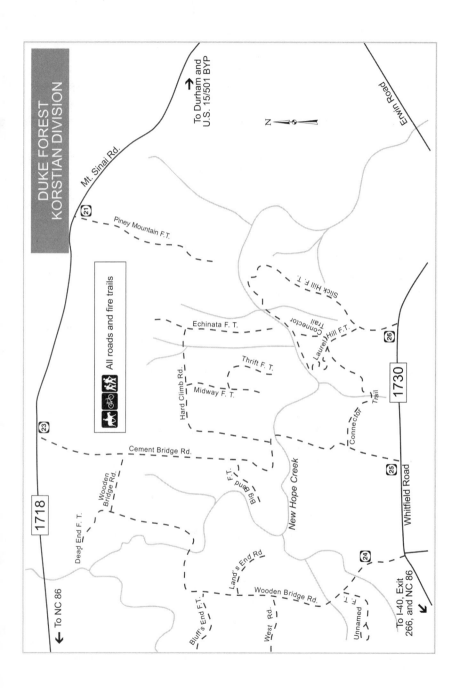

DUKE FOREST KORSTIAN DIVISION

All roads and fire trails

Mt. Sinai Rd.

To Durham and
U.S. 15/501 BYP

N

Erwin Road

Piney Mountain F.T.

21

Slick Hill F.T.

Echinata F. T.

Connector Trail

Laurel Hill F.T.

26

Thrift F. T.

Hard Climb Rd.

Midway F. T.

1730

Connector Trail

23

Cement Bridge Rd.

Big Bend F.T.

New Hope Creek

25

Whitfield Road

1718

Wooden Bridge Rd.

Dead End F. T.

Land's End Rd

Bluff's End F.T.

West Rd.

Wooden Bridge Rd.

F.T.

Unnamed

24

To NC 86

To I-40, Exit
266, and NC 86

under overhanging hardwood trees. Ascend steeply to cross under a Duke Power Company power line at 6.4 miles, then turn right on *Bluff's End Fire Trail* at 6.5 miles. Located on a tranquil and little-traveled ridgeline above the creek, the 0.5-mile trail dead-ends and makes a return to Wooden Bridge Road at 7.0 miles. Pass under the power line again and arrive at *Land's End Road*, located on the left at 7.1 miles. Follow it east, first on a level ridge, then descending southeast toward the rim of the gorge at 7.5 miles. Backtrack and turn left on Wooden Bridge Road.

At 8.0 miles, turn right on *West Road*. Pass under the power line again and reenter the forest at 8.2 miles. Here are red mulberry, black cohosh, buckeye, and redbud. The road ends at the forest property line at 8.3 miles. Backtrack to Wooden Bridge Road and turn right to begin a long descent. Cross an intermittent tributary of New Hope Creek at 8.9 miles. After 225 feet, turn right on an *unnamed fire trail*; it has a cul-de-sac and is a 0.4-mile round-trip. You will continue through a majestic part of the forest, cross a small stream, ascend, and reach a narrow roadside parking area 200 feet beyond Gate #24 at 9.7 miles. It is 0.1 mile on a narrow entrance road to Whitfield Road and 0.5 mile east on the road to roadside parking at Gate #25 at Cement Bridge Road, for a total loop of 10.3 miles. To the west on Whitfield Road, it is 2.1 miles to NC 86 and Exit 266 on I-40.

Gate #26 and Laurel Hill Fire Trail (1.0 mile round-trip; moderate) Slick Hill Fire Trail (1.4 miles round-trip; moderate)

Trailheads and Description: It is 0.3 mile east on Whitfield Road from Gate #25 at Cement Bridge Road to *Laurel Hill Fire Trail*.

Ascend slightly for 0.15 mile to a junction with *Slick Hill Fire Trail* on the right. Continue left on Laurel Hill Fire Trail, descending past a connector trail on the right at 0.2 mile. (The unnamed connector trail descends 0.2 mile to a rocky bluff at New Hope Creek.) At 0.25 mile, there is another connector on the left. (It goes 0.4 mile on the slope to connect with Cement Bridge Road.) At 0.4 mile, the trail arrives at a cul-de-sac and cliffs overlooking the creek. To the right are switchbacks into the New Hope Creek gorge; they lead among rocks to the creek side at 0.5 mile. Backtrack. Another option is to continue downstream on an unnamed connector trail. If following this connector trail, ascend a bluff at 0.2 mile to use or pass another connector to Laurel Hill Fire Trail on the right. If continuing down the creek among scenic rock formations, pass an island, and at 0.6 mile connect with an unnamed trail on the right that leaves the creek and ascends through a young forest to a cul-de-sac at 0.2 mile. Here it connects with Slick Hill Fire Trail. Ascend on the

Children running on Laurel Hill Fire Trail in Duke Forest in Durham

gravel road to reenter a more mature forest and join Laurel Hill Fire Trail at 0.7 mile. Along the way is an understory of huckleberry, downy arrowwood, and dogwood. Return to Whitfield Road at 2.0 miles, if completing the loop rather than making two backtracks.

Gate #21 at Piney Mountain Fire Trail (1.0 mile round-trip; easy)

Trailhead and Description: *Piney Mountain Fire Trail* is on the north side of the Korstian Division at Gate #21, across the road from Mount Sinai Baptist Church on Mount Sinai Road. If traveling from U.S. 15/501 Bypass, take Exit 107 and go 0.3 mile west on Cameron Boulevard. Turn left on Erwin Road at the Duke Forest sign. Follow Erwin Road for 1.9 miles to a junction with Mount Sinai Road on the right. Drive 1.0 mile farther to roadside parking on the left.

This pleasant, grassy fire trail has pine, maple, and oak with an understory of redbud, dogwood, downy arrowwood, and sourwood. After 0.3 mile, the trail reaches a new white-pine plantation, planted in 1975. Wildlife tracks may be visible in some of the shallow roadside ditches. At 0.5 mile, there is a high, breezy rim above New Hope Creek. A picnic table is located here among tall oak trees. Backtrack.

Eno Division (Orange County)

The 519-acre Eno Division is southeast of Hillsborough and west of Eno River State Park, between I-85 and I-40. Stony Creek runs through the division on its way east to the Eno River in Eno River State Park. The main artery in the division is Eno Road from Gate #28 to NC 86. Although *Flat Rock Fire Trail* is scenic and *Oak Hill Fire Trail* is historic, this division does not have many users. All of its pathways are described below.

Gate #28 at Eno Road (1.4 miles, easy)
Flat Rock Fire Trail (0.7 mile round-trip; easy)
Stone Wall Fire Trail (1.3 miles round-trip; easy)
Bivens Fire Trail (0.8 mile round-trip; easy)
Oak Hill Fire Trail (0.7 mile round-trip; easy)
Slick Rock Fire Trail (0.4 mile round-trip; easy)

Trailheads and Description: There are several ways to reach the Eno Division of Duke Forest. If driving west from Durham on I-85, turn north at Exit 170 onto U.S. 70. After 1.3 miles, turn left immediately past the traffic lights onto Old NC 10 (SR 1710). Drive 3.75 miles to the junction with New Hope Church Road (SR 1723); turn left. After 0.4 mile, you will reach Gate #28, on the right.

If driving from the east on I-40, take Exit 263 and follow New Hope Church Road 2.1 miles to Gate #28, on the left; on the way, cross NC 86 at 0.7 mile.

If approaching from the west on I-85, take Exit 165, drive south on NC 86 for 0.4 mile to Old NC 10, on the left; look closely after the I-85 exit because the road is easy to miss. Drive 2.1 miles to the junction with New Hope Church Road and turn right. Drive 0.4 mile to the roadside parking on the right.

From the junction of NC 86 and New Hope Church Road, it is 1.2 miles north on NC 86 to the Hillsborough District of the N.C. Forest Service (right) and Gate #29. This trailhead can also be reached from I-85, Exit 165, by following NC 86 south for 1.6 miles. Because the forest service gate is locked each day at 5 P.M., park outside the forest gate.

From *Gate #28 at Eno Road*, enter a forest of tall trees, then a new forest at 0.4 mile. Cross Stony Creek in an area of tall yellow poplar and low patches of filbert and buckeye, then enter an open area; to the left is evidence of a timber harvest. Gradually ascend to a junction with *Flat Rock Fire Trail*, to the right at 0.6 mile. Follow Flat Rock Fire Trail. At 0.7 mile, cross a

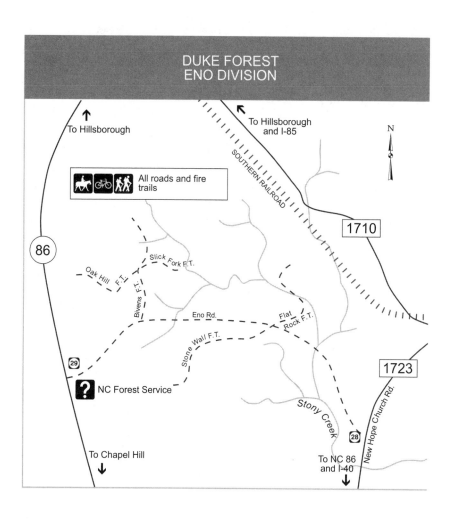

DUKE FOREST
ENO DIVISION

To Hillsborough

To Hillsborough
and I-85

N

SOUTHERN RAILROAD

All roads and fire
trails

1710

86

Slick Fork F.T.

Oak Hill F.T.

Bivens F.T.

Eno Rd.

Flat Rock F.T.

Stone Wall F.T.

29

1723

? NC Forest Service

Stony Creek

New Hope Church Rd.

28

To Chapel Hill

To NC 86
and I-40

footbridge over gurgling, rocky Stony Creek. The ground cover includes mosses, Pinxter, and rattlesnake orchid. You will reach the end of the road at 0.8 mile; backtrack. Turn right at Eno Road. Within 50 feet, turn left on *Stone Wall Fire Trail*, where there may be evidence of timber harvesting, thinning, and a planting process. Colicroot grows on the roadside. Reach a tributary of Stony Creek at 1.9 miles. Backtrack to Eno Road and turn left at 2.5 miles. The road passes through a young forest and descends to enter an older forest. Cross an intermittent stream at 2.9 miles. After this, the trail ascends, passes a timber-management area, located to the left, and arrives at *Bivens Fire Trail* at 3.1 miles.

Turn right on Bivens Fire Trail. Pass through a forest of hardwoods and pine to a junction with *Oak Hill Fire Trail* at 3.3 miles. Turn left and ascend in a pine forest to the rock foundation of a farm building, on the left at 3.4 miles. Cross an imposing level area to reach a hilltop of oak trees at 3.6 miles. Backtrack to Bivens Fire Trail and turn left. After 110 feet, turn right on *Slick Rock Fire Trail*. Descend slightly on a rarely used road to a small stream for a respite among spicebush, jack-in-the-pulpit, and green and gold. Backtrack to Bivens Fire Trail at 4.3 miles. Turn right, descend, and enter a section where timber was harvested in 1996. After crossing a small stream, ascend to the forest boundary at 4.5 miles. Backtrack to Eno Road at 5.0 miles. A right turn leads 0.2 mile to Gate #29 at the maintenance area of the N.C. Forest Service, for a total hike of 5.3 miles. Or you can backtrack another 1.0 mile on Eno Road to Gate #28 for a total of 6.3 miles.

Hillsborough Division (Orange County)

In this 645-acre division, there are old and currently used quarries of blue stone. The division has also been used in timber harvesting, particularly of shortleaf and loblolly pine. Two of the forest roads have trailheads close to each other on U.S. 70. The other road is farther west and off U.S. 70. All are on the west side of Hillsborough. The Eno River flows north to south through the division, and U.S. 70 runs east-west. Only one fire road is open to the public for hiking.

▌ Gate #31 and Wagon Fire Trail (1.2 miles round-trip; easy)

Trailhead and Description: Access to *Gate #31 and Wagon Fire Trail* is on the north side of U.S. 70 (Cornelius Street), 1.5 miles west of the junction with NC 86 (Churston Street) in Hillsborough. From the west, take Exit 161 off I-85 and go 0.9 mile to U.S. 70, then go 1.0 mile east on U.S. 70 to the gate, located on the left near the junction with West Hill Avenue. Enter the gate. Cross a small stream at 0.2 mile in an area damaged by a tornado in 1992. The tornado damage is no longer noticeable. A stand of pine was replanted in 1994. Skullcap, coreopsis, aster, wild indigo, buttercup, and wild rose grow on the road banks. Deer may be seen in the grassy areas. At 0.3 mile, you will enter a forest of tall pine; periwinkle is on the north side of the road. Cross a small stream and reach the trail's end at 0.6 mile. Backtrack for a round-trip hike of 1.2 miles.

Blackwood Division (Orange County)

The Blackwood Division offers unique topography, the forest's highest hill (Bald Mountain, 762 feet in elevation), and part of a swamp known as Meadow Flats. The division is comprised of one large tract and three smaller tracts. In the division's 998 acres, there are 16 compartments and 11 roads and fire trails. Because of restricted research, the routes to seven of these roads and trails are closed north of Eubanks Road (SR 1727). Two other short fire trails have private access in a separate tract near Blackwood Mountain, but the enchanting 1.1-mile *Bald Mountain Fire Trail* described below is open to the public on the west side of Old NC 86.

Bald Mountain Fire Trail (2.2 miles round-trip; easy)

Trailhead and Description: Access to *Bald Mountain Fire Trail* is 4.1 miles south on Old NC 86 (SR 1009) from its junction with Exit 261 at I-85. (There is also an access from I-40 at Exit 266.) Drive west for 3.2 miles on Eubanks Road (SR 1717) to Old NC 86. After a right turn, it is 0.8 mile to the fire trail, on the left (west). Parking is limited, and neighbors discourage parking in their driveways.

Enter the forest on a grassy road and ascend slightly at 0.3 mile. At 0.5 mile, there is a poplar about 15 feet in circumference along with a large patch of crested dwarf iris. Curve around the south slope of Bald Mountain in an oak/hickory forest and follow the edge of the forest boundary markers. Deer, squirrel, raccoon, and owl inhabit the area. At 0.9 mile, cross a ridge in a pristine setting. Descend to the trail's end between pine and hickory at 1.1 miles. Backtrack.

Johnston County Community College
(Johnston County—Smithfield)

Rudolph Howell and Son Environmental Learning Center

Rudolph Howell and Son Environmental Learning Center
6601 Devil's Racetrack Road
Four Oaks, NC 27524
Telephone: 919-938-0015
www.johnstoncc.edu/information/howellwoods/

Johnston County Community College, a large community college in the urban environment of Smithfield, enhances its biological science program at the Rudolph Howell and Son Environmental Learning Center, which is also known as Howell Woods. Located near the Neuse River, the center is part of a 2,856-acre donation made by Rudolph Howell in 1993. Situated about 11 miles south of the college's main campus, it provides a convenient research environment for the faculty and students. A vast network of old roads connects to offer 30 miles of trails, some of which are not open to the public. The preserve is open daily, but the office is open 8:00 A.M. to 5:00 P.M. Monday through Friday. Camping is prohibited. For hunting, fishing, horseback riding, and mountain biking, a fee may be charged. Call in advance for specific information.

The center has 16 trails that have either mowed paths or paths with a sand or gravel base. In heavy rains, flooding may close some roads and trails. (Inquire about the conditions of longer roads, such as River Loop West and East that travel through wetlands near the river.) Researchers have identified 58 species of butterflies, 62 species of dragon- and damselflies, 43 species of reptiles, 42 species of mammals, and 154 species of flora in this biological preserve. Visitors will likely see many of these species in any season. Hikers should wear hiking boots in all seasons. They should use insect repellent in warm or hot weather.

Before starting a hike, hikers should get a map from the office to identify the trails. Individual trail descriptions are waived here because there is so much repetitive information. The trails are listed here in alphabetical order. They offer a total of 8.9 miles of hiking possibilities.

Bartram Trail (0.2 mile, easy, mowed)
Box Turtle Trail (0.3 mile, easy, mowed)
B.W. Wells Trail (0.24 mile, easy, mowed)
Cornell Road (0.3 mile, easy, sand/gravel)
Diversity Trail (0.7 mile, easy, sandy)
Fox Squirrel Trail (0.3 mile, easy, sandy/mowed)
Howell Drive (2.5 miles, easy, improved gravel)
Leopold Trail (0.4 mile, easy, mowed)
Loblolly Lane Trail (0.6 mile, easy, mowed)
Longleaf Lane (0.25 mile, easy, sandy)
Outside Slough Trail (0.2 mile, easy, mowed)
Owl Box Trail (0.1 mile, easy, mowed)
Plantation Road (1.6 miles, easy, improved gravel)
Smokey Trail (0.2 mile, easy, mowed)
Thoreau Trail (0.6 mile, easy, mowed)
Wild Turkey Lane (0.25 mile, easy, sandy)

Trailheads and Description: From Smithfield, drive south on I-95 to Exit 90. Turn right onto U.S. 701 and go over I-95. Turn left onto the access road, which is Devil's Racetrack Road (SR 1009). After 8.0 miles, turn left at the sign.

North Carolina State University

Carl A. Schenck Memorial Forest (Wake County)

Loblolly Trail (6.0 miles, easy)
Frances Liles Interpretive Trail (1.2 miles, easy)

Trailheads and Description: The Carl A. Schenck Memorial Forest is a research laboratory of conifers and broad-leaved trees on the university property between Wade Avenue and Reedy Creek Park Road (SR 1650) in Raleigh. These two trails were covered in detail in Chapter 4 under "Loblolly Trail" in the "Other Raleigh Trails" section of the Raleigh coverage.

Hill Forest (Durham County)

The 2,400-acre Hill Forest is located north of Durham and southeast of Rougemont. The forest is on both sides of the Flat River, which flows into

Lake Michie and then Falls Lake; State Forest Road (SR 1614) provides an access bridge to either side.

The forest has a network of forest roads that may be used by the public for day-hiking. Permission is required; if you cannot reach the caretaker at 919-477-1125, call the N.C. State University Department of Forestry at 919-515-2891. Camping and hunting are not allowed.

Because the forest roads in Hill Forest are not named or numbered, the following trail descriptions are designated as the first, second, third, and fourth nature walks.

First Nature Walk (1.6 miles, easy)
Second Nature Walk (1.2 miles, easy)
Third Nature Walk (3.8 miles, easy)
Fourth Nature Walk (2.9 miles, easy)

Trailheads and Description: To reach the forest from I-85 in Durham, drive 12.5 miles north on U.S. 501 to the Quail Roost community and turn right on Moores Mill Road (SR 1601); from Rougemont, go 2.0 miles south on U.S. 501 and turn left on Moores Mill Road. Turn right immediately on the gravel State Forest Road. The entrance to George K. Slocum Forestry Camp and the caretaker's office is on the left after 0.8 mile. Reserved camping is allowed beyond the office.

For the *First Nature Walk*, continue east on State Forest Road for 0.3 mile from the access to Slocum Forestry Camp, descending to a left curve. On the right of the curve is the forest road entrance; parking in this area is difficult. Ascend on a narrow road and pass through a pine forest planted in 1952 and thinned in 1982; a prescribed burn was done here in 1992. Along the roadside are sensitive pea, selfheal, and wild basil. On the right at 0.2 mile is a young forest of poplar planted in 1978. Cross a rocky stream at 0.4 mile and ascend in an older forest of large white oak. Parts of the roadway are eroded. The road then levels off. At 0.8 mile, enter a pine forest planted in 1962. Descend, pass an old, eroded road (left), and enter a mature loblolly pine forest at 1.4 miles. Pass an area of harvested timber and exit at Quail Roost Road (SR 1615) at 1.6 miles. To the right, it is 1.2 miles to U.S. 501; another right turn leads 0.4 mile to Moores Mill Road, on the right.

The *Second Nature Walk* begins across the Flat River, 0.2 mile from the beginning of the walk described above. Cross the bridge on State Forest Road and ascend steeply in a curve to a forest road on the right. Again, there is only roadside parking. Walk past the gate, which may be open during the summer months. Pass through a loblolly-pine plantation, then enter an open

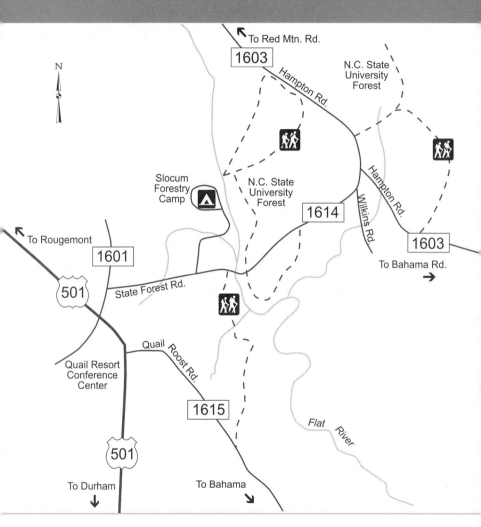

To Red Mtn. Rd.

1603

Hampton Rd.

N.C. State
University
Forest

N

To Rougemont

1601

501

State Forest Rd.

Slocum
Forestry
Camp

N.C. State
University
Forest

1614

Hampton Rd.

Wilkins Rd.

1603

To Bahama Rd.

Quail Roost Rd.

Quail Resort
Conference
Center

1615

Flat River

501

To Durham

To Bahama

space before entering a forest of Virginia yellow pine at 0.2 mile; notice a sign forbidding road usage by equestrians and bikers. Descend to a low area among oak, maple, poplar, and holly. Ascend to a stand of pine on the right and pass an old tobacco barn and other abandoned buildings before exiting to State Forest Road at 1.2 miles. To the left, it is 0.5 mile on the gravel road to where you started.

The *Third Nature Walk*, which may also be hiked as a loop, has an entrance across State Forest Road from where you began the second trail. Enter a narrow, but more frequently used, road and pass through a young forest for 0.4 mile. At 0.75 mile, there is a magnificent stand of white pine planted in 1941 and pruned first in 1965 and more recently in 1984. The road divides at a curve; an extremely sharp curve is to the left. Here, you have an option for completing the loop. If continuing to the right, ascend through a loblolly-pine plantation planted in 1950. At 1.15 miles on the right is a stand of pond pine, infrequent in this part of the state. Pass a private house, to the left, and arrive at Hampton Road (SR 1603) at 1.6 miles. Turn left and follow Hampton Road 0.4 mile to a forest road on the left. You will enter a steel-blue gravel road at 2.0 miles, then pass a large, unique rock formation in the woods to the left. At 2.6 miles, reach a controlled forest burn, right and left; this is a bobwhite and quail management area. Gradually descend; the Flat River is to the right. Curve left, cross a tributary of the Flat River, and complete the loop at 3.0 miles. Turn right and return to the point of origin at State Forest Road at 3.8 miles.

The *Fourth Nature Walk* is farther northeast. From the entrance of the third trail on State Forest Road, drive east 1.0 mile to Wilkins Road (SR 1613). Turn left and drive to the junction with Hampton Road. Follow Hampton Road to the left; after 0.2 mile, look for the forest road to the right. After entering the forest, notice open areas for the first 0.3 mile, then large hardwoods and pine. Descend, cross a small stream, and ascend in a hardwood forest to a road fork at 0.4 mile. If continuing left, enter an area of natural-forest reproduction, then a combination of oak species and Virginia yellow pine. Before reaching the gate and a dead end at 0.9 mile, pass through a rocky area, which has infrequently seen chestnut oaks. Backtrack to the fork and turn left at 1.3 miles. Descend to some white pines planted in 1968. At 1.5 miles, pass an abandoned road (left) and ascend through mature loblolly pine. Descend, then approach a timbered area at 2.1 miles. Turn right at a gravel forest road, which travels among saplings and wildflowers. Arrive at a gate and Hampton Road at 2.3 miles. Turn right on Hampton Road and go 0.6 mile back to the trail's beginning, for a total hike of 2.9 miles.

Goodwin Forest (Moore County)

Although Goodwin Forest offers no developed trails, there are 4.1 miles of single-lane access roads open to hikers.

ACCESS: If approaching from Carthage, go west on NC 22/24/27 for 1.3 miles to the junction with Bethlehem Church Road (SR 1261); turn left. After 1.5 miles, enter Goodwin Forest. Follow the first road to the left or go straight ahead. Permission for hiking is required from the College of Forest Resources, Department of Forestry, NCSU, Box 8002, Raleigh, NC 27695 (919-515-2891).

University of North Carolina at Chapel Hill

N.C. Botanical Garden (Orange County)

N.C. Botanical Garden
University of North Carolina
CB# 3375 Totten Center
Chapel Hill, NC 27599
Telephone: 919-962-0522
www.ncbg.unc.edu

The 600-acre N.C. Botanical Garden is a preserve of Southeastern trees, shrubs, plants, ferns, wildflowers, and herbs. Its self-guided nature trails are open daily; the administrative offices are open Monday through Friday. Guided tours of the garden are offered by prior arrangements to groups of 10 to 60 people. In addition to trails, there are short access points to plant collections, one of which is about poisonous plants. Sculpture and picnic tables are placed among some of the collections.

In 2007, construction began on a new 30,000-square-foot building, which will be used for education with an emphasis on recycling.

The garden's trail system, including the trail connections or unofficial trails, has undergone a transformation. For many years, the units were called the N.C. Botanical Garden Nature Trail. They are now referred to as the *Piedmont Nature Trails* and have subtitles, as well as color-coded markers and arrows.

Streamside Self-Guided Trail (0.5 mile)
Oak-Hickory Trail (0.7 mile)

Length and Difficulty: 1.2 miles combined; easy to moderate
Trailheads and Description: N.C. Botanical Garden is located in east Chapel Hill at Laurel Hill Road (SR 1901) off U.S. 15/501, 0.7 mile south of the junction of U.S. 15/501 and NC 54. Watch for the turn signs.

From the visitor parking area, follow the trail access for 0.1 mile to the yellow-blazed *Streamside Self-Guided Trail*, going right and left. If taking a left, follow the numbered interpretive signs and cross Meeting of the Waters Creek at 0.1 mile. There are benches here. Continue the loop with three passes on the left to red-blazed *Oak-Hickory Trail*. At 0.4 mile, cross the creek again. Return to complete the loop.

To hike the Oak-Hickory Trail, choose any of the access points mentioned above and ascend into a hardwood forest. There are scattered pines and some understory of holly and beech. If taking the first access from the first crossing of Meeting of the Waters Creek, go 0.2 mile to a fork that ascends among some ridge points for a circle around a knob. At 0.4 mile, reach a short connector on the right. Continue straight until connecting with the Streamside Self-Guided Trail for a return to the parking area.

Mason Farm Biological Preserve (Orange County)

Mason Farm Biological Preserve has about 1.5 miles of fire roads that provide easy walking in a natural area. To visit the preserve, request a free permit at the Totten Center. A drive from the botanical garden is 0.7 mile east on Old Mason Farm Road to a right turn on Finley Golf Course Road. Ascend to the clubhouse and drive around the building to the far side where there is a small sign indicating the preserve is to the right. Descend on a narrow gravel road to a gate. From there it is 0.3 mile to a right turn over Morgan Creek on a low-water concrete bridge. Approach the parking space ahead. *Note:* Use caution at the bridge crossing after a rain or during higher-than-normal water levels.

Penny's Bend Nature Preserve (Durham County)

The 84-acre Penny's Bend Nature Preserve is upstream from Falls Lake on the north side of the Eno River. It is managed by the N.C. Botanical Garden under a long-term lease from the U.S. Army Corps of Engineers.

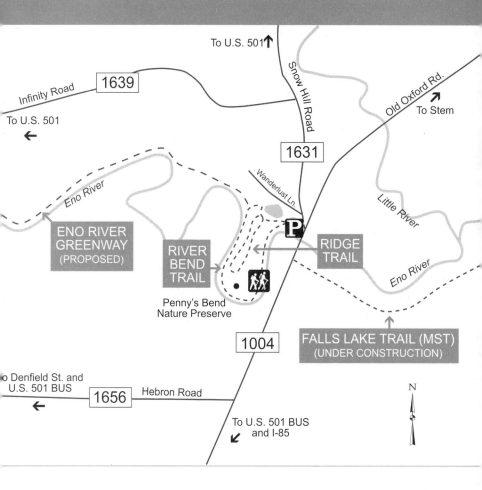

UNIVERSITY OF N.C. AT CHAPEL HILL
PENNY'S BEND NATURE PRESERVE

To U.S. 501↑

Infinity Road

1639

To U.S. 501
←

Snow Hill Road

Old Oxford Rd.

To Stem ↗

1631

Wanderlust Ln.

Eno River

Little River

ENO RIVER
GREENWAY
(PROPOSED)

RIVER
BEND
TRAIL

P

RIDGE
TRAIL

Eno River

Penny's Bend
Nature Preserve

FALLS LAKE TRAIL (MST)
(UNDER CONSTRUCTION)

1004

o Denfield St. and
U.S. 501 BUS
←

1656   Hebron Road

To U.S. 501 BUS
and I-85 ↙

N

The preserve is unique because of its diabase geological structure and unusual vascular flora. The diabase of igneous rock is resistant to erosion, so it deflects the Eno River, causing the river to form an oxbow shape. The rocky slope of the river and the soil on the ridge-top meadows contain wildflowers more common to the prairies of the Midwest than the Southeast.

The preserve's history can be traced to the ancestral plantation of Duncan Cameron in the 1830s. Near the parking area of today's preserve is the site of Cameron's Mill, which served as a gristmill and sawmill. The rich grasslands within the river bend were excellent pasture for the Cameron family's livestock. The source of the bend's name is uncertain.

River Bend Trail (1.8 miles, easy)
Ridge Trail (0.7 mile, easy)

Trailheads and Description: From the junction of I-85 and U.S. 15 Business (Exit 177B, if going west; Exit 177C, if going east), drive north on Roxboro Road for 1.3 miles and turn right on Old Oxford Road. After 3.3 miles, cross the Eno River bridge; turn immediately left to the parking lot on Snow Hill Road (SR 1631).

From the parking area, enter the preserve at the sign to enjoy the wildflower field stations. Some of the stations are for wild blue indigo, wild smooth coneflower, tall larkspur, and hoary puccoon. Follow *River Bend Trail* into the woods and hike by the riverside to a fork at 0.1 mile. Stay left and follow the riverbank among dense oak, elm, walnut, and sycamore. At 1.0 mile, there is a huge grapevine. You will pass a rocky area on the right, then some river rapids. Turn right to ascend a rocky slope covered with wildflowers at 1.4 miles. Turn right at a woods road and enter a field; the caretaker's residence is to the left near a pond. At 1.6 miles, reach a junction with *Ridge Trail*, which forms a loop partly in the field to the right and along the ridge rim of the river. Continuing on River Bend Trail, pass under two large post oak trees, descend, and turn left at a fork at 1.7 miles. Return to the parking lot.

CHAPTER 6

Trails in the Triangle's Neighboring Counties

This chapter describes some distinguished trails that are found in the counties that adjoin the seven-county Triangle. These trails are within a 55-mile radius of the center of the Triangle. The counties included are Person County, which is north of Orange and Durham counties; Halifax County, which adjoins Franklin County; Nash County, which adjoins Franklin and Wake counties; Wilson and Wayne counties, which border Johnston County, and Cumberland County, which adjoins Harnett County.

Outstanding parks located farther west, such as Cedarock Park in Alamance County, are covered in *Trails of the Triad*, a guidebook covering the 12-county region that surrounds Greensboro, Winston-Salem, and High Point.

When visiting these trails, it is suggested that visitors have a state map such as *North Carolina Atlas & Gazetteer*, published by DeLorme. Call in advance if there are questions about camping, trail locations and conditions, and points of interest near the park. Trail users may also consider a visit to more than one location, depending on proximity.

The sections ahead are listed in alphabetical order by city or location.

Fayetteville (Cumberland County)

Cumberland County was founded in 1754; the county seat of Fayetteville was founded in 1762. The county contains part of Fort Bragg in the northwest. The Cape Fear River runs through the county from north to south. The trails mentioned here are found along the river at the Cape Fear Botanical Garden, J. Bayard Clark Nature Center, and the Cape Fear Trail. Because of their proximity, the trails here are described in order going from south to north.

The Fayetteville-Cumberland Parks and Recreation Department, in association with other organizations, has proposed a greenway that will run from the library downtown to Cape Fear Botanical Garden and from J. Bayard Clark Nature Center to the botanical garden.

> **Fayetteville-Cumberland Parks and Recreation Department**
> **122 Lamont Street**
> **Fayetteville, NC 28301**
> **Telephone: 910-433-1547 or 1415; fax: 910-433-1762**

Cape Fear Botanical Garden

> **Cape Fear Botanical Garden**
> **P. O. Box 53485 (mailing)**
> **532 North Eastern Boulevard (physical location)**
> **Fayetteville, NC 28301**
> **Telephone: 910-486-0221; fax: 910-846-4209**
> **www.capefearbg.org**

Cape Fear Botanical Garden encourages environmental stewardship with research, conservation, and preservation, involving the community in the process. Once you visit the natural wonders in these 85 acres, you will know the garden is accomplishing its mission.

Facilities include picnic tables, an amphitheater, a pavilion, restrooms, and charming lawns, which offer perfect settings for weddings. The garden is open daily from 10:00 A.M. to 5:00 P.M. except on Sunday when it is open from 1:00 P.M. to 5:00 P.M. The garden is closed from December 21 to January 1. During April, visitations are free. At other times, the fee is $5 for adults and $4 for military personnel; children can visit for free.

River Trail
Rim Walk-Laurel Loop-Oak Loop Trail

Length and Difficulty: 1.2 miles combined; easy

Trailheads and Description: From the junction of NC 24 and Business I-95/U.S. 301 (North Eastern Boulevard), drive north on Business I-95/U.S. 301 for 0.4 mile and turn right at the sign. If driving south on Business I-95/U.S. 301, slow down after crossing the Cape Fear River and make a hairpen right turn onto a service road. Drive north to pass under the bridge and turn left to enter the parking lot. (This driving arrangement is necessary because there is a barrier in the center of the highway.)

Located between the Neuse River and Cross Creek, the garden has more than 2,000 species of ornamental plants. Hundreds of additional plants are found among the special gardens that include a children's garden. The garden's network of trails runs alongside azaleas, camellias, day lilies, ferns, and native wildflowers—all blended in with the tall hardwoods and pines. You can experience this blend on *River Trail*, which runs along the banks of the Cape Fear River, and on *Rim Walk-Laurel Loop-Oak Loop Trail*, which run along the bluffs of Cross Creek. Taken together, these trails combine for a 1.2-mile walk through an enchanting forest.

J. Bayard Clark Park and Nature Center

J. Bayard Clark Park and Nature Center
631 Sherman Drive
Fayetteville, NC 28301
Telephone: 910-433-1579; fax: 910-488-1437

The 76-acre J. Bayard Clark Park was established in 1959, while the nature center was opened in 1990. Facilities include picnic areas, display exhibits, restrooms, and semi-private tent camping with cold-water bathrooms. Advance reservations are necessary for camping. The center is open from 8:00 A.M. to 4:30 P.M. Monday through Saturday. It is closed on major holidays. Visitors need to be prepared for ticks, mosquitoes, and red bugs during the summer months.

Bear Trail (0.6 mile, easy)
Wetlanders Trail (0.6 mile, easy)
Laurel Trail (0.3 mile, easy)

Trailheads and Description: From U.S. 401 in north Fayetteville, turn east on Sherman Drive and drive 0.4 mile. If beginning at the picnic area near the waterfall, follow *Bear Trail* to a loop that will twice cross a utility line. The trail has two accesses to scenic views of the Cape Fear River. Along the way, there are large loblolly pines. On the return, there is a connection with *Wetlanders Trail*, which has displays of ferns and switch cane. Some of the trail travels over boardwalks. At 0.3 mile, there is a scenic stream crossing. Cross a scenic bridge, then cross the entrance road to reach the nature center. *Laurel Trail*, which begins close to the nature center, is named for the mountain laurel found along the way. It is unusual for this plant to grow this far east of the mountains.

Cape Fear Trail (4.0 miles one-way; easy to moderate)

Trailheads and Description: The southern access to *Cape Fear Trail* is the same as for J. Bayard Clark Park and Nature Center. Its northern trailhead is off U.S. 401 (3.0 miles north of Sherman Drive) on Tree Top Drive. It is 0.5 mile farther to Methodist University's Jordan Soccer Complex.

From the north end of the parking lot at the Clark Park and Nature Center, enter the elegant greenway. This skillfully designed classic trail

Cape Fear River Trail in Fayetteville passing over a waterfall and under a railroad

has historic sites, educational value, a virgin forest, birds and butterflies, mammals and amphibians, water to drink, and more. It passes through a forest of stately trees with some dense understories of buckeye, paw-paw, and mountain laurel. Parts of the trail run along the banks of an ancient river and parallel an active historic railroad. Other parts border floodplains and meander near the edges of entangled swamps—spaces that were rarely explored until the city developed this greenway. Facilities include benches, restrooms, and emergency telephones.

At 0.1 mile, there is a 690-foot boardwalk. Among the wildflower found along the trail are passionflowers, jewelweeds, beauty-bushes, and blue asters. Because the trail creates an open passage through the forest, birds are commonplace. At 0.45 mile, turn right on Eastwood Avenue to cross a railroad. At 0.6 mile, turn left and travel by the riverside. At 1.45 miles, there is a picnic table, restroom, and emergency telephone, followed by an arched bridge over picturesque Evans Creek. At 1.9 miles, cross a bridge over Three River and approach another picnic facility. Pass under a power line at 2.3 miles. At 2.8 miles, begin to follow an elevated boardwalk that goes under a shelter and railroad trestle. To the right, there is a deep ravine and waterfall, which is in contrast to the preceding flat wetlands. At 3.1 miles, there is a bench and restroom. Ascend, level off, and pass a golf course on the right. There is a small pond with water lilies at 3.8 miles. At 4.0 miles, arrive at a bench and information board. This is the end of the greenway. To the right at 4.2 miles are the parking lots for Methodist University's Jordan Soccer Complex, home of the Fayetteville Soccer Association.

Goldsboro (Wayne County)

Founded in 1847, Goldsboro is located on the north side of Neuse River. Southeast of the city is Seymour Johnson Air Force Base. From the base, it is 8.0 miles south (downstream) on NC 111 to the 355-acre Cliffs of the Neuse State Park, which includes a rare and scenic geological formation as well as trails and other recreational features. The *Mountains-to-Sea Trail* is scheduled to follow the Neuse River in this area.

Goldsboro Parks and Recreation Department
P.O. Drawer A
Goldsboro, NC 27533
Telephone: 919-739-7480; fax: 919-734-6201
For information about Cliffs of the Neuse State Park, call 919-778-6234

▌ Stoney Creek Trail (1.8 miles one-way; easy)

Trailhead and Description: To reach *Stoney Creek Trail*, turn south off Bypass U.S. 70/13 at Wayne Memorial Drive and turn at the first left onto Newton Drive. Turn left again on Quail Drive to Quail Park.

From here, begin the hike downstream past the picnic shelter. Trail blazes may be yellow or white. Plant life includes tall river birch, yellow poplar, laurel oak, and ironwood. Among the wildflowers located near the stream are cardinal flower and beauty-bush. The trail is also known for bird-watching. Cross Royall Avenue and go under the railroad trestle at 0.3 mile. At 1.1 miles, cross Ash Street to enter Stoney Creek Park.

Continue downstream, cross Elm Street, and at 1.8 miles arrive at South Slocumb Street. To the left is the entrance to Seymour Johnson Air Force Base. Turn right and go 130 yards to a dead-end street where there is a parking space. (There is a proposal for the *Mountains-to-Sea Trail* to travel conjunctively with Stoney Creek Trail from the trail's entrance to Slocumb Street. The trail crosses the road, descends, and connects with Arrington Bridge over the Neuse River after about 1.5 miles.)

Henderson (Vance County)

Henderson is located east and slightly north of the Triangle area. Like many other towns in the state, Henderson has a historic district, where there is a loop walk that travels among some of the old and cherished residences and businesses. The loop actually follows the street blocks that surround the courthouse square.

> **Henderson/Vance Recreation and Parks Department**
> P.O. Box 1556
> Henderson, NC 27536
> Telephone: 252-431-6093; fax: 252-438-2786

Fox Pond Park

Fox Pond Park has lighted tennis courts, sheltered picnic areas, a children's playground, youth baseball fields, fishing (but no swimming) facilities, and trails. The park is open year-round.

Fox Pond Trail (1.4 miles, easy)
Conoconors Trail (0.6 mile, easy)

Trailheads and Description: From NC 39 (0.4 mile east of U.S. 1 Bypass), turn onto Vicksboro Road (SR 1533) and drive 0.5 mile to the park, on the left.

From the parking lot near the tennis courts, begin *Fox Pond Trail* on the east side of the lake. Cross a floating bridge at the lake's headwaters at 0.5 mile. Cross a service road near a concrete bunker at 0.9 mile. Cross over the stream (near the dam) on a bridge at 1.3 miles and return to the parking lot. East of the parking lot is *Conoconors Trail*, which loops around the tennis courts, while traveling through sweet gum and yellow poplar trees.

Hyco Lake (Caswell County)

Hyco Lake, a reservoir of 3,750 acres, is northwest of Roxboro. The major headwaters for the reservoir are Hyco Creek and Hyco Creek South, which actually flows north.

Sixty-five-acre Hyco Lake Recreation Park, which is located on one of the lake's peninsulas, was opened in 1965. The park has facilities for camping, picnicking, swimming, boating, and fishing, as well as a network of educational trails.

Next to the park is the Natural Learning Area, conceived by the Person-Caswell Lake Authority. The park is open year-round.

> **Person-Caswell Lake Authority**
> P. O. Box 343
> Roxboro, NC 27573-0343

Hyco Lake Natural Learning Area

Beaver Trail (0.5 mile)
Campfire Trail (0.2 mile)
Rockpile Trail (0.2 mile)
Ridge Trail (250 yards)
Shore Trail (0.3 mile)

Length and Difficulty: 1.4 miles combined; easy to moderate

Trailheads and Description: From Roxboro, it is 10 miles northwest on NC 57 to a sign for the lake where you turn left. After 0.8 mile turn right, enter left of a gate, and curve left to ascend to a parking lot for hikers. (The town of Milton is 6.5 miles north on NC 57, near the Dan River and the Virginia state line.)

From the parking area, walk to the edge of the woods at the information booth. Enter the woods and descend on *Beaver Trail*. Along the way, there are Virginia pine, black gum, and dogwood. In open areas, there are blackberry, sumac, and cedar. Pass *Campfire Trail* at 0.1 mile, on the right, followed by *Rockpile Trail*. If following Rockpile Trail, ascend to a colorfully designed blind for observing birds such as titmouse, nuthatch, junco, wren, and blue jay. Descend to rejoin *Beaver Trail* at 0.3 mile. Soon after joining Beaver Trail, *Ridge Trail* goes to the right. Taking Ridge Trail, it is 0.6 mile to a 28-step descent to a scenic picnic area by the lake. Return to Campfire Trail and follow it to connect with *Shore Trail*. At 1.2 miles, ascend right on a service road for a return to the parking area at 1.4 miles.

John H. Kerr Dam and Reservoir

(Granville, Vance, and Warren counties)

Kerr Lake State Recreation Area

Kerr Lake State Recreation Area
6254 Satterwhite Point Road
Henderson, NC 25737
Telephone: 252-438-7791

The 48,900-acre John H. Kerr Reservoir was completed in 1953. It was named for the N. C. congressman whose leadership made the project possible. More than three-fourths of the project is located in the Virginia counties of Charlotte, Halifax, and Mecklenburg. Of the 29 recreation areas, nine are in North Carolina, including 6,200 acres of land that is leased to the state by the U.S. Army Corps of Engineers. The chief activities here are boating, sailing, water skiing, fishing, swimming, picnicking, and camping. The following recreation areas are part of Kerr Lake State Recreation Area: Bullocksville, County Line, Hibernia, Henderson Point, Kimball Point,

Nutbush Bridge, and Satterwhite Point. They offer a total of 700 campsites. All campgrounds are open from April 1 or Easter (whichever comes first). They close the last day of October. Two campgrounds (J. C. Cooper Point at Satterwhite and Nutbush Bridge) are open year-round. All campgrounds have some sites with electrical and water hookups. Three commercial marinas offer full services for fishermen, boaters, and campers. Bullocksville, Hibernia, and Satterwhite Point recreation areas all have hiking trails described here. (*The Trails of Virginia* by Allen de Hart, published by the University of North Carolina Press, has descriptions of the trails on the Virginia side of the reservoir.)

Bullocksville Recreation Area

▦ Old Still Trail (0.5 mile, easy)

Trailhead and Description: The recreation area is 3.3 miles west of Drewry on Bullocksville Road. To reach Drewry from I-85, take Exit 223 and go 2.3 miles west on Mason Road (SR 1237) or take Exit 226 and go 2.4 miles west on Ridgeway Road (SR 1224). Both exits are north of Henderson.

This recreation area has 75 campsites, a baseball field, picnic shelters, a children's playground, a community building, a fishing pier, and a nature trail. *Old Still Trail*, the nature-trail loop, has a trailhead across the road (north) from the baseball field. Hike the right access of the trail first. In an old forest at 0.3 mile, there is a sharp left turn leading to the former ruins of an old liquor still. Complete the loop at 0.5 mile.

Hibernia Recreation Area

▦ Hibernia Plantation Trail (1.1 miles round-trip, easy)

Trailhead and Description: From Henderson, take Exit 214 off I-85 and drive north on NC 39 for 13.7 miles. Turn right onto Hibernia Road (formerly Hargrove Road). After 2.2 miles, enter the gate for the recreation area.

This recreation area is on the west side of Kerr Lake, 5.0 miles south of the Virginia state line. Its facilities include 150 campsites in three major areas and one group camping area. There are also beach sections, a picnic area, and boat ramps.

From the gate, drive 0.5 mile and turn left at the access road to campground area #1 (it has 70 campsites). At the access road, there is a parking area, a public telephone, restrooms, and showers. The trailhead for *Hibernia Plantation Trail* begins at the northeast corner of the parking lot. Cross the main road to an entrance gate. Follow an exceptionally wide old road through the forest. This part of the trail, as with other connections, bears traces of Hibernia Plantation, which is now partly under the waters of Kerr Lake. *Hibernia* is Latin for "Little Ireland." The plantation was begun by Richard Hargrove in 1715. During the early 1950s, the plantation buildings were torn down in preparation for the making of the lake.

The trail has 20 interpretive posts that identify trees. (A brochure at the gate office lists 10 of these identifications, unless the park staff or volunteers have completed the list.) At 0.1 mile, there is a fork. Continue to the right. At 0.25 mile, a trail sign indicates a left turn to complete the loop and a right turn to go to Hargrove cemetery.

If going right, enter a spacious grassy field that is bordered with a cathedral of black walnut and Eastern red cedar. Ahead and through the field, the trail leads to the lapping waters along the lake shoreline. To the left of the field is the cemetery. Graves outside the gate are reburial sites that occurred after construction of the lake. Reading the gravestones provides knowledge of the colonial family. The grave of Colonel John Hargrove (1815-1900) is next to his son Charles, whose engraved tombstone has the verse "no pains, no griefs, no anxious fears can reach our loved one sleeping here."

On the return, follow the old road with the interpretive posts at 0.65 mile. After post #16, reach an old road at 0.9 mile. Turn left. (To the right, there is an access to the main road, where there is a grassy space with a few benches.) At 1.0 mile, complete the loop and turn right for a return to the parking lot.

Satterwhite Point Recreation Area

This recreation area actually has two sections—one at Satterwhite Point Park/J.C. Cooper Campground; the other at Satterwhite Point Marina. The campground has 79 campsites. Both trails described below are near

KERR LAKE STATE RECREATION AREA
HIBERNIA RECREATION AREA
HIBERNIA PLANTATION TRAIL

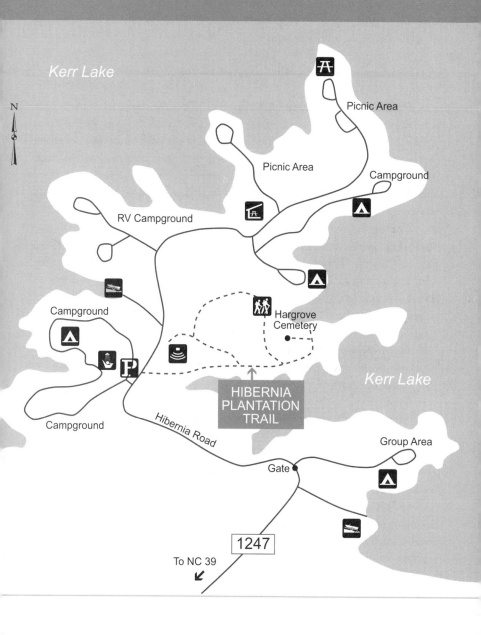

Kerr Lake

N

Picnic Area

Picnic Area

Campground

RV Campground

Campground

Campground

Hargrove Cemetery

HIBERNIA PLANTATION TRAIL

Kerr Lake

Hibernia Road

Group Area

Gate

1247

To NC 39

the campground. Facilities in the campground section include sheltered picnic areas, a beach, a children's playground, a community building, a group campground, and the park office and visitor center. The marina is at the north end of the main entrance road, where there is a marina office, boat service, a fuel dock, a store, and boat ramps.

▌ Henderson Nature Trail (1.5 miles round-trip; easy)

Trailhead and Description: From I-85, take Exit 217 in North Henderson. Turn north onto Satterwhite Road (SR 1319) and go 5.8 miles to the Satterwhite Point area. The trailhead is at the park office/visitor center, on the right, which is 0.1 mile east on the main entrance road across from the J.C. Cooper Campground. A second trailhead option is at the Outdoor Education Area, which is also on the right, 0.1 mile from the park office. If choosing the latter, pass the kiosk and enter the forest at a nature-trail sign.

The red-blazed *Henderson Nature Trail* has interpretive signs for tree identification. After frequent curves, arrive at an old road, going right and left, at 0.4 mile. Turn left and go 0.1 mile to a view of the lake from a red-clay embankment. Backtrack, but stay on the old road leading to a grassy knoll. To the left, there is an amphitheater; to the right, the gravesite of Richard Henderson (1735-85), the founder of Boonesborough, Kentucky, and Nashville, Tennessee.

From the amphitheater, go 0.6 mile to a paved and lighted interpretive walkway leading to the parking area at the visitor center at 0.75 mile. Backtrack or arrange for a shuttle.

▌ Big Poplar Hiking Trail (1.5 miles round-trip; easy)

Trailhead and Description: After entering the J.C. Cooper Campground, you have access to at least four sections of *Big Poplar Hiking Trail* from the campground. (The trail was mainly designed to connect the 123 campsites.) A visitor who only wants to hike the trail can choose a roadside space as long as a campsite is not blocked, or the visitor may park near the restroom/shower facility or the public telephone. If you choose to start from the campground section for sites #111-123, you can hike east from near the shower building.

The trail is used frequently, and its pathway has ribbons of roots that show years of exposure. At 0.1 mile, there is a cove with a streamlet with large American beech trees nearby. Big yellow poplar? Maybe a century ago, but not now. In addition to the beech trees (where tree carvings may have dates from the late 1890s), there are large white oaks, one of which may be the largest

KERR LAKE STATE RECREATION AREA
SATTERWHITE POINT RECREATION AREA
HENDERSON NATURE TRAIL
AND BIG POPLAR HIKING TRAIL

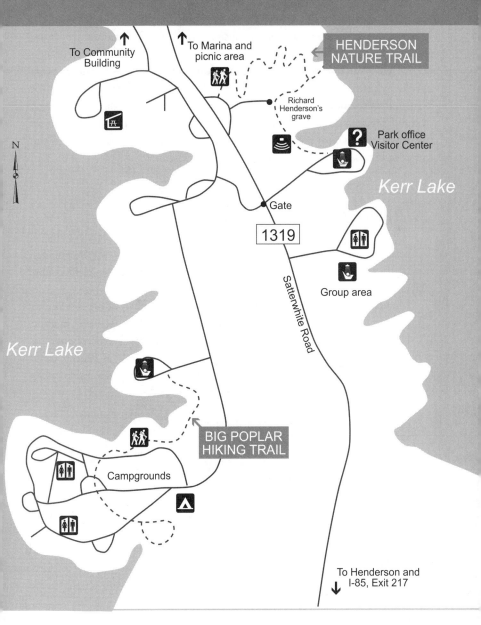

To Community Building

To Marina and picnic area

HENDERSON NATURE TRAIL

Richard Henderson's grave

Park office
Visitor Center

Kerr Lake

Gate

1319

Group area

Satterwhite Road

Kerr Lake

BIG POPLAR HIKING TRAIL

Campgrounds

To Henderson and I-85, Exit 217

N

tree you'll see along the trail. At 0.4 mile, cross a campground entrance road for sites beginning at #1. At 0.55 mile, exit the woods into a large grassy area, where there is a telephone, shower and restroom facilities, campsites for the physically handicapped, and the location for the campground host.

From here, you may not see a trail sign, but the trail continues across the road to a road fork. There is a "no entry" sign on the right and a yield sign on the left. Watch carefully for the trail bearing left. After 0.1 mile, there is a fork. If turning right, access a park road between campsites #74 and #75. Turn left onto the road, then turn left again into the woods near the end of the campsites. Rejoin the loop part of the trail. Turn right and return to the grassy area where the telephone is located at 0.4 mile. Backtrack to the camping section for sites #111-123 at 1.5 miles.

Mayo Lake (Person County)

Mill and May creeks, east of Roxboro, are the two headwater streams for the 2,800-acre Mayo Lake system. Parts of the Person Game Lands surround Mayo Lake.

Mayo Park is located on a peninsula of the lake. N.C. Wildlife Resources Commission operates a boat launch on the lake. Other facilities include RV campsites, platform and primitive tent sites, cabins, picnic shelters, a playground, bathhouses, and an amphitheater. A network of hiking trails makes loops within the park facilities. Annual events include several festivals and special events. The park is open year-round.

> **Person County Parks and Recreation Department**
> **425 Long Avenue**
> **Roxboro, NC 27573**
> **Telephone: 336-597-7806, park office; 336-597-1755,**
> **main office; fax: 336-597-1754**
> **www.visitroxboronc.com/index.htm**

Mayo Park

Lake View Trail (0.3 mile)
Wild Turkey Trail (0.5 mile)
Bridge Trail Loop (0.25 mile)
Eagle Trail (0.2 mile)

Red Tail Hawk Trail (1.9 miles)
Beaver Trail (1.1 miles)
Rocky Trail (0.9 mile)
Sappony Spring Trail (0.1 mile)

Length and Difficulty: 5.35 miles combined, including backtracking; easy to moderate

Trailheads and Description: To access Mayo Park from U.S. 501 in Roxboro, drive northeast on NC 49 for 9.0 miles to Neals Store Road and turn left. (It is 0.7 mile farther on NC 49 to Triple Springs and another 5.5 miles to the Virginia state line at Virgilina, where NC 49 intersects with NC 96.) On Neals Store Road, pass the main park entrance and park at the northwest corner of the boat-launch parking area for access to the trail system. All trails are well-designed with wraparound color blazes on the trees. The trails have numerous educational markers about plants and animals.

Begin the trail network at a display sign near a restroom at the boat-launch parking area. Follow directions for *Lake View Trail* and *Bridge Trail*, which are both loop trails. The forest has hardwoods of oak, yellow poplar, sweet gum, hornbeam, holly, and Virginia pine.

At the east end of the parking area, choose either direction of the lavendar-blazed *Eagle Trail* loop. A family cemetery is on the side nearest the parking area. The trail descends into a hollow of yellow poplar and ground cedar before ascending to cross the main park road. (Picnic shelters are to the left.) Connect with the red-blazed *Red Tail Hawk Trail* that joins with the yellow-blazed *Beaver Trail* to make a southern loop and with the gray-blue-blazed *Rocky Trail* to make a northern loop.

To follow Red Tail Hawk Trail, go right and descend to cross a footbridge over a stream. At 0.2 mile, pass through a beech grove near the lake, on the right, and park cabins, on the left. Ground cedar grows on a slope along the trail. At 0.6 mile, there is a patch of ebony spleenwort on the left. After going through the clear understory of a hardwood forest, pass an educational sign about the red-tailed hawk at 0.8 mile. Pass through scattered wildflowers and wild quinine at a power line at 0.9 mile. A primitive campground is on the left at 1.4 miles. Cross the park office road at 1.5 miles, followed by the brown-blazed *Sappony Spring Trail*, going to the left. After taking the Sappony Spring Trail and backtracking, turn left and complete the loop at 1.9 miles. Use Eagle and Wild Turkey trails for another 0.5 mile to return to the parking area.

Medoc Mountain State Park

(Halifax County)

The 2,286-acre Medoc Mountain State Park is on the granite fall line of the Piedmont, where the coastal-plain zone begins. The area was named for a grape-producing region in France, where a large vineyard operated in the nineteenth century. Although locally called a mountain because of its elevation relative to the rest of the area, at 325 feet above sea level the summit is more like a low ridge. Within the park, there are two main creeks: Little Fishing and Bear Swamp creeks. The creeks carry bluegill, large-mouth and Roanoke bass, redbreast sunfish, and chain pickerel. The forest consists mainly of hardwoods with understories of holly and mountain laurel located near the creeks.

Park rangers provide educational programs and information on the flora, fauna, and geology of the area. Recreational activities include fishing, picnicking, hiking, birding, tent camping, and canoeing. (Contact park staff regarding put-in and take-out points and water levels.) Camping facilities include tables, grills, tent pads, a central water source, and hot showers. Camping facilities for groups and families are available from mid-March through November. Reservations for groups are required. Otherwise, the campground is open year-round. Of the 34 campground sites, 12 have electrical hook-ups and two are handicapped accessible. Groceries and gasoline are available in nearby Hollister.

> **Medoc Mountain State Park**
> **154 Medoc State Park Road**
> **Hollister, NC 27844**
> **252-586-6588; fax: 252-586-1266**
> **www.ncparks.net/memo.html**

Air Awareness Trail (0.3 mile, easy)

Trailhead and Description: From the junction of U.S. 401 North and NC 561 in Louisburg, take NC 561 for 24 miles to the traffic light in Hollister. Turn right on Medoc Mountain Road (SR 1002), drive 2.6 miles to Medoc State Park Road (SR 1322), and turn left. After 0.5 mile, turn right to the campground, picnic area, and main trail access. If going to the park office first, stay on Medoc State Park Road for another mile and turn left. (The road continues another mile to connect with NC 561.)

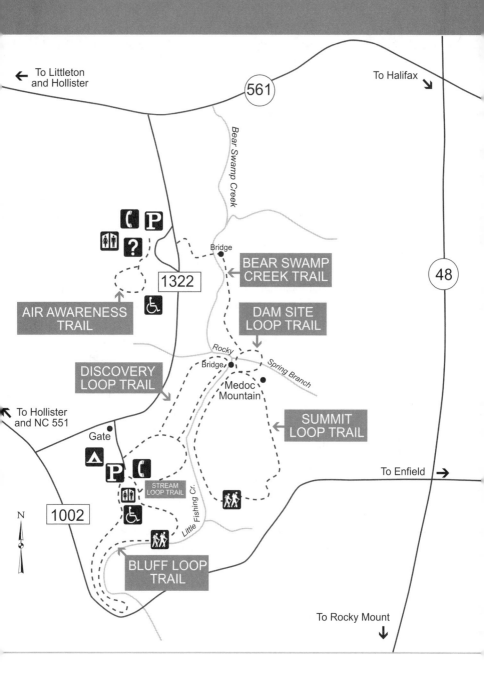

To Littleton and Hollister

To Halifax

561

48

Bear Swamp Creek

Bridge

BEAR SWAMP CREEK TRAIL

1322

AIR AWARENESS TRAIL

DAM SITE LOOP TRAIL

Rocky

Spring Branch

Bridge

DISCOVERY LOOP TRAIL

Medoc Mountain

SUMMIT LOOP TRAIL

To Hollister and NC 551

Gate

STREAM LOOP TRAIL

Little Fishing Cr.

To Enfield

N

1002

BLUFF LOOP TRAIL

To Rocky Mount

The unique *Air Awareness Trail* begins on the left side of the park office. It is a paved loop with six kiosks, which describe such topics as the earth's life-support system, climate, global warming, and air quality. At 0.2 mile, there is a well from an old homesite, which is lit by solar power.

Stream Loop Trail (0.8 mile)
Discovery Loop Trail (1.3 miles)
Bluff Loop Trail (2.9 miles)

Length and Difficulty: 5.0 miles combined with overlaps; easy

Trailheads and Description: From the picnic parking area and kiosk, go between the picnic shelter and restored tobacco barn for 60 yards to the trailhead. Enter the forest where *Stream Loop Trail* goes left and *Bluff Loop Trail* goes right.

If taking Stream Loop Trail, follow a well-designed and well-maintained passage through oak, beech, and loblolly pine with an understory of mountain laurel, holly, and aromatic bayberry. Rattlesnake orchid, partridgeberry, and club moss are part of the ground cover. At 0.2 mile, arrive at Little Fishing Creek and turn upstream. At 0.4 mile, there is a fork where Stream Loop Trail turns left and *Discovery Loop Trail* goes both right and left.

Turning left onto Stream Loop Trail, after 0.1 mile, there is a west loop connection with Discovery Loop Trail. It is 0.3 mile for a return to the parking area.

If continuing on Discovery Loop Trail, turn left near the creek at 0.7 mile. (At the pedestrian bridge over Little Fishing Creek, there is a connection with *Summit Loop Trail* and *Dam Site Loop Trail*, described ahead.) Continue on Discovery Loop Trail to rejoin Stream Loop Trail at 1.3 miles.

After originally entering the forest from the parking lot to the fork of Stream Loop Trail and Bluff Loop Trail, take a right onto Bluff Loop Trail. It is a wide, manicured trail that passes through a former field. At 0.4 mile, turn right (downstream) by Little Fishing Creek. Pass through large loblolly pine, beech, river birch, and oak, then climb to a steep bluff at 1.0 mile. Reach the highest bluff (over 60 feet) at 1.4 miles. Descend, bear right on a return ridge, and cross a stream at 2.6 miles. Return to the parking lot at 2.8 miles.

Bear Swamp Creek Trail (0.6 mile)
Dam Site Loop Trail (1.0 mile)
Summit Loop Trail (2.9 miles)

Length and Difficulty: 5.1 miles combined and backtracked; easy to moderate

Trailheads and Description: These trails can be accessed from *Discovery Trail* described above or by following directions below. To reach the white-blazed *Bear Swamp Creek Trail*, cross the road from the park office to a trail sign. Follow a wide passage into a black-walnut grove. Descend among large oaks and arrive at a steel pedestrian bridge at 0.25 mile. Cross the bridge and ascend a rocky slope of quartz and granite under a concentration of white oaks. (Users may notice the remains of old tobacco rows from a period when this was a farm.) At 0.6 mile, there is a junction with *Dam Site Loop Trail*, which goes to the right and left. (To the right, Dam Site Loop Trail descends easily, crosses a bridge over Spring Branch, and connects with *Summit Loop Trail* after 295 yards. Here, there is a steel footbridge across Little Fishing Creek, which leads to Discovery Trail.)

If taking the white-blazed Dam Site Loop Trail, clockwise users may see sparse plant and animal interpretive signs. Pass the remains of two rock dams; the second is at 0.4 mile. There are patches of holly and dense groves of mountain laurel. Scattered wild ginger and Christmas ferns are along the trail. After crossing two footbridges, ascend among dense mountain laurel on an old road. At 0.8 mile, there is a junction with the red-blazed Summit Loop Trail, which goes sharply right and ahead on the old road. (If making a loop of the Dam Site Loop Trail, turn right, descend to steps, and follow a

Bridge on Bear Creek Trail in Medoc Mountain State Park

switchback to Little Fishing Creek. Turn right, going upstream to a junction, on the left, with Bear Swamp Trail.)

If following Summit Loop Trail, stay ahead and ascend 100 yards to a bench near large oaks and a beautyberry patch. Turn right on an old, wide ridge-top road. At 0.7 mile, watch for a right turn that is easy to miss. Gradually descend in and out of coves and ridges to Little Fishing Creek and a bench at 1.7 miles. Turn right, going upstream; the pathway may be wet or flooded after heavy rains. Holly and mountain laurel intersperse the tall creekside trees. Cross a wooden bridge over a large ravine at 2.2 miles. At 2.6 miles, pass a large rock face with moss and lichens on the right and the steel pedestrian bridge across Little Fishing Creek to the left. At a trail sign, turn right, ascend to a switchback, climb up steps, and return to the point of origin at 2.9 miles. Backtrack to the creek and signs. Turn right. After 295 yards, connect with Bear Swamp Creek Trail on the left.

Rocky Mount (Nash County)

The city of Rocky Mount is located east of Raleigh. The city's parks and recreation department has successfully connected six parks located near the Tar River to create the *Tar River Trail*, which is described ahead.

In addition to the sections of the trail itself, there is a 0.5-mile loop around City Lake at the western trailhead for Tar River Trail. There is a large geyser in the center of the lake. The trailhead also features wildfowl observation sites. At the eastern trailhead, there is a 0.7-mile loop around an impressive landscape at Martin Luther King, Jr., Memorial Park.

Another trail supported by the city's parks and recreation department is the *Tar River Paddling Trail*, which offers camping platforms in the river for those paddling on the river.

> **Rocky Mount Parks and Recreation**
> **P.O. Drawer 1180 (mailing)**
> **331 South Frank Street (physical location)**
> **Rocky Mount, NC 27802**
> **Telephone: 252-972-1151; fax 252-972-1232**
> **www.ci.rocky-mount.nc.us**

Tar River Trail (3.0 miles, easy)

Trailhead and Description: Access to the upstream trailhead (western) is at Sunset Park. To reach Sunset Park from U.S. 64, exit onto U.S. 64

Bridge—the longest of its type in the nation—
on Tar River Trail in Rocky Mount

Business, which becomes Sunset Avenue. Cross U.S. 301 Bypass, and then cross the Tar River bridge. Turn right into City Park parking or continue ahead to turn left on Taylor Street. Go to Gay Street and turn left to access Sunset Park on the right. The trail begins at the corner of Gay Street and River Drive.

To reach the eastern trailhead, turn off U.S. 64 onto Atlantic Avenue. Go south on Atlantic Avenue to cross the Tar River bridge. Turn left on Virginia Avenue and then turn left on Leggett Road to reach Martin Luther King, Jr., Memorial Park.

Tar River Trail is a 3.0-mile, first-class greenway for scenic hiking and bicycling. It passes through old forests, leads to overlooks of the river, goes past historic sites, travels over wetlands, and leads over and under bridges and railroad trestles.

If starting at the western trailhead, the greenway leaves Sunset Park after 0.3 mile. Sunset Park has picnic shelters, tennis and basketball courts, a skate park, and a historic carousel. As the trail leaves the park, it enters the forest.

At 0.8 mile, cross a scenic boardwalk among tall cypress. At 0.9 mile, cross a 620-foot pedestrian bridge over the Tar River. This bridge adjoins the side of the Peachtree Street bridge. After crossing the river, cross Peachtree Street and then cross Falls Road to go into 54-acre Battle Park. To the left, there is a small parking area and farther to the left, there is a view of the Confederate Memorial. The memorial is near the entrance and parking areas on Battle Park Lane.

For the next 0.7 mile, the views of the river dam, rock formations, and forest are impressive. The long concrete-and-stone dam and the natural stones in the river that make the "Great Falls of the Tar River" can be viewed from the trail, from large boulders, or from a sheltered gazebo. Across the river, you can see Rocky Mount (Cotton) Mill, built in 1818 by Joel Battle. Although destroyed during the Civil War, the mill was rebuilt. It operated until 1998.

The trail passes under Church Street bridge at 2.2 miles. It then passes under a railroad trestle. At 2.6 miles, cross the Tar River on the longest (227 feet) single-span, wood-laminated bridge in the United States. Cross under the Atlantic Avenue bridge to a platform overlooking the river. Leave the river and curve left around Tom Stith and Talbert Park, which has top-quality athletic fields. Cross Leggett Road to the parking area at Martin Luther King, Jr., Memorial Park at 3.0 miles.

Roxboro (Person County)

Piedmont Community College

The city of Roxboro is located north of Durham. Piedmont Community College offers hiking trails on the college's forest property located between the main campus and Marlowe Creek. This area provides an outstanding opportunity for the study of the area's flora and fauna. The forest consists mainly of hardwood, with sections of conifers. It also offers scenic rock formations and wetlands. Hiking during daylight hours is allowed on a network of trails described ahead. The network, which consists of 10 individual trails, is called *Piedmont Community College Nature Trail*. Large groups using the trails should contact the college's director of physical facilities.

Piedmont Community College
P.O. Box 1197
Roxboro, NC 27573
Telephone: 336-599-1181; fax 336-597-3817
www.piedmontcc.edu

General Trail
Wildflower Trail
Conservation Trail
Observation Trail
Geology Trail
Wildlife Trail
Forestry Trail
Connector Trail
Spring Connector Trail

Length and Difficulty: 2.5 miles round-trip and combined; easy to moderate

Trailheads and Description: At the junction of U.S. 501 and NC 49 in north Roxboro, drive north 1.0 mile to Memorial Drive and turn left. After 0.5 mile, turn right and go 0.7 mile to the college. Park at the northwest end of parking lot #4, near a sign.

From parking lot #4, enter the forest on *General Trail*, a red-blazed major loop. From the hillsides, it connects with the other trails in the network, except for *Wildflower Trail*, which is outside the loop. Within the loop are spur or connecting trails where routing may not have identifying signs. If beginning on General Trail going counterclockwise from the entrance, descend to a grassy ridge and turn right. At 0.1 mile, *Conservation Trail* and *Observation Trail* are on the left. *Geology Trail* branches off from Conservation Trail to reconnect with General Trail. From General Trail, pass *Wildlife Trail* on a descent, followed by *Forestry Trail*. At 0.7 mile, notice an amphitheater on the left. Arrive at the bank of Marlowe Creek and follow the trail parallel to the creek upstream. Cross a small footbridge. At 1.0 mile, turn left at a scenic area with large boulders, cascades, and pools. After crossing the small stream above the cascades, temporarily leave the creek. Return to the creek area after a few yards (this route is outside the General Trail loop.) This is *Wildflower Trail*, which may not have a sign. After rejoining General Trail, make a steep ascent on which you pass *Connector Trail* and *Spring Connector Trail*. To complete the loop, either end where you started, exit after 2.0 miles, or exit on a right spur that preceeds the original entry to reach the parking lot.

Wilson (Wilson County)

The city of Wilson is located southeast of Raleigh. In the nearly 30 parks either within the city limits or nearby, there are a number of trails that are 1.0 mile or less. Regardless of the season, trail users are likely to see wildlife. Examples are beavers, raccoons, wood ducks, mallards, herons, and red-tailed hawks.

There are a few short trails that are favorite havens for wildlife. Merrimont Park, located at 2516 Buckingham Road, has a 0.5-mile creekside path, which runs through the park.

Recreation Park and Community Center at 200 Sunset Road has a 0.75-mile nature trail that runs from Ripley Road to Ward Boulevard.

Between Tilghman Road and Ward Boulevard, there is a 0.9-mile greenway in the Deerfield Subdivision.

Some of the longer trails are described in more detail. They are listed in order of their length from shortest to longest.

> **Wilson Parks and Recreation Department**
> P.O. Box 10
> Wilson, NC 27894
> Telephone: 252-399-2262; fax: 252-399-2196

Hominy Canal Trail (0.9 mile, easy)

Trailhead and Description: Access for parking is available at Williams Day Camp on Mount Vernon Drive.

Hominy Canal Trail, recently restructured after a closure, is a path between Ward Boulevard and the junction of Kincaid Avenue and Canal Drive. Along the way are tall loblolly pines, willows, live oaks, sweet gums, and river birches.

Toisnot Lake Trail (1.8 miles, easy)

Trailhead and Description: Access to Toisnot Park is on Corbett Avenue and Lawndale Drive, near a junction with Ward Boulevard (NC 58/42).

Toisnot Lake Trail circles the lake for 1.2 miles and extends for another 0.6 mile into the hardwood forest downstream to the Seaboard Coast Railroad.

Lake Buckhorn Trail (2.0 miles currently completed; easy)

Trailheads and Description: The trailheads are accessed at the boat dock west of Wilson on NC 42. To reach them, turn right at Buckhorn Crossroads. After 2.0 miles, turn left on Rock Ridge School Road (Wilkerson Crossroads). It is about 1.7 miles to the dock. For access to the multi-use trail, continue on NC 42 from Buckhorn Crossroads for 2.5 miles and turn right (near the county line) on Hawley Road. After 1.5 miles, turn right on Bailey Road to a fork with Sullivan Road. The two trailheads are at the ends of both of these roads.

The city of Wilson purchased 100 acres for a park at Lake Buckhorn. Plans call for a baseball complex, six soccer fields, boat ramps, and a boat dock, some of which is already in place. Construction is underway on a 9.0-mile multi-use trail. Two miles have been completed between the ends of Sullivan and Bailey roads. (Call the parks and recreation department for an update.)

Lake Wilson Trail

Length and Difficulty: 2.3 miles combined or 4.5 miles backtracked; easy

Trailhead and Description: To access the trail from NC 58/42, drive north on Corbett Avenue for 3.3 miles, turn left on Lake Wilson Road (SR 1327) at Dunn Crossroads, and go 0.5 mile to the lake on the right.

From the parking lot, either go right or left at the dam. If going left, cross the dam and spillway to follow an old road through a forest of river birch, tag alder, sweet gum, and holly. (This is also a good bird-watching trail.) At 0.8 mile, bear right, going off the old road, and enter a swampy area to follow the yellow blazes. There may be evidence of beavers in the area. The trail ends at 1.0 mile. Backtrack.

If hiking from the dam on the right side, follow an old road upstream. On the left are marshy areas, which offer habitats for birds, buttonbush, and swamp candle. (There used to be a boardwalk to connect the trail here.) The end of the trail is at 1.25 miles. Backtrack.

Mountains-to-Sea Trail Appendix

The *Mountains-to-Sea Trail* (MST), an officially designated state trail, passes through the Triangle on its way from Clingmans Dome and the *Appalachian Trail* in Great Smoky Mountains National Park to Jockey's Ridge State Park on the Atlantic Coast. Of the proposed 935 miles, nearly 500 miles have already been officially designated part of the trail or are in the process of final inspections for the official recognition. On its way, the trail passes through 40 small towns and 37 counties. In the Triangle area, the trail has sections in Orange, Durham, Wake, and Johnston counties. When completed, approximately 125 miles of trail will pass through the Triangle. About 55 miles are already complete.

The information offered here is about the trail's history, government guidelines, expectation for its future, and its significance. Upon completion, it will be the longest single natural-surface footpath in the Triangle, and even in the state. The trail is recognizable by the 3-inch white dots blazed along the way. Hikers may also notice the red-white-and-blue logos denoting the U.S. Interior and Agriculture departments' recognition as a National Recreation Trail. Another impressive fact about the trail is that its construction is provided mainly by dedicated volunteers.

From Dreams to Legal Reality

Long-distance trails in North Carolina are not new. Native Americans had trade routes from the Gulf Coast through what is now North Carolina going to the Potomac River. Some archaeologists have found evidence to support this in the Triangle area, and particularly in Orange County. John Lawson, surveyor-general for North Carolina in 1700, followed many of the Native American trails, including some used by the Occaneechi tribe in the Triangle area.

Over the years, many highways have followed these routes. As transportation changed and asphalt took away the feeling of being close to nature, there were those who desired to restore the tradition of walking long distances in the woods.

There is uncertainty about where the name "Mountains-to-Sea Trail" originated as the official name for North Carolina's state trail. Some officials at the N. C. Department of Transportation think it came from the leaders who established the Mountains-to-Sea Bicycle Trail. Other officials state that the N. C. Department of Natural Resources and Community Development (NCDNRCD) had the idea first. There are documents that show the dream floated freely among government agencies from 1972 through the summer of 1973, when the N.C. General Assembly passed the Trails System Act. Legislative records show the use of such terms as "from the mountains to the coast," and "mountains to the seashore." The original abbreviation for the trail was MTST but it was shortened to MST in the late 1980s.

One of the Trails System Act's statutes explains that "in order to provide for the ever-increasing outdoor recreation needs of an expanded population and in order to promote public access to, travel within, and enjoyment and appreciation of the outdoors...trails should be established in natural scenic areas of the state, and in and near urban areas." After the general assembly passed the act, the staff of NCDNRCD began brainstorming about the future of trails in the state. Instrumental in the outset of their discussion was *Resources for Trails in North Carolina*, written by staff member Bob Buckner in 1972. With fresh ideas about trail purposes and usage, staff planners such as Alan Eaks and Jim Hallsey inspired others to move forward in implementing the act.

Which Mountain and Which Beach?

After receiving overwhelming support from the general assembly and allied support from county and local agencies for more trails and especially for a special trail that would run from the mountains to the sea, questions arose about the trail route. Would it start at Mount Mitchell, the state's highest elevation, or at a small community, like Ranger, in the southwestern tip of the state? Would it go to Knotts Island on the coast, making the trail more than 1,000 miles long, or would it end somewhere else?

As excitement turned to pragmatic issues, planners realized that it was important to incorporate federal and state properties. The national parks and forests were basic to the blueprint. The question arose whether the trail should pass through metropolitan areas, where parks and trails were cultural points of interest, or should it follow the countryside where real estate would be less expensive to acquire for new trail construction. Early in the discussions, there was a strong movement to choose a point on the *Appalachian Trail* for the western terminus. Discussion about the location for the eastern trailhead centered on using a historic site or wildlife refuge. Cape Hatteras Lighthouse was a strong contender, as was the Wright Brothers National Monument.

The Appalachian Trail at Clingmans Dome in the Great Smoky Mountains National Park was finally chosen as the western terminus. Originally, the coastal terminus was the community of Whalebone because it was the northern end of the 70-mile *Cape Hatteras Beach Trail*. Later, that terminus was changed to Jockey's Ridge State Park. That located the trailhead on the highest sand dunes on the East Coast. The trail route leading to Jockey's Ridge passed near the Wright Brothers National Monument, through the Pea Island National Refuge, by Cape Hatteras Lighthouse, and through Ocracoke Island. The two ferry rides needed to connect the locations were welcome respites.

Because the Blue Ridge Parkway was already a gem of a passage through the mountain region, its entire route from the Oconaluftee River to Stone Mountain State Park was used as a corridor for following old trails or building new ones. The decision to use the parkway left out the Uwharrie National Forest, but it included three other national forests—Nantahala, Pisgah, and Croatan. The MST also included Mt. Mitchell, Pilot Mountain, Hanging Rock, and Cliffs of the Neuse state parks. The general conclusion was that the trail would go through or near Raleigh. The trail route would also touch the Triad area of north Greensboro. New Bern and other towns along the Neuse River would be ports of call before the adventurous passage through Croatan National Forest.

Jim Hallsey, who was on the staff of the N.C. Division of Parks and Recreation (NCDPR) during this momentous time, recommended that the entire trail have options of passage within a 20-mile-wide corridor, depending on having volunteer organizations to assist in construction, incorporating historic and cultural places, arranging favorable financial options, and overcoming environmental issues. Twenty-five years since agreeing on its original blueprint, the corridor has shifted only twice. One shift included leaving the Blue Ridge Parkway route for the magnificent views of Bald Knob from the North Fork of the Catawba River and then passing through the Linville Gorge; this 70-mile route has already been designated. The other change is a proposal to shift the trail route from north of Burlington to south of the city along the Haw River before returning to the original path along the Eno River.

The Call to Action

During the mid-1970s, any discussion about the MST was influenced by comprehensive trail plans for urban areas, which included plans for greenways. At the time, regional councils and county governments were also proposing canoe trails and trail connections. Arch Nichols of the Carolina Mountain Club was proposing a 60-mile hiking trail along the Blue Ridge Parkway from Mount Pisgah to Mount Mitchell. The North Carolina Trails Committee (NCTC), a seven-member citizen's advisory board, began discussions of these and many other exciting ideas with state government staff in January 1974. I was fortunate to be an appointed member of that board.

Louise Chatfield of Greensboro was the board's first chair, followed by John Falter of Apex in 1976, and Dr. Doris B. Hammett of Waynesville in 1977. It was Dr. Hammett who led a planning committee for the Fourth National Trails Symposium, held at Lake Junaluska from September 7-10, 1977. Among the distinguished speakers was Howard N. Lee, secretary of NCDNRCD and former mayor of Chapel Hill. Near the end of his speech, Lee said, "I think the time has come for us to consider the feasibility of establishing a state trail between the mountains and the seashore in North Carolina." He explained that he wanted the NCTC to plan a trail that would utilize the National Park Service, the U. S. Forest Service, state parks, city and county properties, and the property of private landowners "willing to give an easement over a small portion of their land on a legacy to future generations. I don't think we should be locked into the traditional concept of a trail with woods on both sides. . . . I think it would be a trail that would help—like the first primitive trails—bring us together. . . . It would depend on trail enthusiasts for maintenance. . . . Beyond that, how great it would be if other states would follow suit and that the state trails could be linked nationally."

After the conference, Curtis Yates of the N. C. Department of Transportation (NCDOT) sent Lee a map of the Mountains-to-Sea Bike

Route #2 from Murphy to Manteo. Yates raised the question whether that bike route as well as other official bike routes, could be used for part of the MST corridor where there was not a foot trail in place. Currently, part of NCDOT Bike Route #4 from Stone Mountain State Park to Danbury, Route #2 from Raleigh to Wilson, and Route #7 from Wilson to Cedar Island Ferry (except for 20 miles through Croatan National Forest) are all being used.

Secretary Lee later became a state senator and was the prime sponsor for Senate Bill #1311 that was ratified by the general assembly on July 22, 2000. That bill authorized the N.C. Department of Environment and Natural Resources (NCDENR), previously the NCDNRCD, to incorporate the Mountains-to-Sea Trail into the state park system under the auspices of the NCDPR. The prime sponsor for corresponding House Bill #1603 was Pryor Gibson III.

Plans Become More Defined

Responding to the state leadership, citizen task forces began organizing to negotiate easements and design, construct, and maintain segments of the "dream trail." Between 1979 and 1981, the NCDNRCD signed cooperative planning agreements with the National Park Service, the U.S. Forest Service, and the United States Fish and Wildlife Service for the MST to pass through federal properties. Another agreement was signed in 1985 pledging a cooperative effort to share resources for the state's longest proposed trail.

"Trek-A-State"

In April 1982, trail organizations such as the N.C. Trails Association began a "Trek-A-State" program, modeled on the nation's bicentennial "Hike-A-Nation." Among the leaders of the trek were Larkin Kirkman, Louise Chatfield, Kathy Chatfield, and Kay Scott. The project included hikers, bicyclists, equestrians, and canoeists. The record-setting hiker was Lee Price, who hiked a continuous journey from Soco Gap in the mountains to a spot near Smithfield east of Raleigh.

Keeping the Dream Alive

In 1989, the NCDPR's trail staff had undergone changes, but hopes of keeping the dream alive produced *Mountains-to-Sea Trail Proposed Trail Routing and Plan of Action.* Its purpose was to incorporate hiking, biking, horseback riding, and canoeing in the passage across the state. The proposal was not acceptable to all parties. The plan was never fully implemented because priority went to rail trails, greenways, and river trails, yet the river trails could not be contiguous. Furthermore, the MST had successful arrangements with equestrians and hikers on the *Sauratown Trail*, and with bicyclists on more than 250 miles that used bicycle routes. Interest and action began to decline with the demise of the N.C. Trails Association in 1989. At the June 23 and September 15, 1995, meetings of the NCTC, the practicality of having a continuous trail across the state was discussed again. NCDPR director Phillip McKnelly reaffirmed the MST concept and his support for a hiking trail across the state. He encouraged the state trails staff to open discussions with the NCDOT to work together to create an arrangement using highway bike routes in sections where foot trails had not been completed.

Time for Details

By the summers of 1995 and 1996, I researched a potential routing that would connect the segments of the MST that were under construction or that had been completed and officially designated. In cooperation with the NCDPR, a continuous route was established. Parts of the routing would follow official state or county bicycle routes and a few other segments would be on connecting backroads within the generally accepted corridor. After the research was compiled, I organized a new citizen's group called Friends of the Mountains-to-Sea Trail. Its organizing statement said that "this Corporation is organized to promote the concept, research and provide information, advocate cooperative efforts among allied government offices and citizens, and support task forces and trail organizations for the benefit of a cross-state trail known officially by the NCDPR as the Mountains-to-Sea Trail." The charter was incorporated by the State of North Carolina on August 5, 1997.

Meanwhile, I chose Alan Householder, a fellow-hiker of the Appalachian Trail, to be my cross-state hiking companion to hike the entire MST from April 18-June 12, 1997. Using a diary from this journey, I prepared a 371-page guidebook, which was published as *Hiking North Carolina's Mountains-to-Sea Trail* in 2000.

Where the MST is Today

Following the original plans, the MST now uses pre-existing trails in Great Smoky Mountains National Park to reach the Cherokee Nation's property and the Blue Ridge Parkway. It follows the Blue Ridge Parkway on a new trail until reaching Nantahala National Forest, where it alternates between the parkway and Pisgah National Forest on its way north.

From Mount Pisgah on the Blue Ridge Parkway, it follows the parkway's corridor to the Mount Mitchell State Park entrance road before entering the Appalachian Ranger District of Pisgah National Forest. The trail then goes through Mount Mitchell State Park, followed by a descent into the Toecane Station of the Appalachian Ranger District leading to Black Mountain Campground. It then returns to parallel the Blue Ridge Parkway for a short distance before leaving the parkway near NC 80 and going into the Grandfather Ranger District of Pisgah National Forest. After crossing Woods Mountain and descending to U.S. 221, it continues east to cross the North Fork of the Catawba and Linville rivers, Harper and Wilson creeks, and return to the parkway at Beacon Heights (near Grandfather Mountain). From there, it follows the 13.4-mile *Tanawah Trail* on parkway property to Julian Price Memorial Park and to U.S. 321 in Blowing Rock.

The route from Blowing Rock to Glendale Springs is now being designed and approved by archaeologists. The 30 miles from Glendale Springs to Stone Mountain State Park has been completed. Other sections that have been completed include: a segment from Pilot Mountain State Park through Hanging Rock State Park; a 20-mile section across north Greensboro; more than 55 miles in the Triangle; the route through Croatan National Forest near New Bern; and the section from Cedar Point (at the ferry terminal) to Ocracoke Island and on to Jockey's Ridge.

On May 6, 2006, a 10.6-mile segment from the North Fork of the Catawba River pedestrian bridge to the Pinnacle near the west rim of Linville Gorge was officially designated. It was a distinctive milestone because it completed 230 miles of contiguous trail from the parkway's Balsam Gap south of Waynesville to Julian Price Memorial Park near Blowing Rock.

Whatever the trail's final eastern route, the trails in Hillsborough and Eno River State Park will be used going toward Durham. From Durham, the trail will follow a route already planned and under construction that will connect with the eastern section of *Falls Lake Trail* in Raleigh. From Raleigh, it will follow the floodplain corridor of the Neuse River through Johnston and Wayne counties to Cliffs of the Neuse State Park and on through Lenoir County. It will leave the Neuse River to enter Croatan National Forest, where 21 miles of the *Neusiok Trail* is complete. It will then follow roads in Pamlico and Carteret counties. At Cedar Island, hikers now take a state ferry to Ocracoke to begin the final 114 miles of the trail. It follows Cape Hatteras Beach Trail, which was the first section of the MST to be officially designated, on through Cape Hatteras National Seashore for a finish at a high sand dune in Jockey's Ridge State Park.

Triangle Homework

In 2006, Jeff Brewer, in his capacity as president of the board of directors of the Friends of the Mountains-to-Sea Trail, negotiated a *Memorandum of Agreement* between the NCDPR, the U.S. Army Corps of Engineers, N.C. Wildlife Resources Commission, and Durham Open Space and Trails Commission for construction of approximately 25 miles of the MST. This segment would travel westward from NC 50 in Wake County to Durham's West Point on the Eno Park. The work on this section required a cooperative understanding unlike any of the other efforts needed to construct the trail over a period of nearly 20 years.

The NCDENR prepared a conceptual plan that would combine 246 miles of land and water trails from Falls Lake Trail in north Raleigh to Cedar Island and the Ocracoke Ferry in Carteret County. The routing would follow a corridor along the Neuse River most of those miles.

The Trail Next Door

Currently the Mountains-to-Sea Trail may be closer to Triangle residents than they know. Completed segments that connect trails, as well as future plans are described ahead.

The proposed passage through Hillsborough will follow the *Historic Occoneechee Speedway Trail* for about 0.6 mile on the south side of the Eno River. (Visitors to that trail may notice a sign noting that intention.) Downstream from there, the trail now has a gap to Eno River State Park that will need to use private property. New construction of about 5.0 miles will be necessary to complete the connection from the Historic Occoneechee Speedway Trail to the two trails already open to the public in Eno River State Park—a section of *Pump Gap Station Trail* and all of the 2.5-mile *Laurel Bluff Trail*. The latter trail ends on the south side of the river at Guess Road Bridge (NC 157). From there, the MST crosses the bridge to the north side and enters the West Point on the Eno Park, where it follows 1.8 miles of the scenic *Eagle Trail*. Eagle Trail connects with a new construction project that will lead to Penny's Bend Nature Preserve.

It may take as long as 10 years for the design, inspection, and construction (including bridge building) of the approximately 25 miles from Penny's Bend Preserve to NC 50 (Creedmoor Road). Creedmoor Road is where 26.1 miles of the MST/Falls Lake Trail comes from Falls of Neuse Road downstream to Falls Lake Dam. (For more details about Falls Lake Trail, see Chapter 1.) Financial assistance and volunteer labor could shorten the time needed to complete this long-range project. On January 6, 2007, construction began on the first 10.0-mile phase from NC 50 west to Rolling View Recreation Area.

At the base of the Falls Lake Dam, the MST will jointly follow *Neuse River Trail* (greenway) downriver to Anderson Point and beyond to the Johnston County line north of Clayton. This segment may involve from 8 to 18 miles of construction. Raleigh's Department of Parks and Recreation already has the first phase from Falls of Neuse Road east to Perry Creek Road on its master plan. This section is included in the conceptual plan for the eastern section of the trail, which was described above.

For more information about the MST, go to www.ncmst.org, see additional information under "Resource Information Appendix," or email me at adh4771@aol.com. Hopefully, now that Triangle residents know more about the dreamers, the action leaders, and the volunteers who have worked to make the MST a reality, they will join us on a journey not far from their doorsteps.

Resource Information Appendix

The names and addresses listed below of national, state, and Triangle organizations associated with trails are intended to supplement those given in the text. Because many hikers and walkers are bikers, information for bikers is included here. New residents of the Triangle may wish to know about trail clubs and special groups interested in outdoor activities.

National Organizations

American Birding Association
4945 North 30th Street, Suite 200
Colorado Springs, CO 80919
800-850-2473 or 719-578-9703
www.americanbirding.org

American Hiking Society
1422 Fenwick Lane
Silver Spring, MD 20910
301-565-6704
www.americanhiking.org

Appalachian Trail Conference
P.O. Box 807
799 Washington Street
Harpers Ferry, WV 25425
304-535-6331
www.appalachiantrail.org

Boy Scouts of America (national)
P.O. Box 152079
Irving, TX 75015
www.scouting.org

Friends of the Earth
1717 Washington Avenue, NW, #600
Washington, DC 20036
877-843-8687
www.foe.org

Girl Scouts of the USA
420 Fifth Avenue
New York, NY 10018
800-478-7248
www.girlscouts.org

National Wildlife Federation
11100 Wildlife Center Drive
Reston, VA 20190
800-822-9919
www.nwf.org

North Carolina Governmental Agencies

N.C. Department of Commerce
Division of Tourism, Film, and Sports
   Development
301 North Wilmington Street

Raleigh, NC 27601
919-733-4171
www.visitnc.com

N. C. Department of Environment and
  Natural Resources (NCDENR)
1601 Mail Service Center
Raleigh, NC 27699
512 North Salisbury Street
Archdale Building
Raleigh, NC 27611
919-733-4984
www.enr.state.nc.us/

N.C. Department of Transportation
  (NCDOT)
Division of Bicycle & Pedestrian
  Transportation
1552 Mail Service Center
Raleigh, NC 27699
401 Oberlin Road, Suite 250
Raleigh, NC 27605
919-807-0777
www.ncdot.org

N.C. Division of Parks & Recreation
1615 Mail Service Center
Raleigh, NC 27699
512 North Salisbury Street
Archdale Building, 7th Floor, Room 732
Raleigh, NC 27611
919-733-4181

N.C. State University
College of Natural Resources
Department of Parks, Recreation and
  Tourism Management
P.O. Box 8004
Biltmore Hall, NCSU
Raleigh, NC 27695
919-515-3276
www2.ncsu.edu/ncsu/forest_
  resources/rrs.html

N.C. Wildlife Resources Commission
NCSU Centennial Campus
1751 Varsity Drive
Raleigh, NC 27606
919-707-0010
www.ncwildlife.org

North Carolina Citizens' Groups
(chiefly in the Triangle area)

Duke Law School Hiking Club
5700 Barbee Chapel Road
Chapel Hill, NC 27514

Eno River Association
4419 Guess Road
Durham, NC 27712
919-620-9099
www.enoriver.org

Eno River Racers (cyclists)
900 West Main Street
Durham, NC 27701
919-544-3948

Friends of Mountains-to-Sea Trail
3585 U.S. 401 South
Louisburg, NC 27549
919-496-4771
www.ncmst.org

Friends of State Parks
P.O. Box 37655
Raleigh, NC 27627
www.rasman.com/fsp/

Nature Conservancy-N.C. Chapter
Suite 209, 4705 University Drive
Durham, NC 27707
919-403-8558
www.nature.org/wherewework/
  northamerica/states/northcarolina

N.C. Bicycle Club
4908 Lily Atkins Road
Cary, NC 27611
919-851-9256
www.ncbikeclub.org

N.C. Governor's Council on Physical
Fitness and Health
1907 Mail Service Center
Raleigh, NC 27699
1300 St. Mary's Street, Room G-2
Raleigh, NC 27605
919-733-9615

N.C. Horse Council
4904 Waters Edge Drive, Suite 290
Raleigh, NC 27606
919-854-1990
www.nchorsecouncil.com

N.C. Native Plant Society
Margaret Reid Chapter (Triangle)
708 Brent Road
Raleigh, NC 27606
919-859-1187
www.ncwildflower.org

N.C. Rail Trails
P.O. Box 61348
Durham, NC 27715
www.ncrail-trails.org

N. C. Recreation and Park Society
883 Washington Street
Raleigh, NC 27605
910-832-5868

N.C. Sierra Club
112 South Blount Street
Raleigh, NC 27601
919-833-8467
http://nc.sierraclub.org

Neuse River Foundation
112 South Blount Street
Raleigh, NC 27601
919-856-1180

Outing Club
Campus Recreation, NCSU
P.O. Box 8111
Raleigh, NC 27695
919-515-3161

Outing Club of Duke University
Office of Student Affairs
101-3 Bryan Center
Duke University
Durham, NC 27706

Recreation Resources Service
Box 8004, NCSU
Raleigh, NC 27695
919-513-3937

Sierra Club (Capital Group)
P.O. Box 6076
Raleigh, NC 27628
http://nc.sierraclub.org/capital/index.
html

Sierra Club (Headwaters Group)
58 Newton Drive
Durham, NC 27707
919-490-1566
http://nc.sierraclub.org/headwaters/
index.html

Sierra Club (Medoc Group)
http://nc.sierraclub.org/medoc/index.
html

Sierra Club (Orange-Chatham Group)
http://nc.sierraclub.org/ocg/index.
html

The Umstead Coalition
P.O. Box 10654
Raleigh, NC 27605
919-852-2268
http://umsteadcoalition.org

Triangle Greenways Council
P.O. Box 2746
Raleigh, NC 27602
www.trianglegreenways.org

Triangle Land Conservancy
1101 Haynes Street, Suite 205
Raleigh, NC 27604
919-833-3662
www.tlc-nc.org

Triangle Mountain Biking
www.trianglemtb.com

Triangle Off-Road Cyclists
www.torc-nc.org

Triangle Rails-to-Trails Conservancy
www.triangletrails.org

Triangle Trailblazers (Volkswalkers)
www.triangletrailblazers.org

UNC-Chapel Hill Outing Club
Box 16, Carolina Union, 065-A
Chapel Hill, NC 27514

Wake County Audubon Society
P.O. Box 12452
Raleigh, NC 27605
www.wakeaudubon.org

Special Trails Appendix

Although there is something of interest on every Triangle trail, there are some trails with special characteristics. Listed below are trails that are particularly appealing to families; trails specifically made for mountain bikers; and trails catering to equestrians.

Trails and Parks for the Family

The trails and parks listed here are likely to have family appeal. One particular trail is worth noting—Thanks Trail. Its name is an acronym for the slogan "Trail for Health, Art, and Nature for Kids and Seniors." The trail makes a circle on the campus of Central Carolina Community College in Pittsboro.

Air Awareness Trail (Medoc Mountain State Park)
American Beech Nature Trail (Raven Rock State Park)
American Tobacco Trail (the section from the south trailhead parking area in the New Hope Game Lands at Jordan Lake north to the Wimberly Road parking area in Wake County)
Bass Lake Greenway (Holly Springs)
Battle Branch Trail and connecting trails (Chapel Hill)
Beaverdam Loop Interpretive Trail (Beaverdam Recreation Area, Falls Lake)
Bentonville Battleground Historic Site (Johnston County)
Black Creek Greenway (Cary)
Bolin Creek Greenway (Chapel Hill)
Bond Nature Trail (Fred G. Bond Metro Park System, Cary)

Cape Fear Botanical Garden (Fayetteville)

Carrboro Nature Trail (Carrboro Park)

Carroll Howard Johnson Environmental Education Park (Fuquay-Varina)

Center for Environmental Education (Blue Jay Point County Park, Wake County)

Chavis Heights Park (Raleigh)

Children's Bamboo Trail and connecting trails (DeHart Botanical Gardens, Franklin County)

Clayton Community Park (Clayton)

Clemmons Talking Tree Trail (Clemmons Educational State Forest)

Community Center Park (Chapel Hill)

Community Park Greenway and connecting trails (Apex Community Park)

Crabtree Creek Greenway (between Capital Boulevard and Raleigh Boulevard on Middle Crabtree Trail in Raleigh)

Crowder District Park (Wake County)

Dry Creek Trail (Chapel Hill)

Durant Nature Park (Raleigh)

Eno Nature Trail and other trails (Eno River State Park)

Falls Lake U.S. Army Corps of Engineers Visitor Center (Raleigh)

Harris Lake County Park (for its special mountain-biking trails for children and its environmental education programs)

Hemlock Bluffs Nature Preserve (Wake County)

Historic Occoneechee Speedway (Orange County)

Hinshaw Greenway (MacDonald Woods Park and Kids Together Park, Cary)

Hyco Lake Natural Learning Center (Caswell County)

J. Bayard Clark Park & Nature Center (Fayetteville)

Johnson Mill Nature Preserve (Orange County)

Jo Peller Nature Trail (Cedar Falls Park, Chapel Hill)

Joyner Park and Nature Trail (Louisburg)

Jordan Lake U.S. Army Corps of Engineers Visitor Center (Chatham County)

Jordan Lake Educational State Forest (Chatham County)

Lake Johnson Nature Park (Raleigh)

Lake Lynn Trail (Raleigh)

Laurel Hill Fire Trail (Duke Forest)

Mayo Park (Person County)

Miller Park Nature Trail (Wake Forest)

Millpond Trail (Historic Yates Mill County Park, Wake County)

Morrisville Community Park (Morrisville)

Muir Nature Trail (and other trails at San-Lee Park and Outdoor Educational Center, Sanford)

Neuse River Nature Trail (Smithfield)

Neuse River Trail and Anderson Point Park (Raleigh)

New Hope Bottomland Trail (Durham)

New Hope Overlook Trail (Jordan Lake)

North Carolina Botanical Garden (Chapel Hill)

Oak Rock Trail and connecting trails (William B. Umstead State Park)

Occoneechee Mountain State Natural Area (Hillsborough)

Old Beech Nature Trail (Lake Crabtree County Park, Wake County)

Penny's Bend Nature Preserve (Durham)

Pirates Cove Greenway (Cary)

Pump Station Trail and Laurel Bluff Trail (Eno River State Park)

Reedy Creek Greenway (section from east edge of Meredith College through properties of North Carolina Museum of Art, Raleigh)

Ridge Trail and North River Loop Trail (Little River Regional Park and Natural Area, Durham/Orange counties)

Rock Quarry Trail and connecting trails (Durham)

Rocky Branch Greenway at Pullen Park (Raleigh)

Rolesville Main Street Park (Rolesville)

Rolling View Recreation Area (Falls Lake)

Rudolph Howell and Son Environmental Learning Center (Johnston County Community College)

Sarah B. Duke Memorial Gardens (Durham)

Seaforth Recreation Area (Jordan Lake)

Sears Farm Road Park (Cary)

Shelley Lake-Sertoma Park (Raleigh)

Swift Creek Recycled Greenway (Cary)

Symphony Lake Greenway (Cary)

Tar River River Trail (Rocky Mount)

Thanks Trail (Central Carolina Community College, Pittsboro)

Upper Warren Creek Trail (Whippoorwill Park, Durham)

Vista Point Recreation Area (Jordan Lake)

Walnut Creek Trail at Legacy Garden (Raleigh)

West Point on the Eno Park (Durham)

White Oak Creek Greenway (section by White Oak Creek Conservation Area, west from NC 55 to Green Level Church Road, Cary)

White Oak Nature Trail (Chatham County)

Woodland Nature Trail (Sandling Beach Recreation Area, Falls Lake)

Mountain-Bike Trails

Bicycling trails are plentiful in the Triangle. Almost all the greenways are open to hikers, walkers, runners, strollers, and general bicyclists, but not many trails in the Triangle are designed for mountain bikers. The following mountain-biking trails are open to the public:

Beaverdam Recreation Area (Falls Lake)
Harris Lake County Park (New Hill area in Wake County)
Hilliard Creek Trail (Garner Recreation Park in Garner)
Lake Crabtree County Park (Wake County)
Legend Park (Clayton)
Little River Regional Park and Natural Area (Orange/Durham counties)
San-Lee Park and Outdoor Educational Center (Sanford)

Equestrian Trails

As with mountain bikers, specific areas for public horseback riding seem limited in the Triangle. Two popular equestrian areas in the Triangle that are open to the public are as follows:

American Tobacco Trail (nearly 10 miles on south end)
Duke Forest (on maintained fire roads where designated)
Raven Rock State Park (the north side of the Cape Fear River)
William B. Umstead State Park (central entry and report station off U.S. 70)

Trail Index

Sign at current end of Beaver Creek Greenway in Apex